D0593682

MY LIFE AND *The Times*

My Life and The Times

TURNER CATLEDGE

HARPER & ROW, PUBLISHERS

NEW YORK, EVANSTON
AND LONDON

1817

Portions of "Notes and Comments," by John Bainbridge, originally published in *The New Yorker*, April 13, 1963, are reprinted by permission; © 1963 The New Yorker Magazine, Inc.

MY LIFE AND THE TIMES. Copyright © 1971 *by Turner Catledge. Printed in the United States of America. All rights reserved. No part of this book may be used or reproduced in any manner whatsoever without written permission except in the case of brief quotations embodied in critical articles and reviews. For information address Harper & Row, Publishers, Incorporated, 49 East 33rd Street, New York, N.Y. 10016. Published simultaneously in Canada by Fitzhenry & Whiteside Limited, Toronto.*

FIRST EDITION

LIBRARY OF CONGRESS CATALOG CARD NUMBER: 73-123919

PN
4874
.C32
A3

71C981

To My Wife

ABBY RAY CATLEDGE

Dexter Library
Northland College
Ashland, Wisconsin 54806

Acknowledgments

THIS book is in large measure a response to many friends who over the years have urged me to put down in writing those stories of my life which I liked most to tell. I am deeply indebted to all of them. I owe a special debt, however, to those who more recently have helped me distill from my abundant store of recollections and memoranda this running account of the high points of an interesting life. Among them:

Cass Canfield, senior editor of Harper & Row, for originating the idea of this particular book and for his gentle but persistent prodding, without which it might not have come about.

Thomas B. Congdon, Jr., editor of Harper, whose painstaking, competent, and firm editorial guidance was responsible for keeping the total story in manageable proportions and in the groove of auto-biography.

Patrick Anderson, for his highly valuable assistance in selecting and molding the various episodes gushing from my memory into a more orderly account of my life, and for his great help in preparing the manuscript.

Arthur Krock, my former chief in the *New York Times* Washington bureau, for his characteristic graciousness in giving me carte blanche permission to draw on his own recently published *Memoirs*, and correspondence that passed between us, in supplementing and checking the accuracy of my own recollections.

Dexter Library
Northland College
Ashland, Wisconsin 54806

Will Lissner of the *New York Times* staff for helping me reconstruct an accurate account of the Eastland Committee episode.

A. H. Raskin, assistant editorial-page editor and former chief labor reporter of the *New York Times,* for his assistance in recalling details of the paper's labor troubles, especially the 114-day strike of 1962-63.

Tad Szulc, presently a member of the *New York Times* Washington staff but a man of many missions, for his help in checking details of the Bay of Pigs story, in which he participated intimately as a reporter.

Iris Turner Kelso, New Orleans television commentator for her helpful criticism of the early draft and especially her comments on the parts relating to the king-size Turner family of Philadelphia, Mississippi, in which we were two of forty-two first cousins.

Herbert Andree and Joseph Romanello, my valued office assistants, for their patient and competent assistance in transcribing the manuscript, and for keeping my office files in such perfect order that by the time I sat down to write I had before me an effective diary spanning the last twenty-five years. And special thanks to Herbert Andree for his ever-frank and helpful appraisal of items as we went along.

T.C.

Contents

A section of illustrations follows page 144

Introduction

A TRUE newspaperman spends his life wanting to see and to tell. That was my overwhelming desire during forty-eight years in the newspaper business, and I found that the urge continued after my retirement from the *New York Times* early in 1970. I also found myself with some unaccustomed leisure to think and to write, and this book is the result.

In this memoir I look back, allowing myself the benefit of hindsight, upon an immensely exciting and rewarding career. My purpose is not to tell how things should have been or could have been, but how they were. I will say a little about my youth in Philadelphia, Mississippi, where I was first bitten by the newspaper bug, and also about my early experience on little county weeklies in Mississippi, and then about my first big-city experience, with the Memphis *Commercial Appeal*. Neither my little home town nor the rip-roaring newspaper style of the twenties endures today as I once knew them, and I hope to recapture something of them in these pages. They have changed, just as I have changed.

Looking back over my life, nothing impresses me more than the inevitability, the speed, and the pervasiveness of change. I can remember the first automobile I saw. I was sixteen when I first saw an airplane; a half century later I was an executive of a newspaper that reported the landing of men on the moon. The magnitude of the social, political, and scientific change that occurs in one lifetime staggers the imagination, yet we in the newspaper business must report it on a day-to-day basis. Amid such flux I found it unwise to set out rigid rules of behavior. I tried to be flexible and pragmatic.

As a political reporter in the 1930s and early 1940s I knew most of the leading national figures of the era, and I'll here indulge myself in a few recollections of them—men like Herbert Hoover (who got me my job on the *Times*), Franklin Roosevelt, Huey Long, Pat Harrison, Jimmy Byrnes, Ed Crump, John Nance Garner, Wendell Willkie, and others. There may be more rogues than statesmen in my gallery, but I confess I always enjoyed the rogues more.

Early in 1945 I gave up the life of a roving political correspondent and went to New York as an assistant managing editor of the *Times*. Later I became managing editor, executive editor, and finally vice president of the *Times*. As an executive of the newspaper, I had to make hard decisions concerning our news coverage and our employees. My life changed when I became a top editor of the *Times*, and I think the tone of this book changes, too, when I reach that point in the narrative.

The job of a modern newspaper editor is often misunderstood. The movies and television traditionally picture a crusading editor running the rascals out of city hall, or facing down a lynch mob, or something equally dramatic. My career was not without drama, but the hardest decisions tended to be those within the organization, within the family, decisions regarding policy and people, decisions that demanded a crusading spirit less often than a careful balancing of complex issues.

What do you do when a valued reporter seems no longer able to write objectively about an important issue? How does a tradition-minded newspaper make the changes necessary if it is to survive in the era of television? What do you do when you have information about a secret government operation, but one of your most senior editors insists that to print the story would be against the national interest? What do you do when you appoint a critic, or a bureau chief, only to find that you have made a mistake, that the man cannot do the job you want done? What do you do if the owner of a newspaper, or a member of his family, insists on a course of action you think will harm the newspaper?

These are the sort of problems I had to deal with as an editor of the *Times*. I was not dealing with abstractions, but with people, talented, sensitive, ambitious men and women. I had to work with and through them. I had to get them to do what I wanted done, not by force but by persuasion.

During my editorship, the *Times* covered many major news stories—the use of the first atomic bomb, the coming of Fidel Castro, the Bay of Pigs invasion, the war in Vietnam, the civil-rights revolution, the culture explosion, and many others. I want to discuss those stories, but equally important I want to get at the story behind the stories, the story of how hundreds of talented men and women work together to get out a great newspaper.

I used to say that when I switched from reporter to editor I traded my one by-line for thirty or forty by-lines, for I learned to feel a vicarious pleasure when my reporters wrote the stories I'd once written. One of my goals in this book is to give the reader some vicarious sense of what it is like to hold one of the most challenging, demanding, frustrating, rewarding jobs in the newspaper world, that of the top news editor of the *New York Times*.

In telling that story, I have had to face the same questions I faced daily at the *Times*—what news is "fit to print"? I am not interested in gossip, but I am interested in candor, and I have tried to draw the proper line between the two. I have quoted from letters and memoranda that passed between me and the publisher and others, for that seems a good way to make clear the specific problems and policy issues I faced as an editor. Inevitably, I have spent a lot of time discussing the problems I confronted. There were many good times too, many joys and rewards, but the fact remains that an editor must expend most of his energies solving problems. I stress, however, that, when I discuss any shortcomings of the *Times*, they are the shortcomings of what I believe is the finest newspaper in the world. Most other newspapers, I suspect, would be happy to have the *Times*'s problems.

MY LIFE AND *The Times*

I

A Youth in Mississippi

I WAS born on March 17, 1901, on my Grandfather Catledge's three-hundred-acre farm near the little community of New Prospect, in Choctaw County, in central Mississippi. My parents lived there until I was three, when we moved to Philadelphia, Mississippi, and thereafter I would often return for visits to the farm. As a boy, it seemed to me that I knew two very different and distinct worlds. One was my Grandfather Catledge's farm, where I felt free and independent, where I could do as I pleased with no one looking over my shoulder. The other world was Philadelphia, where, as part of a small Southern community and of my mother's large, closely-knit family, I was subject to influences that did much to make me the man I became.

My parents were Lee Johnston Catledge and Willie Anna Turner. I was their second child; my sister Bessie preceded me by about eighteen months. My parents had been married in 1898, when my father was twenty-seven and my mother thirty-one. I am almost certain my parents met at church, there in the New Prospect community, for both were quite devout. It happened that he was a Baptist and she a Presbyterian, and they might never have met except that my father sometimes "crossed over" and attended the Presbyterian church because his mother was one.

Both my grandfathers served in the Confederate Army as very young men. My mother's parents were James Andrew Turner and

Mary Hanna Turner. They were married while still in their teens, soon after he returned from the war. At age fifteen or so he had joined General Nathan Bedford Forrest's Third Army, taking with him his own horse, a saber he had forged in his father's blacksmith shop, and two sides of salt pork. His mother, my great-grandmother, used to tell how Jimmy rode off to war, his legs sticking out over the two sides of bacon.

Jim and Mary Turner had fourteen children, all of whom survived to a ripe age. My mother was their first child, and in time she became a kind of "deputy mother" to her thirteen younger brothers and sisters. This responsibility was one reason she did not marry until she was thirty-one.

My Grandmother Turner's people, the Hannas, had been small slaveholders; she inherited several slaves just before the Civil War began, but they were soon freed by proclamation. My Grandfather Catledge's people were farmers but not slaveholders. Thus, in the community where my parents lived, there were several Negro families named Hanna and Turner, but none named Catledge. My Grandfather Catledge was what was called a subsistence farmer, which meant that his farm produced almost everything he needed. He slaughtered his own meat, grew his own fruits and vegetables (he was noted for his fruit, especially his peaches and watermelon), produced his own soap and sugar, even operated his own blacksmith shop. He was contemptuous of money; if he couldn't produce something himself, he didn't want it. He had, to my knowledge, only three indulgences, roasted peanuts, chewing tobacco, and stick candy.

My father grew up on the farm, but he didn't like farm work. He attended only a small church college, but he was a sensitive and well-read man, and had an abiding interest in politics and public issues. He taught school for a few years before his marriage, and he had several types of jobs throughout his life, but he never really found his niche. I think this was due partly to ill-health and partly to his temperament. Several times in his early years, when some venture had not worked out, he would return to the security of his father's farm as he did at the time of my birth.

When I was three, our family moved to Philadelphia, where two of my mother's brothers were opening a hardware store. Two other Turner brothers had successfully operated a hardware store in the little town of McCool, in Attala County, so two younger brothers decided to try their luck in Philadelphia. It was then a community of less than a thousand people, and because it was on a new railroad line, the town was expected to boom.

The Turner brothers offered my father a job as clerk and book-keeper in their new store, primarily because they wanted their beloved older sister with them. My father accepted the offer and we set out by horse and wagon on the two-day trip to Neshoba County. We camped at night beside a stream and set lines to catch fish for breakfast. We had plenty of fresh milk on our journey, because we'd brought our cow with us.

The Philadelphia we had moved to was a rough, raw town. A few wooden houses were perched up on a red clay hill, and down by the new railroad tracks was a Negro section called Froggy Bottom. There were no sidewalks, nor water nor sewage system, and pigs roamed the streets. Yet Philadelphia was growing; my mother would recall that when we first arrived she could hear a constant beat of carpenters' hammers throughout the town. In addition to my father's job in the hardware store, it had been arranged that we would live in, and my mother operate, a small boardinghouse. It would cater to the swarms of salesmen, politicians, merchants, and other travelers who we thought would be coming to Philadelphia.

Neither the boardinghouse nor my father's job in the hardware store worked out as anticipated. The boardinghouse didn't succeed because there simply weren't as many travelers as we'd hoped. My father's lack of success at the hardware store is more complicated.

The muted conflict between my father and my uncles, the Turner brothers, was an important influence on my youth. They were very different sorts of men. The Turners were hard working, tight-lipped, frugal men, men who knew what they wanted and how to get it. My father was not like that. My uncles regarded him as a ne'er-do-well and some of them were bitter that he didn't provide better for their beloved sister. They were fine men, and I respected them, but they were not tolerant or always tactful and I often overheard their scathing remarks to one another about my father. It was a hard position for a young boy. The Turner brothers prospered while my family stayed poor. All this, combined with my mother's high hopes for my future, early instilled in me an intense desire to prove myself, to show the Turners that a Catledge could succeed as well as they had.

My mother, I hasten to say, always stood by my father in our muted family disputes. She said that ill-health was the cause of his difficulties, and it is true that he died of a heart disorder at age fifty-two, and his six brothers also died at relatively early ages—two in infancy.

My father was a tall, thin, handsome man who always wore a

mustache. He and his brothers were quite musical, and the Catledge Brothers Quartet was well known in our community's churches for its gospel singing. I don't know where he acquired the talent, but he was somewhat of a tap dancer; at my Grandfather's farm the few Negroes who lived around would often plead, "Mr. Lee, show us some steps," and he would oblige them with the few steps in his routine. But that was about as close as he got to frivolity. He was a religious man and served as superintendent of the Baptist Sunday school in Philadelphia. He rarely took a drink and I never heard him utter a word of profanity.

He was one of the two or three best-informed men in our town. He read the Memphis *Commercial Appeal* every day to keep abreast of current issues and he discussed politics with anyone who'd take him on. None of these qualities, however, helped him succeed in my uncles' terms and in a short time he withdrew from the hardware store.

After that, for some years, he often wasn't working. He spent a lot of his time at the courthouse, talking politics with the other men who hung out there. Before his marriage back in Choctaw County, he had worked as a deputy sheriff and had run unsuccessfully for sheriff. When I was about six he was elected the first mayor of Philadelphia. Besides prestige, the job provided a $25-a-month salary, which the Catledge family was glad to have. He was elected to a second term but for some reason—I never knew the story—he resigned before the term was up. As mayor he was the town's chief judicial officer, and on Monday mornings he'd hand out $2 and $5 fines to all the Negroes and poor whites who'd been tossed in jail on Saturday night for drinking or brawling. As mayor, he was empowered to perform weddings; I remember going with him one Sunday morning to a Negro wedding for which he received the grand fee of fifty cents.

After he quit as mayor, he continued to spend most of his time at the courthouse, talking politics, sometimes working in the courthouse offices. He was quite an expert on deeds, property records, and other courthouse affairs. He could add two rows of figures at the same time. During the First World War, he went to work as a clerk at the railroad station. He became a fervent union member, and he stayed at that job until ill-health forced his retirement. He died in 1924.

My mother was very unlike my father. As the oldest of fourteen children she learned at an early age to be a leader. She was a tireless worker. After our boardinghouse ceased to make much money she took in sewing—for she was an expert seamstress. We were poor people but my mother substituted pride for money—in that sense, there was no one richer than my mother.

She dominated my father and, by her force of character, she became a leading figure in the community. She was always heard from when a family or community decision was being made. She was a sentimental woman, quick to shed tears about other people's troubles, but rarely about her own. A strict Presbyterian and a firm believer in predestination, she believed that everything in her life had been written in the Book at the beginning of time. Among other things, this made her entirely fearless; if a cyclone came through the town, as they often did, she would simply ignore it. If the Lord wanted her, he would take her, and His will was not to be challenged. One of her favorite hymns began, "What a friend we have in Jesus," and she meant that literally, for she considered the Lord a close personal friend.

As more and more of my mother's younger brothers and sisters moved to Philadelphia, she remained the center of Turner family life. She was always on call during births and sicknesses, and she was as free with her advice as with her assistance. In later life, she raised the children of three of her brothers whose wives had died. I suppose some of her in-laws resented her, but her own kin loved her and were in awe of her. I remember when my Uncle Joe Turner, then a middle-aged man, took up smoking, he'd always dispose of his cigarette if my mother was coming. Once she appeared unexpectedly and he stuck his burning cigarette into his pocket and set his pants afire.

My mother thought her family could do no wrong, and few outsiders could, in her mind, measure up to our standards. She could be highly critical of other people and, for all her goodness, she was lacking in tolerance. She had little use for people who indulged in drinking, smoking, gambling, or idleness. Dancing to her was a mortal sin, at least so far as it involved the body contact of opposite sexes.

In the years after 1903, Philadelphia began to fill with Turners. Eventually, all of my mother's five sisters and all but one of her eight brothers settled there—and the missing brother settled in a nearby community. All of them married except one sister, and I was one of forty-two first cousins, some thirty of whom are still living. In 1912, my Grandmother and Grandfather Turner moved over from McCool, officially making Philadelphia the family base of operations.

My mother and her brothers and sisters had grown up poor and they yearned for financial security. Unlike my father—or me—the Turners were not interested in politics, only in the church and material success. They achieved it. All of the brothers, as they arrived in town, worked in the hardware store—for a time they even operated two hardware stores, across the street from each other. Then, as they became settled, most of them branched out into other businesses. My Uncle Jim owned a drugstore, Homer and Joe ran a grocery. Sam had the Ford agency. Homer, after returning from World War I, branched out into the lumber business with his father-in-law.

To this day, the Turners are prominent people in Philadelphia. I have kept in close touch with many of them over the years, although my career has taken me far from Mississippi. Perhaps I got to know them better in 1963, when our little town attracted world-wide attention because some of its Ku Klux Klansmen murdered three civil-rights workers. At that time, I was shocked and saddened to see that the good people of Philadelphia, certain members of my family included, did not step forward to condemn the murderers. I felt that I had misread their natures, that I had changed but they had not, and that in many ways I had romanticized the little town where I grew up. As I wrote then to a friend in Philadelphia, Florence Mars, one of the few citizens who was carrying the banner of decency, "Where oh where are those decent people I used to know? Most, of course, are over there on the hill, but where are their descendants?" And yet, in honesty, I had to ask myself what I would have done in their place, under the same pressures, and sometimes I'd almost break into a cold sweat thinking about that question.

I grew up, of course, under a system of total segregation and it did not occur to me to challenge that system, nor did it to many people in that time and place. Yet I was always taught to treat Negroes with respect. If I used the word "nigger," for example when I was playing with Negro children, I'd get a licking, and I was taught to regard whites who did use that word as themselves inferior. We were taught to call older Negroes "uncle" and "aunt"; that sounds paternalistic today but we meant it as a sign of respect and affection. We considered many Negroes our friends. They were as poor as we, as Southern as we, as religious as we, and we valued them despite the great social barrier between us.

The Negroes were subject to terrible cruelty from what we called the white trash. To these poor, ignorant whites, it was a sign of manhood to mistreat helpless Negroes. In the twenties and later, the

Negroes' greatest fear was of course the Ku Klux Klan. My father always despised the Klan and the politicians who catered to it—in our house the name of Bilbo, then a state politician and later the famous racist Senator, was a dirty word. I remember once when a pro-Klan preacher came to town for a revival meeting, and during the service six Klansmen walked in dressed in their full regalia and made a contribution. My father stood up and walked out and about half the congregation followed him.

I am not by nature a crusader. I thought very little about the plight of Negroes during my early newspaper career. Separate but equal was the law of the land and it did not occur to me to challenge it. My thinking changed slowly, as did the nation's. When the great Supreme Court decisions of the 1950's came down, outlawing various forms of segregation, I realized that they were right, that segregation in public institutions and facilities cannot be tolerated.

I served as managing editor and executive editor of the *New York Times* in 1951-64, some of the most turbulent years of the Negro revolution. Other men wrote the editorials, but I saw it as my job to ensure that the *Times* printed the fullest possible presentation of the facts about the racial situation in America. But I will say more about that later.

When I look back on my boyhood, it is the good memories I recall, not the problems. I was a poor boy but I didn't know it. There were people in our town who owned big houses or automobiles but I didn't think much about that or ever feel resentful. Even though we were poor my mother's standing in the community made us "quality folk." The church was a great leveler in small Southern communities; rich and poor stood the same there. The church was also a great disciplinary force. If I missed church, I felt terribly guilty about it. Our community churches were active in the prohibition cause, and I must have signed the temperance pledge a dozen times before I was twelve years old, but I fear that all these vows of sobriety only made me all the more curious about that forbidden fruit called whiskey.

I remember the first time I got really drunk. I was home on a college vacation and had gone over to the Neshoba County Fair where I ran into some fellows who had a fruit jar of moonshine liquor. I don't know what an LSD trip is like, but it can't be much more debilitating than a young man's first encounter with corn whiskey. My uncles later found out about my spree but they never told my mother about it.

When I was ten or so, I started working at part-time jobs. That was one way my uncles would help my mother indirectly, by seeing that I had a job on weekends and in the summers. So I skipped around from the grocery store to the hardware store to the drugstore to the automobile agency. Few of the Turners ever worked for anyone else; it was a sort of tribal system with the family determined to take care of its own.

Most often I worked at the grocery store owned by my uncles Homer and Joe. They were the youngest of the brothers and the ones I was the closest to. Uncle Joe never went past the seventh grade in school but he became the wealthiest of the Turners. I remember when I eventually left Philadelphia, to start my newspaper career, Joe took me to the station, and as the train came in he handed me a checkbook. "Don't ever borrow money," he said. "If you need money, write a check on me." That was the way it was with him and his brothers: each one took care of the others. I often needed money in the next few years but I never wrote that check. My uncles Joe and Homer were as good friends as I ever had, but I was finished with living off my uncles.

My schooling, by Mississippi standards, was quite good. Schools then were entirely autonomous; whether they were good or bad depended on the quality of the teachers the community could attract. Fortunately, the Philadelphia high school in my time was one of the best in the state. The principal was a man named Orvis Van Cleave, a graduate of Columbia, and he had assembled an excellent faculty, most of them college graduates. Thus, in high school I was able to study Latin, German, physics, and other courses that might not have been available elsewhere. My father always encouraged me to take the hardest courses they offered. Latin was a must.

I was always a good student. I had a quick and retentive mind and I was a hard worker. I enjoyed school, particularly English composition, in which I made my best grades, but I must admit that I was driven less by a pure quest for knowledge than by a desire to please and be praised by my teachers, my family, and our friends. I could never forget how my mother was counting on me. My success would compensate for my father's failures. I was her pride and joy, her hope of security in years to come.

My obligation seemed even greater after an eye disease struck my older sister, Bessie, when she was twelve, leaving her nearly blind. She had to go to the state institute for the blind, in Jackson, to continue her schooling. She was, like our mother, a brave and religious person, who never complained or showed self-pity. Eventually her eyesight improved and she married and bore two children.

I had to drop out of school and work one semester when my father was ill and make up the lost courses by taking a double load the next year. And in my senior year my Uncle Homer was drafted into the army and I was "drafted" to do the bookkeeping at his grocery store, but I managed to juggle that job and my schoolwork too. I was helped by the fact that I was never an athlete, so if I wasn't working I could spend my time studying.

There were, of course, many hours in my childhood when I was neither working nor studying—hours I spent enjoying the wonderful variety of people in that little town. As a storyteller, which I've been accused of being, I got a lot of mileage out of Philadelphia. There were an abundance of colorful characters and memorable events there, or so it seemed to a boy who had never known any other world.

Because of my father, I grew up interested in politics and I liked to spend my spare time at the courthouse watching trials; before I was bitten by the newspaper bug, I thought I would become a lawyer. Sometimes at the courthouse I would encounter a boy of about my age named Jim Eastland, the future Senator, who would be with his father, Woods Eastland, the district attorney for our area. Besides the trials, I remember vividly the scene twice each year, at the opening of the court terms, when the traveling horse traders came to town with long strings of horses to trade and sell. We called the traders "gypsies" because they camped on the outskirts of town, and everyone was suspicious of them. The horse trading often led to angry words and fights. Yet almost everyone was lured on by the hope of a bargain. Mississippi's greatest storyteller, William Faulkner, captured the flavor of these events perfectly in one of his most famous stories, "Spotted Horses."

One of the great heroes of my youth was a man named Adam Byrd, a successful lawyer who later became a Chancery Court Judge and after that a Congressman. Byrd lived for a while in our boardinghouse and I first came to admire him one day when my father was about to give me a licking for something and Byrd talked him out of it—in fact, he simply ordered him not to whip me.

He was a large, fine-looking man with a reddish complexion and high cheekbones that bespoke his Indian blood—his mother was one-fourth Indian. Philadelphia was in the heart of the old Choctaw nation. Most of the Choctaws had gone to Oklahoma under the terms of the Dancing Rabbit Treaty, but some had stayed behind and others returned and Byrd was their champion. Quite a few white families in that area had Indian blood and they made no attempt to hide the fact. They hoped (vainly, it turned out) that the federal government would repay the Choctaws for the lands taken from them by the Dancing Rabbit Treaty.

I loved to watch Adam Byrd defend his Indian friends in court. He seemed to me the most exciting man in our community; when I was ten or twelve he was my idol of greatness. When I prayed—as I did every night and at least twice Sundays—the visage of God I saw in my mind's eye was not the white-robed, bearded Deity of the Sunday-school books, but the ruddy Choctaw face of Adam Byrd.

My friend Byrd impressed me a great deal more than the first President of the United States I ever saw. That was in 1908 when my father took me to Jackson to see President William Howard Taft, who was visiting the state fair. My father was invited because he was mayor of Philadelphia. On the train ride to Jackson, people kept telling me, "Young man, you're going to see the President." Finally I asked my father what a President was. Knowing I enjoyed fairy tales, my father told me that a President was the same as a king.

I couldn't sleep that night thinking I would see a king the next day. The next morning my father took us up on the top floor of the tallest building in Jackson, an insurance-company building that was three stories high. From that vast height we watched out a window as the parade started up Capitol Street. I was looking anxiously for the king—a man with a gold-and-diamond crown on his head and a scarlet, fleece-lined robe.

I didn't see him, although there was a fine parade in progress, with marching soldiers and a band and horse-drawn carriages, as automobiles could not be trusted in parades at that time. But where was the king? I kept asking my father until finally he pointed and said, "There he is—that big fat man." I saw the man he meant—for President Taft was very fat—in an open carriage waving to everyone. And I was crestfallen. According to my father, I said disgustedly, "Ah, shucks, he's just a man," and crawled down out of the window.

Years later, in Washington, I told that story to President Taft's son, Senator Robert Taft, and he often asked me to repeat to his friends—"Ah, shucks, he's just a man."

Sometimes I think that encounter when I learned the President was just a man may have left a mark on me, for throughout my newspaper career I was never much awed by great political figures. I tried to treat them with respect, as I did everyone, but I kept in mind that they were just men like me, and I think that attitude helped me along as a Washington correspondent. After all, I had known Adam Byrd.

My Grandfather Turner was an extraordinarily silent man. He could go days hardly uttering a word. On many Sunday afternoons my sister and I were made to share in his meditation. We would sit with him as he rocked in his rocking chair, chewing tobacco but rarely speaking. I hated those silent Sunday afternoons, but looking back I guess the discipline did me no harm.

There were many stories about my grandfather's odd ways—I think today we would call him alienated. When one of his daughters was being married at his home he refused to join the ceremony; he just sat on the porch until it was over. At church he used to terrify visiting preachers by sitting in a corner pew and staring them down. What he was thinking as he sat so silently, we never knew. He never told us.

We older grandchildren were often terrified of him; our parents used to warn that if we weren't good they'd send us to have a talk with Grandpa. Yet I have some happy memories of him too. He used to love to go to the Confederate reunions that would be held in the summers throughout our region of Mississippi, and one summer he took me along as a companion and errand boy. I loved hearing the old-timers describe their exploits in battle, although I sensed that many of the tales were imaginary. My grandfather never told a single story, although he would grin with delight whenever an eye-witness would explode someone's tall tale. It was wonderful listening to those old men, especially when someone would break out a jug of liquor and they would laugh and sing as they recalled the distant battles of their youths.

My grandfather never took a swig with the others. That was another of his peculiarities. He only drank on one day of the year, Christmas. Then he would allow one of his daughters to mix him some eggnog. He would give a nip of it to his sons-in-law, but never to his own sons. Apparently he was willing to corrupt other men's sons but not his own.

One character in my home town was our lone Republican, whom I'll call Mr. Eustace Eubank. Mr. Eubank was an odd individual in many ways. For one thing, he always attended strictly to his own business, which quickly set him apart in our community. But the oddest thing about this old man was his being a Republican. He never admitted being a Republican, but every four years one Republican vote would turn up in the local ballot box and we never doubted who had cast it. And in those days, in Philadelphia, Mississippi, a Republican was as much an oddity as a Communist would be today.

He had other peculiarities. He read books, quoted Shakespeare, and discussed poetry with Brother Arnett, the Presbyterian preacher,

and politics with my father. My father respected Mr. Eubank's learning but had some reservations about him because he took a nip now
and then.

Mr. Eubank lived over west of the railroad tracks in a little un-
painted house with his second wife and three daughters. One of his
daughters was in school with me. She was very smart and I'm certain she won most of the literary contests we had at school. But she
never got the prize, because the teachers didn't think it would be
right to give prizes to a Republican's daughter. Eubank's only work
was his gardening, and he grew the biggest tomatoes in Philadelphia.
They would slice out as big as saucers. My Uncle Homer used to sell
those tomatoes in his grocery store, but he never told customers
who'd grown them, as he figured no one would want to eat a Republican tomato. Eubank walked with a limp which, the town legend said,
was because he had a wooden leg. The story went that Eubank had
been a Union soldier at the battle of Shiloh and had his leg shot off.
His fellow Yankees—as we told the story—had run off and left him,
but he had been so fortunate as to survive and make his way to our
compassionate little community. And yet he'd repaid us by casting
that lone Republican vote every four years!

Such was the situation one hot summer, when Eustace Eubank's
saga came to a close. That summer my uncles Homer and Joe had
bought a Ford car and converted it into a truck. They'd taught me to
drive and I was having a wonderful time delivering groceries in it.
One hot July day, about noon, I was out in front of the grocery,
polishing the Ford, when a Negro boy who worked for us said that
my Uncle Joe wanted to see me. I went inside the store and found
a gathering of the local power structure: the town marshal, the
county sheriff, the owner of the furniture store, a livery-stable keeper,
our leading physician, and my Uncle Joe.

I took one look at this assembly and decided they were going to
arrest me for speeding. The marshal, Lon Welsh, had been after me
several times about exceeding the ten-mile-an-hour speed limit
around the courthouse square. So I was ready for the worst when my
Uncle Joe put his hand on my shoulder and said, "Turner, Mr.
Eubank was found dead in his bed this morning, and I want you to
take the truck, go over to his house, get the remains and take them
out to the cemetery."

Suddenly the reason for this assembly became clear. The town
elders wanted to ensure that our lone Republican was properly laid
to rest; they wanted it done promptly, for it was a ghastly hot day.
I felt proud to be part of this ceremony, which combined civic,

political, and religious significance. A younger boy, Clifford Sanford, was to assist me, and two Negroes from his father's livery stable would dig the grave, but I was in charge. Clifford and I jumped into the Ford, went by Mr. Spivey's furniture store for a coffin, and then I drove us out to the Eubank house. His family led me into a little front room, where a body was lying on a bed under a heavy quilt. I lifted the quilt and there he was, our lone Republican, stiff and cold. I had been born and bred a Democrat, and I couldn't suppress a moment of triumph at the sight.

Our first problem was that Mr. Eubank's body was longer than our coffin, but finally we were able to bend his legs enough to get the lid screwed down. But when we got the coffin out to the Ford truck, I faced another problem. The Eubank family would be coming to the cemetery in a wagon drawn by little mules. Should I drive the Ford slowly, so the mules could keep up in a funeral procession, or should I hurry on to the cemetery and let the family follow as best it could? It was Philadelphia's first motorized funeral, so I had no precedent to follow.

I decided to respect tradition and have a funeral procession. So I drove very slowly, and soon the Ford began heating up. I had to stop every five or ten minutes and run into someone's house for water. Then the fanbelt broke. Meanwhile, I was wondering what sort of religious ceremony would be held. Mr. Eubank had never been seen in church, and we assumed that, being a Republican, he was bound to be an atheist too. So, as our little funeral procession approached the graveyard, I wondered if Mr. Eubank would be laid to rest in the respectable part of the graveyard or across a little gravel road in the Potter's Field. I was pleased to find the mourners waiting around a newly-dug grave in the respectable part of the cemetery, although only three feet from the gravel road.

Standing at the head of the grave was Brother Arnett, the Presbyterian preacher who'd liked to talk about poetry with Mr. Eubank. Brother Arnett led us in a hymn, and read from the Psalms, and then read Tennyson's "Crossing the Bar." Then we lowered the coffin into the grave and everyone present helped shovel dirt onto the coffin. It was a sort of community project. Finally there was the question of a headmarker for the grave. No one seemed very worried about it, now that Mr. Eubank was underground, so I made a marker out of a couple pieces of wood that were in the back of the truck and wrote his name and dates on it, and stuck it in the dirt at the head of the grave.

Then I drove the Ford back to the grocery store, where a lot of people came around to congratulate me on a job well done. A great sense of relief came over the entire community. The Lord had taken away our Republican, and we were pure again.

Thus things stood until November of that year, when the balloting was held in the Presidential election. The balloting was held under a chinaberry tree in the courthouse yard. Not many voters turned out for the general elections, because all the important decisions were made in the Democratic primaries. But the election that fall was important to the Catledge family because my father was earning a dollar and a half as one of the election judges.

I was standing in front of my uncles' grocery, eating some of their cheese and crackers, when I noticed a commotion in the courthouse yard. In those days, when you heard shouting at the courthouse on election day, you waited for the shooting to begin. I was worried about my father's safety. Then, suddenly, I saw the chancery clerk break out of the crowd, race across the courthouse yard, jump over the fence, and come running into my uncles' store, waving his arms and shouting.

"My God, my God," he cried, "that Republican vote has showed up again!"

We had buried the wrong man. Forever after, the community had to live with guilt and shame. The Republican, whoever he was, was not our departed friend Eustace Eubank. He was still in our midst, and we would never know who he was, and everyone was suspected.

There was never any doubt in my mind that I would go to college. I had done well in high school, and I had set my sights on being a professional man, a doctor or a lawyer. My father wanted me to be a lawyer, and I'm sure my mother wanted me to be a Presbyterian preacher. But there was the question of money. The state's finest university, Ole Miss, at Oxford, was too expensive for me. My Uncle Joe would have readily loaned me the money but I didn't want to be that much in debt to anyone. So I chose Mississippi A & M, now known as Mississippi State University, which was located sixty miles from Philadelphia on a beautiful two-thousand-acre campus near Starkville.

At A & M rooms were free and I could earn my meals by working in the dining hall. It was a military school and I would not have to worry about buying clothes because everyone wore a uniform, supplied from World War I surpluses. I arrived on campus in September, 1918, and went right to work in the mess hall. My job was to serve the food to two tables of twelve boys each; I did this three times a day, seven days a week, for two years. By then I had learned touch-system typing and was able to trade the mess-hall job for one as secretary to one of the deans.

I was just getting settled in my dormitory, an old building known as Polecat Alley (because skunks sometimes occupied its basement), when the great influenza epidemic of 1918 struck the campus. I was among the first to catch the flu and luckily I got over it quickly. But the epidemic spread fast among the three or four thousand students and soon some were dying.

One day an army sergeant rounded up several of us freshmen for emergency duty in the school hospital. We knew boys had been dying there, for we had seen the coffins coming out. The sergeant took us to a big first-floor ward. A nurse was trying to hold down a delirious patient on a bed near the door. "Hold that man," the sergeant ordered me and Peter Minyard, who became my close friend. "He won't last long." The man was a regular soldier, perhaps twenty years old, and even sick and delirious he was strong as a bull. We held him for about an hour until his struggles began to weaken and he died.

Peter and I were quickly assigned to another patient. There was only one doctor in the place; a local veterinarian was helping him. I saw three men die that day. They wouldn't let Peter and me leave. We had gained too much needed experience. After three days I was assigned to be assistant to the undertaker. By then I wanted out of there, so I faked a faint. I didn't know how people fainted so I fell to the floor and kicked my feet. The undertaker reluctantly released me.

Fifty-two people in the college died in that epidemic and by then I was ready to end my college career before it got started. But there was no way to leave; a military school during wartime was like a prison; we couldn't even use a telephone, much less go off the campus. So I went back to waiting tables. There was little academic work that fall, because of the epidemic, the war, and finally the Armistice on November 11. Another unpleasant factor was the hazing that was common in military schools then. The upperclassmen beat us with big saber belts. I hated that—but I did my share of the whipping the next year.

Hundreds of students didn't return to A & M after that awful fall semester, and I was almost one of them. But I knew my parents would be heartbroken if I quit, and I knew it would be wrong for me in the long run, so I went back.

A & M was a land-grant college—a "people's college"—with stress on agricultural and engineering courses. It had four schools: agriculture, science, business, and engineering. While I was there, however, a professor began an "academic course," stressing literature, history, government, and languages, and I took all of those courses I could, although technically I was a business major. Eventually I graduated with honors and an average above 85; much of the credit for my record goes to the instruction I had received in the Philadelphia school.

Being able to type got me a job as secretary to Fitzjohn Wadell, the head of the academic department. He then helped get me a job as assistant to the school's agricultural editor, who sent bulletins on agricultural topics to the state's farmers. I helped write, edit, and distribute these bulletins. It was valuable experience for me and, even more important, in my senior year my classmates elected me editor of the college yearbook.

I think that one reason for my election was that the editorship was a moneymaking post and they knew I needed the money. The editor and business manager got to keep whatever profits they might make from the yearbook, so my senior year was a financial success. I had entered college with $90 loaned to me by my Uncle Joe; I graduated in 1922 with $300.

I was a campus politician from my first day at A & M. The mess-hall job was no fun, but it did help me get to know a lot of people. By the time I became an upperclassman, if a student wanted to be elected to anything at A & M, he was wise to have a talk with four young men: Turner Catledge; Jimmy Ewing, who later became president of a junior college in Mississippi; John Stennis, the future Senator; and Stennis Little, John's cousin, who was captain of the football team.

I was not surprised when John Stennis entered politics and became a Senator. He was an outstanding student, a persuasive speaker, and a born politician even at age seventeen. It happened that John had the best wardrobe of civilian clothes on the campus. Many of us, when we had dates with girls in nearby towns, would borrow John's clothes, and this generosity didn't hurt his popularity.

When I graduated from college I was not prepared for any particular line of work, and there were no corporate recruiters clamoring to hire me. I thought I wanted to go on for further education, preferably in law. The most important thing I had learned in college was simply that, even away from the Turner clan, I could get along with people and usually get them to like me and listen to me.

But there remained the matter of making a living. My uncles assumed I would follow them into business, and they arranged a job for me with a large wholesale hardware firm in Memphis. This was agreeable with me, for I had it in mind to take the job and study law at night. But a depression struck the South that year and one of its casualties was my job in Memphis. After a brief and unsuccessful fling as a door-to-door salesman of aluminum pots and pans in Middle Tennessee, I was back in Philadelphia working for my uncles and wondering if I would spend the rest of my life there. That was what my mother was counting on. My father had by then retired from his railroad job because of his health, and was bedridden most of the time. I was restless and uncertain; I wanted to get out of Philadelphia but I didn't know how to break away. It was then that Clayton Rand, the publisher of our little county paper, the *Neshoba Democrat*, offered me the job that started me on my career as a newspaperman.

I I

Apprentice

CLAYTON Rand was one of the most remarkable men I ever knew. He came from the little town of Bond, Mississippi, and was the son of a sawmill worker. He preceded me at Mississippi A & M, where he worked his way through school selling peanuts. Rand is still active today as a publisher and columnist, and in a column published in the New Orleans *Times-Picayune* in December of 1969 he explained that when he arrived at A & M "the only job available was milking cows at eight cents an hour. Having some experience, I didn't want to milk my way through, so I got the more profitable peanut concession and was a peanut vendor for four years. I made more money the last year than the president of the college and there was no income tax."

Rand was a gifted orator. While at A & M he won the state oratorical contest, and in his senior year he wrote to Harvard requesting a fellowship in public speaking. The story was that he told the Harvard officials they were probably lacking in Southern orators and he was just the man to fill the gap. He got the fellowship, hoboed to Cambridge, and graduated from both Harvard College and Harvard Law School in three years. He then returned to practice law in Jackson, and soon became involved in a land-development project that brought him to Philadelphia in about 1918.

Perhaps it was inevitable that Rand, with his salesmanship, his civic-mindedness, and his love of public affairs, would be drawn to the newspaper business. After arriving in Philadelphia he wrote a few articles for our little weekly, the *Neshoba Democrat,* and when its owner decided to sell out, Rand had just made some money in a land deal, and he bought the paper. As I recall, he bought the *Democrat* for about $3,000 and sold it five years later for $20,000, which was typical of Rand's skill as a businessman.

Rand and I met and he took a liking to me. I was attending his old college, and I acted in some amateur play he directed. Also, I had had a little experience with the *Democrat* before Rand bought it. Its former owner, Lamar Ray, knew he wasn't much of a writer, and he sometimes called me in to write articles because he knew I had excelled in composition in high school. I had also tried my hand at setting type. I loved the newspaper business from the first. All of it—not just the writing. I loved the way the printing shop smelled, and the excitement of getting the paper out, and also the thrill of writing things that all my friends would read. Still, I never worked regularly for Lamar Ray; I would go to his office for excitement, but I would return to my uncles' stores to earn my spending money.

The summer before my junior year in college I was working in Uncle Sam's Ford agency and Rand asked me to write some "locals" for him—births, marriages, visitors to town, and the like. I set up a system of calling the town's four or five doctors each week to get the names of new babies. In fact, I got the doctors to calling me, for they liked the publicity.

The next summer I worked for Rand full time. He wanted me to travel about the country soliciting subscriptions, which I did, but I also began gathering news from the people I met. Before the summer ended I was being invited everywhere to eat and gossip. I would go out early in the week, in Rand's Model T, and come back Friday, our press day, loaded with tidbits of news and farm produce.

On Fridays I helped get out the paper. I was learning to set type and run a job press, and in time I learned to operate Rand's ancient printing press—a Campbell or "humpback" press, we called it, because of its shape. There was no electricity in Philadelphia then, so the old humpback press was powered by a gasoline engine. The press didn't have a brake on it, so if I put the paper in crooked I'd have to throw the belt and grab the flywheel to try to stop the press before the paper got jammed around the ink rollers. I wasn't very big then and in time there came to be a kind of shiny spot on the wall where I'd been tossed against it by that flywheel.

I'd feed papers through the old press at a rate of about five hundred an hour, then turn them over and put the other side through. I once tried to calculate how long it would take to print our Sunday *New York Times,* with its several hundred pages and circulation of over a million, on the old humpback press. My estimate was about one hundred and sixty-five years.

The *Democrat's* circulation was about twelve hundred. After we ran off the papers, I hauled them to the post office in a pushcart. Occasionally we'd send a copy to everyone who had a post office or rural letter box, then bill them later, hoping they'd pay. It was amazing how often they would pay up and continue to take the paper.

I didn't earn much money that summer. As I recall, Rand gave me $50 when I returned to college. But I gained experience both in reporting and production that I would use the rest of my life. Lessons I learned from Jim Yates, Rand's printer, and other printers I knew later in Tunica and Tupelo, were still important to me twenty-five years later when I became responsible for the production of the *New York Times.* The *Times* printing plant was a thousand times bigger and more complicated than the ones I learned on, but I found that printers still spoke the same language and still respected a white-collar man who could speak it with them.

In the summer of 1922 Rand offered me a full-time job. He was expanding. He had bought the weekly in nearby Kemper County, and now he was buying the weekly in Tunica, just south of Memphis, and he wanted me to go run it for him. He said he could pay me only $12.50 a week, but if the paper did well he'd give me more. I doubted that I could live on $12.50 a week; I told him I'd talk to my family about his offer.

I didn't know what to do. The issue wasn't money but what I was to do with my life. I knew that I wanted to get out of Philadelphia and that I loved the newspaper business. I was beginning to fear that I'd spend the rest of my life in the hardware or grocery business. Yet it was very hard to imagine leaving my mother and the security of my family. Also, my father's health was failing rapidly.

I went to see my uncles Homer and Joe, only to learn that Rand had already talked to them—he knew how the Turner family operated. Before we had talked very long, one of my uncles said, "Take the job whatever it pays you. There are too many Turners in this town and you ought to get away."

As much as I thought I wanted to get out of Philadelphia, I was crushed. I felt as if I were being ejected from my family. Yet that was the best advice they could have given. They assured me that they'd provide for my mother and would even help me out if necessary. I talked to my mother that night. She hated to see me go, but she did not question her brothers' judgment.

She talked to my father, who was sick in bed, and he quickly agreed that I should strike out on my own. I felt he wanted to get me out from the domination of my mother. So I accepted Rand's offer.

Tunica was the county seat of Tunica County, which was then a community of about 25,000, perhaps 23,000 of whom were black. The depression had hit many of Tunica County's cotton plantations hard that year. This made life even more difficult for the Negroes who lived and worked on the plantations, and many of them were heading north in search of better opportunities. This upset the local whites for two reasons. First, cheap and abundant Negro labor was the basis of the local economy. Second, the planters had a paternalistic attitude, and they simply didn't want "their" Negroes to leave home.

The town fathers had hired themselves a full-time Chamber of Commerce man, hoping he could bring some stability to the community. He stabilized his own situation by marrying a rich widow; his next move was to bring Rand to town. Rand had made a name for himself in Neshoba and Kemper counties as a newspaper wizard and a real civic tub thumper, and the Chamber of Commerce fellow figured Tunica's tub was in desperate need of thumping. So he arranged for Rand to speak at a Chamber dinner.

At the dinner Rand made his usual tremendous impression. Before the first evening was over, Rand had agreed to buy the Tunica *Times* and make it into the greatest little paper in the land, and the leading citizens of Tunica had promised him $1,000 worth of new subscriptions. Implicit in the deal was an understanding that the new, revitalized Tunica *Times* would encourage Negroes to stay at home.

The Tunica *Times* had nowhere to go but up. Its owner was a fellow named Billy Barlow, who stood about four feet ten and lived in the newspaper office with fifteen or twenty cats. His family had owned the *Times* for many years, and by the time Rand arrived he had the circulation down to less than a hundred copies a week. To get Little Billy out of the way, the town fathers made a deal with their Congressman whereby he was appointed the local postmaster. Eventually he got the post-office money mixed up with his own and wound up in jail. In later years, I'd sometimes see Little Billy in Memphis, where, having settled his debt to society, he ran a sidewalk newsstand, and we'd talk about the good old days in Tunica.

Rand had pledged to get the *Times'* circulation up to a thousand, so I had my work cut out for me. First, we had to find a new printing plant. He bought one for a thousand dollars from a printer in Meridian who was leaving the state because his political hero, Senator James K. Vardaman, had been defeated in a recent election.

I was assigned to get our new printing plant to Tunica. It was a beautiful batch of machinery. The brass rules shone like gold, the type and "furniture" were immaculately clean; the two job presses ran like clockwork. It took me two weeks to get it all packed and into a railroad car, and it took another two weeks for the boxcar to travel the two hundred miles to Tunica. I'll never forget my shock when I opened that boxcar on its arrival. There had been some kind of a train wreck and our beautiful new machinery was scattered all over the floor of a Yazoo and Mississippi Valley Railway boxcar. I wanted to cry, but instead I got busy cleaning up the mess.

Rand had rented a building that formerly housed a bakery for our printing shop and offices. One of my first moves was to hire some local girls to unscramble our type. I planned to teach them to set type, although I was not an expert typesetter. Fortunately, a tramp printer happened through town about then—actually, he was a combination printer-preacher, but I didn't need his spiritual services—and he showed the girls how to set type. He tried to show them some other things, too, until his young wife intervened.

Rand had bought a linotype machine and hired a man named Ernest Sheffield to operate it. Ernest was a light-hearted fellow who liked to drink and shoot dice, and often on Saturday nights he'd get drunk and lose his week's pay in a crap game an hour after he'd drawn it. He was a wonderful, droll fellow, and we had many good times together. Rand hired a printer as well, Harry Wood, who had worked in the shop in Starkville that printed our college newspaper. Harry was quite erudite and took tremendous pride in this. I learned a great deal from him.

Rand had also bought an old Babcock cylinder printing press and at last we went to work on our first edition of the Tunica Times. It was to be printed on a Wednesday, but there were innumerable breakdowns. I then learned an enduring lesson about new equipment in a printing plant: nothing ever works as planned. Finally we got out a respectable-looking paper, and there followed thirteen months of invaluable experience for me.

I was in a state of euphoria to be running my own newspaper. Rand stayed over a few days to instruct me in selling, advertising, and bookkeeping; then I was on my own.

In those early months we had wonderful cooperation from the local people. There were two power centers in Tunica, the merchants in town and the planters on their outlying plantations. At the start, both were behind us. The merchants gave us advertising and the planters bought hundreds of subscriptions, both for themselves and for their Negro tenants.

In return, we shamelessly propagandized the Negro about the joys of Tunica. We introduced a "colored column" written by a crippled Negro who ran a pressing shop. One startling innovation of this column was the use of "Mr." and "Mrs." in referring to Negroes. Some whites were up in arms at this until we explained it was part of our pacification program. The "Mr." and "Mrs." for Negroes, incidentally, was strictly confined to the colored column.

One day soon after I arrived the county attorney dropped in to inform me that I was to be the county coroner and ranger. The two jobs had been consolidated by state law and were generally held by the local newspaper editor. The ranger's main duty was to locate the owners of stray horses, cattle, and other animals. The idea was that the newspaper editor could run a notice when an animal was found, and when the owner turned up the editor could collect the fee for printing the notice, the expenses of whoever had found the stock, and his rangers fee of $2 a head. As coroner I was to conduct an inquest into any sudden, suspicious, or violent death in the county. My predecessor, Billy Barlow, had surrendered the coroner-ranger post because he had no stomach for corpses. I didn't either but each inquest involved a $5 fee and a man on a $12.50 salary couldn't turn down an opportunity like that.

I hadn't been in Tunica long before I realized that a bitter division was developing among the community leaders and that our paper was caught squarely in the middle. Rand had conducted little research before buying the *Times*—his principal research was the Chamber of Commerce's joyous reception to his speech. And he declined to move to Tunica, preferring to pop in and out from time to time as an honored guest. So he was not aware, as I soon came to be, of the heated disagreement between certain numbers of the town's two great economic groups, the merchants and the planters, on the Negro issue. The matter came to a head when the Ku Klux Klan began trying to organize in Tunica.

It was inevitable that there would be strong racial feelings among whites in a county that was 90 percent black. A form of segregation existed in the downtown streets of Tunica, for example, that I have never seen elsewhere: two sets of sidewalks, one for each race, with the whites' a few inches higher than the other.

There were at least two reasons for the conflict between the planters and the merchants. One was purely economic—the two groups were competing for the Negroes' dollars. The planters had for years operated "plantation stores" to "furnish" food, clothing, and supplies to the blacks on their plantations, and the merchants of course wanted the blacks to come to town to buy their merchandise.

The other reason had more to do with emotion and tradition. The planters represented largely what was left of Southern aristocrats who for generations had felt a traditional paternalism toward "their" Negroes. They believed they understood the Negro and could work things out with him. They felt nothing but contempt for the poor whites in the Klan, and emphatically did not want the Klan coming in and driving their work force off to Detroit or Chicago. The merchants, on the other hand, had less personal feeling for the Negro, and were often ripe for the Klan's racist, white-supremacy appeals.

Such was the state of Tunica after I'd been there a few months: we were trying to encourage Negroes to stay, the Klan was trying to organize, some of the leading merchants were supporting the Klan, the planters were fighting it—and at that point Rand jumped in the middle of the melee by writing a series of fiery anti-Klan articles.

There had been some murders by Klansmen in Louisiana and Rand, moved both by a hatred of the Klan and a love of the sensational, hurried over to investigate. He was as vigorous a writer as he was a speaker, and he sent back some reports that were guaranteed to curl the readers' hair. He ordered his series printed in all three of his papers, over a period of several weeks, and I did as he said, fully expecting a violent reaction from our readers.

After the first article appeared, some of our advertising merchants began stopping me on the street to say they didn't much care for Rand's slant on the Klan.

After the second article, they scheduled a Klan rally in the high-school auditorium and imported a Klan notable to speak. I attended the rally and was shocked to see some of our leading advertisers there. The speaker spent most of the evening denouncing Rand and his newspapers, and if dirty looks could kill they'd have carried me out of there feet first.

There was even dissension within our little staff. Our printer, Harry Wood, became cool toward me and highly critical of Rand. At least I had a supporter in Ernest Sheffield, the hard-drinking linotype operator. His brother had recently run for sheriff in Calhoun County and been beaten by Klan opposition, so Ernest was happy to see them under fire.

Rand eventually came to Tunica to confer with me. Our money was low, our advertising drying up, and our job printing had disappeared. He wouldn't accept my explanation that his anti-Klan articles had caused our troubles. He demanded more vigorous salesmanship from me. He told me to confront the merchants and remind them that they had promised to support us and were behind in redeeming their commitments with linage. We were in heated debate when four leading businessmen appeared and asked Rand to step outside, I went with him. It was, I recall, a balmy fall night with a full moon, but the merchants were not mellowed by the setting. They came to the point. They didn't like what Rand had written about the Klan. Rand was just as blunt. He demanded to know what had happened to the advertising they had promised him. He asked if they were honorable men. If so, why didn't they keep their promise? He didn't bother to suggest that the advertising might help their business; everyone understood it was a subsidy.

The merchants said he had an obligation too, an obligation to please them—in particular, to lay off the Klan. Rand began a great flight of oratory. He said that before he'd be intimidated he'd see that "beautiful little gem" (he pointed to our office) go up in smoke. His life's blood was in that paper, he declared, and he would not let it be defiled by their threats. "Get that through your heads," he shouted. "I've got plenty of money to see me through if you won't support me, but I'll publicize the fact that you've broken your promises. If you want to be held up to scorn before this community, it's up to you!"

To underscore his point he raised his leg and broke wind with a resounding blast. Then he turned on his heel and majestically marched away.

It was a noble gesture ignobly executed but I was not amused. I knew Rand would be gone the next day but I would still have to live with these people. That was what happened. Rand was seen in Tunica less and less. But he saw that his great plans for the Tunica *Times* had gone awry and he began to strip down our printing plant. He had me ship our linotype to Philadelphia for the *Neshoba Democrat* to use. Our local advertising and our job printing were about gone. All we had left was a bit of national advertising, for patent medicines and stock feed. I was barely making our payroll. I had raised myself from $12.50 to $17.50 a week but I couldn't afford to pay me. The planters were still behind us, and they controlled the county courthouse. They increased the fee we received for printing the proceedings of the Board of Supervisors, but that just wasn't enough. We couldn't survive without advertising and it was controlled by the merchants.

One night I had a few drinks of some kind of awful brew with Harry Wood, our pro-Klan printer, and he confided that he expected new ownership of the *Times* before very long. The good people of Tunica were disenchanted with Rand, he said, and someone was going to "take over" the *Times* before long. I suddenly remembered that often recently certain townspeople had been dropping by our office to talk to Harry. It was clear he knew more than I did.

I called Rand the next morning. Not trusting the local switch-board operators, I took a train to Memphis and called from there. Rand told me to sit tight and see what happened. A few nights later, Harry confided to me that a prospective buyer was coming to town soon. I called Rand, who didn't know he was a prospective seller, and he arrived on the scene two days later. He'd hardly been there an hour when the newspaper publisher from a nearby town came in and said he wanted to buy the *Times*.

I hoped Rand would sell. I wanted to get out of there. It wasn't that I feared for my safety, but it was nonetheless clear that my future was not bright in Tunica.

"Brother Rand," the other publisher said, "why don't you sell me this plant? I'm only thirty miles away and I can run two papers together. You're two hundred miles away. Be sensible."

"I'm not interested in selling this little gem." Rand declared. "I'm engaged in a great cause."

Rand made one of his long and flamboyant speeches. The other man pleaded with him to name his price—no doubt the merchants had promised him the sort of support they'd promised us a year before. But Rand maintained that he wouldn't sell at any price. As I recall, their negotiations ended with Rand getting $4,200 for a paper in which he had a remaining investment of less than $2,000 and which was losing money every day. A few months later the news-paper office burned to the ground.

So I was out of a job. I might have worked for one of Rand's other papers, but I didn't want to return to Philadelphia or go to nearby Kemper County. As it happened, another newspaper job was offered me. I knew a fellow whose father owned the biweekly paper in Tupelo. The father was having a lot of trouble keeping a staff, so his son suggested I come help run the paper. So I was off to Tupelo with visions of new worlds to conquer.

I rated a $22.50 salary in Tupelo, but I found I was in another bad situation. The owner of the paper was deep in debt, and his financial records were a mess: I moved eagerly to untangle his affairs, too eagerly, it developed. Among my mistakes was sending bills to some of his friends and creditors he didn't want to send bills to. After three months he fired me for overdiligence. But I didn't care. I was ready to try the big leagues of Southern journalism—Memphis.

III

Memphis

I ARRIVED in Memphis during a blizzard early one Monday morning in February of 1924, with $2.07 in my pocket. I had come to find a newspaper job but I lacked the courage to apply to the paper I most admired, the *Commercial Appeal*. Instead, I took a streetcar uptown to the Memphis *Press*, a Scripps-Howard paper, where I arrived about seven o'clock, shivering for want of an overcoat.

The *Press*'s big front door seemed too imposing for me to enter, but I saw a man going in a side door and asked him where the "printing office" was. Part of my fear was because I really didn't know what I wanted to do. In Tunica and Tupelo I'd been jack-of-all-trades—reporter, salesman, printer—and I had no idea how big papers were organized. Given a choice, I might have ended up in the printing plant, for I spoke the printer's language and loved getting a paper out.

But the man I hailed pointed me up a flight of stairs. At the top, a huge handsome man behind a rolltop desk asked what I wanted.

"A job," I declared.

A miracle then occurred. This man was the new managing editor, Walter Morrow. He had arrived scarcely an hour before and was anxious to assert his authority by hiring or firing someone. There I was, a golden opportunity, and he hired me at $20 a week for a two-week trial period; after that, he said, he'd either fire me or raise me to $25.

He introduced me to the city editor, who was busy clipping society notes, obituaries, and other local items out of the morning's *Commercial Appeal.* He handed me these clippings and told me to rewrite them. He said I didn't need to check the facts because the *Commercial Appeal* was a very reliable newspaper.

I finished the assignment quickly, aided by my touch typing, which was a rarity then and attracted the attention of the staff. Then our first edition came up. The morning's big story was the blizzard. We had one item about an icicle almost as big as a man's body. The city editor clipped our lead story, on the weather, and told me: "Get me an add on this story. Call up some coal companies, railroads, and truckers, and see what troubles they're having." He told me to use the phone in the editor's office since he was away that day.

An "add" in newsroom parlance is short for "addition"; that is, for more information, but I hadn't learned that in Tunica or Tupelo. Still, once someone showed me how to use the yellow pages of the phone book, I got busy on my big assignment.

I called several companies and I was doing fine until someone asked me the rate. I called to the city editor: "What's the rate here?"

"The what?" he asked.

"The rate," I repeated. "How much do you get per inch for an advertisement?"

"That has nothing to do with you," the city editor said.

"Yes, it does," I insisted. "I have a man on the phone who wants to know."

"What are you doing?" the editor asked.

"What you told me to," I said. "I'm getting some ads for this story."

I had confused "add" with "ad." But I was doing exactly what I would have done in Tunica. I would know the coal companies were having good business that morning and I'd try to share in their prosperity. And I'd been having considerable success. Until the man asked me the rate, I'd sold three or four ads, amounting to some $130. One was to the Missouri Pacific Railroad, which had never before advertised in the *Press.*

Some of the reporters started laughing but neither Morrow nor the city editor thought my mistake was funny. Finally they called the business office to take over my new ads, then the city editor quite kindly explained to me what he meant by an add. Fortunately, in soliciting the "ads," I'd picked up a good deal of information, so I was able then to provide the "add" they wanted.

I finished my first week on the *Press* without further incident, but on Sunday one of my uncles called and said my father was fast failing. I called the city editor, who promised to hold my job, then I caught a train to Philadelphia. My father was dead when I arrived. My mother accepted his death with her usual stoicism. Her brothers were a great comfort to her.

My Uncle Homer said to me: "Don't let this upset your plans. You go back to Memphis, and we'll take care of your mother."

I stayed in Philadelphia for a week, then I returned to Memphis for my second week on the *Press*.

I was assigned on Monday to help a hard-drinking older reporter cover a sensational murder trial. On Wednesday the reporter turned up drunk and the city editor told me to take over for him. I did a good job for the rest of the week but on Saturday I found that my pay was still $20. I reminded Morrow that he'd promised me a raise after two weeks. He said he'd meant two consecutive weeks—my father's death had intervened.

I thought that was a dirty trick but I couldn't argue. I needed the job, even at $20. My father was dead, taxes were due on our house, and I needed the money to send to my mother. My attitude toward my work was changing. As a boy, I hadn't known I was poor. In Tunica and Tupelo, newspapering had been sort of a frolic, a wonderful game. Now, however, I wanted security and the only visible road to security was success as a newspaperman.

But my success was not to come on the Memphis *Press*. After another three weeks, Morrow called me over. Once again, he felt a need to assert himself. Before he hired me, this time he fired me. "I think you'd do better at the *Commercial Appeal*," he told me.

He needn't have bothered. I was dying to work for the *Commercial Appeal*. Within minutes I was in its editorial offices, asking to see Mr. Mooney.

Mr. Mooney was Charles Patrick Joseph Mooney, the greatest Southern editor of his day, and people didn't just barge in on him. But I was young, ignorant, and desperate, so I marched into his office, where I encountered a short, stout man reading a newspaper through his thick glasses.

"What do you want?" he snapped.

I told Mooney my story at considerable length and with considerable heat. I told him how I'd been hired, refused a promised raise, and fired by the *Press*. I told him of my schooling, of my experience on small-town papers in Mississippi, of my ambition to be a newspaperman, and of my lifelong admiration for the *Commercial Appeal*.

"Those dirty sons of bitches," he said when I finished, with reference to my former employers at the *Press*. Then: "Young man, I'll tell you what you do. Go out the door and turn left. In the big room turn left again and over by the window you'll see a red-haired Jew. Tell him I said to put you to work."

I followed his directions and found myself face to face with a man with a mop of bright red hair. He asked what I wanted.

"Mr. Mooney said for you to put me to work."

"Mr. Mooney said what?"

"For you to put me to work."

"Exactly what did Mr. Mooney tell you?" the man asked.

"He told me to walk out his door and turn left, to go to the middle of the room and turn left again, and there by the window I'd see a red-headed Jew and to tell him he said to put me to work."

The redhead began to laugh. "Well, I guess that's enough," he said, and he put me to work.

The redhead was Sam Kahn, the city editor, and after I'd worked for him a few months, I never again saw a human transaction that didn't interest me. Sam had a great instinct for news, for what people are interested in, and he taught me that there are stories everywhere if a reporter has the imagination to see them. On slow days, Sam would send a reporter to check the local hotels, for Memphis was a crossroad city, and he knew there would often be newsworthy people there to be interviewed. He tested his reporters in that manner. On my second day with the paper he sent me down to the Gayaso Hotel and I discovered that a Mississippi Congressman I knew was there. I went up to his room unannounced, and he came to the door in the raw, and I glimpsed in the bed a young woman similarly attired. I couldn't convince him I'd just dropped by for an interview—he was sure I was spying on behalf of his enemies. He finally called Sam Kahn, who convinced him that all we wanted was some statesmanlike comments on world affairs—not his personal affairs. When I later arrived in Washington, working for the *New York Times*, this Congressman was still there, and I think he still feared me as a possible blackmailer. Eventually he became a federal judge.

C. P. J. Mooney was to be one of the great influences on my professional life. We became very close, and our association did not end until the day he lay down and died on a couch in his office at the *Commercial Appeal*, nearly three years after he had hired me. By then I was a confirmed newspaperman, and Mooney was my ideal of what a great newspaper editor should be.

Mooney had been a schoolteacher in Kentucky, and before that he had learned telegraphy in the railroad station at Bardstown Junction. He moved to Pine Bluff, Arkansas, as a railroad telegraph operator, and there he would receive the Saturday Associated Press wire reports for a local newspaper. He began spending his spare time at the paper and filling in for copyeditors who were out sick or drunk. Next he began writing editorials for the paper, and they captured statewide attention. This led him to a job with the Memphis *Avalanche,* where he became an outstanding editor and caught the eye of Frank Munsey. Munsey was an entrepreneur who made a fortune buying and selling newspapers, and closing down those he thought could not make money. He was hated by newspapermen. When he died, William Allen White wrote a column that said: "Frank Munsey, the great publisher, is dead. Frank Munsey contributed to the journalism of his day the great talent of a meat packer, the morals of a money changer and the manners of an undertaker. He and his kind have about succeeded in transforming a once noble profession into an eight per-cent security. May he rest in trust."

Mooney ran the editorial in the *Commercial Appeal* under the heading, "These Are Our Sentiments." He had worked for Munsey's New York *Sun* only a few months when they had a violent argument. Mooney's editorials on the Spanish-American War, however, had impressed William Randolph Hearst, and Hearst hired him as editor of the New York *Journal* and later sent him to Chicago as editor of the *Herald-Examiner.* It was from Chicago that Mooney accepted an offer to return to Memphis as editor of the newly-consolidated *Commercial Appeal.* The paper was owned by several prominent Memphis families, and as far as I know they left Mooney free to set editorial policy as he thought best. Boss Crump often said that the reason the *Commercial Appeal* fought him was that he favored publicly owned utilities and some of the owners of the *Commercial Appeal* had large interests in private utilities. But I believe Mooney loathed Crump purely on the issue of bossism, and the utilities had little if anything to do with it.

Mooney eventually was named president of the publishing company, but he never let his official title be anything but Managing Editor. He hated ostentation and had no desire for personal celebrity. When occasionally he would agree to address some civic group, the *Commercial Appeal* could never say more than "C. P. J. Mooney, Managing Editor of the *Commercial Appeal,* also spoke." He loathed organization men and groups like the Rotary and Kiwanis and he rarely appeared in public. He believed that the greatest contribution he could make to the community was to run a good and fearless newspaper. His salary was never more than $18,000, but he loved his work and the power he wielded.

He was a fine writer. He used short, vivid sentences, a style perhaps influenced by his years as a telegraph operator. His blistering editorial attacks on the Ku Klux Klan won him and the *Commercial Appeal* a Pulitzer Prize in 1923.

Mooney was a man of many peculiarities and contradictions. There was a combination of toughness and kindness about him. In that he reminded me of Edwin L. James, my predecessor as managing editor of the *Times*; both men put a tough outer crust over a warm and generous nature. Mooney was Irish and pugnacious. The forefinger of his right hand was missing and the office legend was that it had been chewed off in a fight during his youth. We sometimes called him "the gunner" because one night he shot at some rogue who burst into the office and attacked him. We all lived in fear of him, yet he could be a great jokester. In both his humor and anger he could be quite profane. He had an elderly and devoted secretary, Miss Emma Haskins, to whom he would dictate his editorials each evening. That kind lady never understood the reporters' laughter when he would call to her, "Come on, Miss Emma, let's knock off another little piece before you go."

He could be ruthless with political opponents but he was generous to his employees and stood by them when they were under fire. He was sentimental about the newspaper business and had a policy of always giving a few days' work to the itinerant newspapermen—"snowbirds," we called them—who often passed through Memphis on the way from Chicago to New Orleans. Mooney was a staunch prohibitionist, so much so that, although a Catholic, he favored the prohibitionist William Jennings Bryan over his fellow Catholic, Al Smith, for the Democratic nomination in 1924. He wrote an editorial during the deadlock convention in New York suggesting Bryan as the logical choice. Yet he remained tolerant of reporters with a drinking problem. Some of his older reporters claimed the only way they could get a raise in pay was to get drunk and be fired, then come back to Mooney and cry and plead for the job back.

He'd join them in a good cry and always rehire them and raise their pay.

Mooney saw whiskey at the root of most evil. He had little sympathy for the men who produced it, and he was extremely interested when a famous Tennessee distiller went on trial for murder in St.

Louis. It was charged that the distiller had been drinking during a train trip, became angry at a porter and shot at him, missed the porter but killed a conductor. The jury disagreed, however, and acquitted the distiller. Mooney was outraged at this decision, and wrote an editorial about it that concluded, "O tempora, O mores, O hell!"

I was bursting with pride at being hired by the *Commercial Appeal,* the paper my father and I had read and trusted as far back as I could remember. I liked to write letters on *Commercial Appeal* stationery to people back in Philadelphia. To thousands of people like us, throughout Tennessee, Mississippi, and Arkansas, the *Commercial Appeal* was not just a newspaper—Mooney had made it an institution. People in the tristate area felt possessive about it. When Mooney once assigned some rewrite men to transform the folksy style of our rural correspondents into a more short and snappy prose, the readers revolted. "You can't do this to our paper," they said, and Mooney agreed that it was their paper too, so the folksy style returned.

We were a controversial newspaper. We fought Crump and we fought the Klan. Therefore, we were always looking for stories that showed we had "heart," and that we were the friend of the common man. If an old lady in Senatobia, Mississippi, broke her leg, or a farmer in the flatlands of Arkansas found an unusually big snake, Sam Kahn would have someone call our stringer on the spot. We had over one hundred string correspondents. One of our most famous features was "Hambone," a Negro character in a cartoon series, who many years later would be discontinued in consideration of the feelings of Negro readers.

One Saturday night, after three weeks of delirious joy in my new job, I was told by Sam Kahn he would have to let me go. He explained that one of his star reporters had been off on a binge but he had finally returned under one of Mr. Mooney's dispensations and Sam was over his quota of reporters. He told me to come in the next Monday to see if anything turned up. I did, but nothing had. I was despondent. I had to have a job. I almost went to work writing fake testimonials for patent medicine at a local advertising agency, but I decided to hold out a few more days, and on Friday I got word that Sam was looking for me.

I raced to the office and he asked if I knew anything about layout. I'd handled some layout on the Mississippi papers so I said I knew all about layout. Kahn explained that the society editor was sick and he wanted me to get out the Sunday society page. I jimmied open the society editor's desk drawer and found a lot of pictures and captions. I didn't know any of the people, but one picture caught my eye. It was of an elderly couple posing with their daughter, a tall, voluptuous blonde. The caption said the old couple were celebrating their fiftieth wedding anniversary and that the blonde woman was their daughter and had given a party for them at her home on Front Street. The caption said the parents had come up from Mississippi, which naturally won them my affection. I was also impressed that the woman lived on Front Street, a row of fine old Southern mansions overlooking the river. In those days I rather romanticized the Southern way of life, so I sat down and wrote a flowery story about these beautiful people and their elegant party.

The picture and story appeared on Sunday and then the trouble started. Unbeknown to me, that stately blonde lady was one of Memphis' leading madams and the mansion on Front Street was the city's plushest whorehouse. It was true that she'd given a party and sent the pictures in, but the regular society editor hadn't had the slightest intention of printing them.

When I came in Monday morning I was told that Sam Kahn was looking for me, fit to be tied. When I appeared he dragged me into Mooney's office. The old man was doubled up with laughter. He looked at me and roared. "Serves 'em right," he said. "Goddamn 'em, it serves 'em right. That's the kind of society news I like to see in this paper." It was the first time he'd paid any attention to me since he hired me, and to my and Sam's amazement, he didn't fire me.

As might be expected, the picture of the madam attracted wide attention. I might have expected to become the butt of jokes because of my act of stupidity. Instead, I became a hero. People thought I'd run the picture as a practical joke, and they admired my audacity.

An incident a little later got me back in Sam Kahn's favor. One night Mooney was writing an editorial about the boll weevil—he was against it—and he came storming out of his office demanding to know the word for people who study bugs. He quizzed each reporter and, when they confessed they didn't know the word, made scathing remarks about their ignorance. (He wasn't bothered by his own ignorance; he was the editor.) I knew the word—at Mississippi A & M they trained those bug experts—but I was afraid to speak up. Mooney was about to call on Sam Kahn, who clearly didn't know what the word was, when I called out:

"Entomologist."

"Who said that?" Mooney demanded. Someone pointed to me. "Spell it," Mooney ordered and I did. A few minutes later he called me into his office to take down his editorial on the typewriter and he was impressed by my touch typing. That was the beginning of our friendship. He was mad at me a few times after that, but I never again thought my job on the *Commercial Appeal* was in danger.

Memphis was a wide-open, violent city in those days. Recently I saw a revival of *The Front Page*, the classic play by Ben Hecht and Charles McArthur about newspapering in Chicago in the 1920s, and it reminded me vividly of my own experiences in Memphis in the same era. We reporters were a wild bunch. We drank a lot and had a lot of fun and didn't worry much about the morality of things —that was for the editorial writers. Today's young reporters are better-educated and more serious than we were then. They are far more concerned with social issues, reflecting a nation that is now far more concerned with those issues. In the twenties, we reporters worried more about murders and fires than we did about slum housing and welfare policies.

Memphis was the murder capital of America, perhaps of the world. For the decade ending in 1910, the national average for cities was 7.2 homicides per 100,000 population. Memphis led the nation with a rate of 47.1—more than six times the national average. In 1916, Memphis had 134 homicides, giving it a rate of 89.9 per 100,000, more than double the rate in Atlanta, the next-ranking city.

All this was deplorable but it made a lot of news. Each year in December our paper would carry a front-page box showing the number of homicides that year as compared to the year before, much as papers in other cities carried charts on auto accidents or charitable donations. I was never entirely sure if civic pride demanded that the rate go up or down, but the chart was a much-talked-about feature.

By late one December we had a total of ninety-five homicides as compared with one hundred the year before, and it seemed as if the tide might be turning. Then on New Year's Eve a railroad trainman came home unexpectedly to find his wife entertaining her boy friend and some others. The railroadman got out his Winchester and killed six people, himself included, thereby knocking our box score all to pieces. I arrived with the police and there were bodies everywhere. When we thought we'd found them all, a policeman opened a closet door and two more fell out.

Another time I was at the police station with our police reporter when word came that the son of a leading Memphis family had been killed down in a tenderloin district. A tough old fuzzy police captain was on duty, and he asked our reporter if he'd call the boy's mother and break the news. "Now, you be gentle with that poor little lady," the captain urged. But when the reporter got the mother on the phone he couldn't bring himself to speak, so the old captain grabbed the receiver and blurted out: "Lady, some nigger wench just blowed your boy's head off!"

Mooney had been a Hearst editor, he had an eye for the sensational, and he demanded fiercely aggressive reporting. I pulled many stunts in those days for which I'd have been fired on most newspapers, and for which I hope to gain absolution by these confessions now. Among other things, I became known as an expert picture snatcher. Whenever there was a murder or other sensational story, Mooney and Kahn wanted pictures—of the victims, of the accused, of their families—and the best way to get the pictures was just to snatch them off the walls and tables and mantles and out of family albums at the scene of the action. In the confusion after a homicide you generally could get away with it.

I was a pre-emptive picture snatcher. If I got to the scene first I would grab every picture in sight, including the Christmas calendars off the walls, so nothing would be left for the other papers. Mooney never instructed me to snatch pictures, but when you got back with all those exclusive photographs you could see that.he was pleased.

One night in north Memphis a spurned suitor shot his girl friend and then himself in front of her whole family. When word of the shooting reached our office, Sam Kahn sent me, Dave Bloom, and Sam Bledsoe to the scene, and the last thing we heard as we rushed out the door was Kahn yelling, "Get pictures, get pictures!"

But, when we arrived, the police wouldn't let us in the house. A large crowd had gathered out front. We walked around to the back of the house. It was on a hill, with the back rooms on stilts six or eight feet off the ground. Dave Bloom was the smallest of us, so Sam and I hoisted him up on our shoulders and he crawled in an open window. He found several pictures on the piano and he tossed them out the window to us.

One was of a girl and another of a young man. We took the pictures around front and several women in the crowd readily identified the girl as the victim of the shooting. They weren't so sure if the young man was the spurned boy friend, but someone said she had seen the young man visiting at the house.

Intent on identification, I took the picture to the funeral home to compare it with the corpse. The funeral director, a fine old man named John Collins, told me the police had said not to let anyone see the body. But we reporters stood pretty well with the undertakers, because we always mentioned their names in homicide cases and obituaries. So Collins said, "You know, it could be that you didn't see me," and I sneaked on back to the morgue. A boy was lying there under a sheet. He had been shot in the temple and identification was not easy. I held the picture beside his head and decided they were the same man. We printed the picture and identified the young man as the slayer-suicide. Then we were informed that he was in fact a cousin of the family who was a ministerial student at a nearby Baptist seminary.

Once I learned of my mistake I expected to be fired. But Mooney wanted aggressive reporting, and he was willing to pay a price for it now and then. He headed off a libel suit by printing a profuse apology and agreeing to donate about $1,500 to the young man's church when he became a pastor. The other reporters and I were called into Mooney's office on Monday, after the young man's lawyer had been there and the settlement had been agreed to, and he gave us a long lecture, but he finally said, "Well, mistakes will be made" and "That was an aggressive job you gentlemen did— you were sure in there scratching and snatching." And he sighed and added, "And we ran them in the paper."

After that, he would sometimes say to me, "Well, Catledge, you're certainly a great friend of the Baptists. You may have embarrassed the *Commercial Appeal,* but you did a great job for the Lord."

We didn't bother much with libel suits in those days. We had a rule, for instance, that if a white man was identified as a Negro in a petty crime story—and Negroes were always identified as such— we would pay the man $150 to sign a release and settle the matter immediately. Racial identification could be a tricky business. A white man who happened to be dark-skinned, or have a dirty face, which petty criminals usually had, might be marked down by the desk sergeant as a Negro. Then the police reporter, never actually seeing the man, might copy off the police blotter that so-and-so, Negro, had been arrested for such-and-such. But shyster lawyers watched for this very carefully. If a white man had been described as Negro in the paper, they'd visit him in jail, fast-talk him into signing a paper, collect $150 from us, give the fellow in jail $50 or so, pay his fine, and pocket the rest.

After I left Memphis, one of our police reporters got into a racket with a police sergeant and several shady lawyers whereby wrong designations would be put down deliberately. The racket was uncovered, however, and Boss Crump cleaned house. The desk sergeant was jailed, a police captain was fired for negligence of duty, and the lawyers were disbarred. Mr. Crump was, in his fashion, a very righteous man.

One of the first things I learned as a reporter on the *Commercial Appeal* was that I needed all the contacts I could get, from bootleggers to bank presidents. Most reporters will write the news about the same way; the ones who get ahead are those with a talent for getting the news, so I set out to acquire all the sources I could.

To do so was instinctive with me. Even as a boy back in Philadelphia, my family used to say that I would barge right up and make friends with any stranger I saw. I was aggressive and ambitious, perhaps a little brash. I liked people and I wanted them to like me, and most often they did. I liked to joke and tell stories. I never ran from a bottle of whiskey, and despite the best efforts of the Prebyterian church, I wasn't overly famous for my piety. Once I was delivering a package of paper to Mr. Mooney and happened upon him and his friend Isaac B. Tigrett, a bank and railroad president, having a two-man birthday party—they shared the same birthday— and lustily singing gospel songs. Tigrett's father had been a Baptist preacher. Mooney called me in and said, "Colonel Catledge, do you know any hymns?" "Yes, sir," I said, for I knew dozens, so I spent the rest of the evening singing hymns for them. Mooney was so taken by my talent that afterward he'd occasionally call me into his office and ask me the verse to some old hymn he wanted to quote in an editorial.

One of the most important friends I made in Memphis was a wealthy banker, real-estate owner, sportsman, and civic leader named Brinkley Snowden. Mooney and Snowden were great friends, and Mooney was always pressing Sam Kahn to have one of his reporters get to know Snowden, who was among the best-informed men in Memphis. The trouble was that Snowden didn't like inquisitive reporters. Sam would send one to see him, and the reporter would never be granted a second appointment.

One day Mooney suggested to Sam that he send me over to see if I could get along with Snowden. Sam made it clear that this assignment was as big a challenge as I'd face on the *Commercial Appeal*. I don't remember the details of my conquest of Brinkley Snowden. I remember telling him that we had a mutual interest— I needed information and he had information.

My mission was successful, and soon I got in the habit of dropping by his office every day or two. If he was busy, or didn't seem pleased to see me, I'd leave. After a few weeks, Mooney told me that Snowden wanted me to go down to New Orleans with him to see the races. Mooney was impressed and he worked out some sort of assignment to justify my expenses. It was a most enjoyable trip and Snowden became one of my best news sources. Sometimes I'd "assign" him to get information for me, and he enjoyed it.

One day Snowden told me that a teller in his bank, after several months of fancy bookkeeping, had skipped town and that about $400,000 was missing. A few days later, Snowden told me that the teller, a very religious young man who unfortunately had become involved in a scheme to produce automobile wax, had sent a letter in which he listed the seven accounts he had tampered with and begged forgiveness for his sins.

I craved that letter, but Snowden would not let me have it. He agreed to let me read it but said I could not copy what it said. I was particularly interested in the figures—how much money he had stolen from whose bank accounts—but Snowden said he would only give that information to the bank examiners.

So I stood there reading the letter, forbidden to make notes on it, and suddenly I realized that I could memorize it. Which I did— and rushed back to the *Commercial Appeal* and wrote it out with only one or two minor revisions and we published it the next morning. When I arrived at work the next day, Mooney was already looking for me. "Brinkley Snowden says you double-crossed him, that you stole a letter from him."

"No, I didn't," I protested. "He was sitting right there and he saw that I didn't copy the letter."

"Then how did you get it?" Mooney asked.

"I memorized it."

Mooney demanded an explanation, and I told him that at A & M part of the hazing we freshmen got from upperclassmen was being required to sing the words on a laundry slip, or an equation out of geometry to the tune of the school song. We got a paddling if we failed, so I became adept at memorizing things by singing them. That was what I'd done in Snowden's office. I'd sung the A & M song in my mind and memorized the embezzler's letter to its tune. Then I came back to the office, sat down at my typewriter, and began singing out the words of the letter.

"That's incredible," Mooney said when I'd finished.

He picked up the phone and called Snowden. "Brinkley," he said, "I'm sending Catledge over to see you. He's done an amazing thing, but I don't think he stole that letter."

I hurried to the bank and told my story to Mr. Snowden.

My offense was bad enough—memorizing the note although I knew he didn't want it published—but at least I'd not stolen it, as he suspected. When I finished my explanation, Snowden challenged me to demonstrate my method. So I stood there in his office and sang that embezzler's letter for him. Just as I finished, the bank president came in and I was obliged to sing it again. Then they called another bank executive and I put on my concert again and they all roared with laughter at the spectacle of those bank-account figures sung to the tune of the A & M fight song. So I managed to sing my way back into Brinkley Snowden's favor and we remained friends for many years.

IV

Mr. Crump

ONE of my most important news sources in Memphis was Edward Hull Crump—Boss Crump, or Mister Crump, as we always called him.

A couple of years before I arrived in Memphis there'd been a truce of sorts between Crump and the *Commercial Appeal*, which had opposed him since he first ran for mayor in 1909. The truce came during their joint attack on the Ku Klux Klan. Mooney opposed the Klan on principle, and especially since he was Catholic. Crump, we assumed, hated the Klan not only on principle but as a rival political force.

The anti-Klan war was about over when I arrived in 1924, but I recall one example of how we worked together. A Klan initiation ceremony was being held in a park and several reporters were sent to write down the license numbers of their cars. The county sheriff, a Crump man, put the county records at our disposal so we could print the Klansmen's names the next morning, or suggest we had them. That was enough to prevent further public ceremonies, for individual members couldn't stand being exposed.

Mooney and Crump hated one another. The anti-Klan crusade never brought them together personally. It was said that Crump would not walk on the same side of the street the *Commercial Appeal* building was on. It happened that both men frequently lunched at the Tennessee Club, but the waiters knew to seat them at opposite sides of the room.

It is often forgotten that Crump first entered politics as a reformer. He was an aggressive and popular young businessman who spearheaded a group that wanted to clean up Memphis—the prostitution, the gambling, the bootlegging, the graft, and the high incidence of homicide and other violence. The *Commercial Appeal* opposed these reformers on the ground that they were hypocrites and anti-establishment. After Crump had served a time as mayor, the newspaper recognized his dictatorial desires and fought him on that count.

Ed Crump was essentially a highly moral man, and Memphis was an exceedingly sinful city. The city challenged Crump's zeal and piety. He wanted to remake it in his own image—honest, moral, efficient. The problem was that Crump believed so passionately in his own purity that he thought his noble ends justified whatever ignoble means he chose to employ. So he became a pious, but very ruthless dictator.

The *Commercial Appeal*, needless to say, believed in the righteousness of its cause as completely as Crump did in his. Any slip that any city employee made was put on the front page and blamed on Crump—who, incidentally, resigned as mayor in 1915 while the state legislature was threatening to have him ousted.

For the next twelve years Crump was compelled to share formal control of City Hall with various anti-Crump factions, but he established absolute sway over the county (Shelby) and hand-picked the county delegation to the state legislature in Nashville. (One he hand-picked in the mid-twenties was Mr. Mooney's son, C. P. J., Jr.). So to all intents and purposes Crump called the shots in Memphis and even sought to extend his influence to eastern Arkansas and northwestern Mississippi. He felt a particular obligation to these neighboring communities because the gamblers he chased out of Memphis retreated there and continued to serve the Memphis trade. On at least one occasion Crump had Tennessee state troopers sent into Mississippi to raid and demolish gambling roadhouses, much to the approval of the good churchgoing people, who further justified this excursion on the ground that Crump after all was a native Mississippian.

At the time I joined the paper, the brief truce between Crump and Mooney was still in effect. They'd both been pallbearers at the funeral of a mutual friend, and one or the other of them had made a friendly overture. It was about that time that I was assigned to cultivate Crump. I was given the assignment because I'd gotten a reputation for being able to get along with the hard cases, and for our paper there wasn't any harder case than Crump. Also, it helped that I had been assigned to cover local real-estate news, and Crump in addition to being a politician was a partner in a real-estate and loan company.

Crump and I got along well. He was from Holly Springs, Mississippi, and liked to talk about cornbread and potlikker, yellow-legged chickens and revival meetings, and of course I could speak that same bucolic language. It helped too that in his youth he, like me, had worked as a printer's devil and as a clerk in a small-town store. He was a self-made man who liked ambitious young men.

When we had a critical story about Crump I was often the reporter who called him for comment. Sometimes I was embarrassed at the questions I had to ask—they tended to be of the "Is it true that you've quit beating your wife" variety. I never gave much thought to whether Crump was a good or a bad political influence; if my paper was against him, that was enough for me. And yet I really liked him. So I'd call him and he'd laugh and say, "Well, boy, I know what your paper is going to print." Then, after a raucous guffaw he'd launch a long tirade against himself. "But here are the facts," he'd continue, and give me his side of the issue. Many times I'd wind up arguing Crump's point of view to Sam Kahn, my city editor, who also harbored a secret admiration for Crump.

My most memorable encounter with Crump was an episode that began during the Democratic primary of 1926. Early on election day we got a report at the paper that Crump's henchmen were voting black Republicans in the Democratic primary in some of the Negro precincts of South Memphis. Another reporter, a photographer, and I hurried to the area, where we found the reports were quite true. Crump's men would take Negroes who had voted in the Republican primary, give them phony poll-tax receipts, and run them through the Democratic line.

One photographer started taking pictures and we reporters began interviewing the voters and inspecting their poll-tax receipts. We were getting quite a story when Crump's henchmen descended on us. They arrived in a black Packard owned by the sheriff's office, and their leader was a Crump lieutenant named Willie Gerber. Gerber was a young lawyer, who served Crump for many years and later became highly controversial as Crump's political hatchetman. In 1926 he was an assistant attorney general (county prosecutor) who had a reputation for doing anything Crump told him to and some things he didn't. I knew Willie disliked me because several times when I'd called on or visited Crump he'd told Willie to leave the office while we talked.

Gerber and his goons surrounded the three of us. Gerber began cursing me, then slapping me around. The others joined in and all three of us were beaten rather badly. When they finally left us, battered and bleeding, we limped back to the *Commercial Appeal*. Mooney was furious. He had our pictures taken, and had us prepare affidavits on the attack. All this was printed in the paper the next day, Tuesday.

On Thursday I went to see Crump. I was angry and I wanted him to know it. This was no way to treat a fellow Mississippian. I found him sitting behind his desk wearing a huge straw hat.

In his youth Crump had fiery red hair, but now, at age fifty-two, it was snow white and very long and full. He was vain about his appearance. His clothes were always neat and elegant, and his big desk was always tidy. He usually kept two or three rows of chairs in his office, where he could lecture to politicians and hangers-on as if they were schoolboys, but this day the chairs were empty.

"Come in, Catledge," he roared to me. Then, taking note of my cuts and bruises, he added: "What in the world has happened to you? Have you been in an automobile accident?"

I played along with his game. "No, Mr. Crump, I was beaten up."

"What do you mean?" he said, as if amazed.

I told him I'd been attacked on election day.

"Were you one of those boys in that fight down in South Memphis?"

I confessed I was indeed one of those boys.

"Boy, tell me who did this to you," he said. "Nobody can do this to a friend of mine and get away with it."

I was overjoyed. I was going to get my revenge. Mr. Crump was my friend after all.

"Willie Gerbert did it to me," I explained.

"We've got to do something about this," he added. "What do you suggest?"

I drew myself to my full height and shouted: "Fire the son of a bitch!"

Mr. Crump looked at me thoughtfully. "Oh no, boy, that's not enough," he said. "We've got to do something more than that."

I could smell old Willie's flesh burning at the stake.

"I'll tell you what we're going to do, Catledge," he said finally. He pushed his hat back on his head and pointed a long finger at me.

"From now on, you stay away from places like that or else someday you may really get hurt!"

My humiliation was complete. His thugs had beaten me and he had made a fool of me. Yet before I left his office we were friends again. Several years later, when he was serving in Congress and I was a *New York Times* correspondent in Washington, he was one of my best sources. Often I'd tell the story of my "revenge" on Willie Gerber and Crump would roar with delight.

I don't know what history will make of Crump. He did some good things for Memphis but he made himself a dictator in order to do them. I could never stay mad at him for long. He had his job to do and I had mine, and all things considered we got along pretty well. I never thought of him as a crusader or a moralist, but as a reporter, and I knew my job would have been a lot less exciting without him. He ran the city and county with iron-fisted efficiency and low cost.

Mr. Mooney died in the fall of 1926 a few days before he would have achieved his dream of starting an afternoon newspaper as a companion to the *Commercial Appeal*. He arrived in his office one morning with what he took to be a case of indigestion. He called to his secretary, "Miss Emma, I think I ate too many 'taters last night." Then he lay down on his couch and was dead ten minutes later.

Once I heard the news—Miss Emma called me at home—I knew my days with the *Commercial Appeal* were numbered. To me Mr. Mooney was the *Commercial Appeal*, and it would never be the same without him. And, as I feared, the families who owned the paper, tempted by a huge profit, sold it to a group from Nashville. I was ready to go, but I didn't know where. Then an act of God arranged my future for me. A great flood surged down the Mississippi River in the spring of 1927, and one of the many items of flotsam and jetsam swept along by its raging waters was my career. It was because of that flood that I met a reporter who arranged my job with the Baltimore *Sun*, and also that I met Herbert Hoover, whose interest in me later resulted in my joining the *New York Times*.

Mr. Hoover was then President Coolidge's Secretary of Commerce, and he had been sent South to supervise relief programs for victims of the flood. I had been covering the flood for two weeks before Hoover arrived. I first met it in Cairo, Illinois, then I followed it down to Columbus, Kentucky, where three hundred towns-people—the entire population—had sought refuge in the hills.

Memphis itself was not in danger, for it sits on a bluff high above the river, so I followed the flood on down to the Mississippi Delta country. There had been a break in the levee at a little place called Stop's Landing, just above Greenville, and the waters had swept through and flooded Greenville. I flew over the scene in a small plane piloted by a man named Vernon Omley. I took pictures and gathered information for the reports I was phoning back to Memphis from a landing strip east of Greenville. I stayed around Greenville for two days before returning to Memphis on Sunday. I wrote a couple of stories for the paper, delivered a report over the *Commercial Appeal*'s radio station, and then went home and fell into bed, dog-tired.

I was still sleeping the next morning when Hoover arrived in a special train, accompanied by a dozen or so Eastern reporters. Hoover was anxious to get busy, and he asked the mayor of Memphis for the names of people who could tell him about the flood and the plight of the refugees. The mayor mentioned that a young reporter named Catledge had been all over the flood area and Hoover immediately said he wanted to see me.

Thus a few minutes later, two city detectives were beating on the door of the apartment I rented on Eastmoreland Avenue. My mother was living with me then, and when she came to awaken me she was sure I was being arrested. But the detectives only rushed me to Hoover's suite at the Peabody Hotel. He started firing questions at me, and as I fired back the answers, he listened intently.

One thing I told him about was the refugee camp the American Legion had organized at the Tri-State Fairgrounds in Memphis. Hoover called for a car and said I was to take him on a tour of the camp. So I took him out and showed him hundreds of refugees, most of them Negro sharecroppers, who'd been brought in by freight cars from the lowlands, mostly from the Arkansas Delta. They were being housed in the fairground's vast livestock barns. Men and women had been separated, and the refugees had been organized to serve up their own meals and otherwise take care of themselves. There was even a sort of zoo for the chickens, pigs, dogs, possums— even a pet coon—the refugees had brought out. Considering the circumstances, the Legion had done quite a job. "This is an astounding piece of organization," Hoover declared.

We returned to the hotel, where I met his press secretary, George Akerson, a big handsome Swedish-American who was to become my close friend. Sam Kahn was also there. After a while, Hoover said he wanted me to accompany him on his boat trip down the river. We left that night and the next morning arrived in Greenville, where Hoover met a group of citizens led by William Alexander Percy, the noted Southern poet and author.

I didn't know how long Mr. Hoover wanted me to stay with him, so I arranged for an amphibious plane to fly to Greenville to take me back to Memphis. Hoover and I were standing on the deck of the river boat when the plane landed on the river. I ventured a little joke. "Mr. Hoover, Noah sent out a dove to see how far his Ark was from land; I'll be your dove and fly out in my plane and bring you back a willow branch."

Hoover chuckled. He was not outwardly a jolly man, certainly not in these circumstances, and to make him laugh always seemed a challenge to my sense of humor. He insisted, however, that I stay with his tour and I agreed. That night, just outside of Vicksburg, a group of New Orleans leaders came out in a small boat to meet us. The people of their city were in terror of the flood waters, which had reached the tops of the levees, so that as you walked on Canal Street you looked up and saw ships sailing by above you. My wife, who was a girl in New Orleans at the time, remembers her father showing her and her mother how to use a dining-room table as a raft if the flood struck.

The delegation hoped to persuade Hoover to have the levee below New Orleans, in Plaquemines Parish, blown up to draw off the rising waters from their city. Hoover said firmly: "Gentlemen, that's none of my business. I'm not here as an engineer but as a relief administrator. You'll have to discuss your project with General Jadwin. He's in charge of the river." General Jadwin, the chief of the Army Corps of Engineers, was accompanying Hoover, and eventually he agreed to dynamite the levee in Plaquemines Parish—to "cut the levee" as it was called. The cutting of the levee was to become one of the great fiascos of my career.

The explosion was to be at noon. I was to write a story for the *Commercial Appeal*'s new afternoon paper, the *Evening Appeal*. I was going to watch the explosion from a Coast Guard cutter, and because of the time problem, I wrote my story in advance and put it on the wire to Memphis. It was a most dramatic story. It began, "With one thunderous roar, like the crack of doom, earth flying heavenward, the City of New Orleans was relieved." It went on in that vein at some length.

My story written, I went to see the event myself. The scene at the levee was a dramatic one. There were many boats filled with people who had come out to watch the explosion. The press was there too in great numbers. Since no one could get too close to the doomed levee, the famous Jim West of the A.P. had stationed himself on a telephone pole, with a telegraph ticker, to send three ticks when the levee went skyward. The INS man was hovering above the scene in a small plane, ready to release a roll of toilet paper over the side as a signal when the levee blew.

The trouble was the levee never blew. Unknown to all of us, the engineers in charge of the operation were getting gun shy. They were afraid they had brought too much dynamite and might blow half the Delta to Kingdom Come. So they kept reducing the explosive, until when they finally triggered the fuse there was only a timid little "pop." Not a drop of water went through the levee until late that afternoon, and it was days before workmen with pick and shovel could enlarge the hole enough to make any difference, by which time the water was receding on its own.

Meanwhile, the *Evening Appeal* was on the newsstands with my signed dramatic story about the "thunderous roar," and I was stuck in a boat four hours away from a telegraph office.

Fortunately for me, Sam Kahn understood the problem. He had wanted an advance story filed and he knew there was nothing I could have done about about the nonexplosion.

When I returned to New Orleans that night, I filed a humorous story, telling exactly what had happened and why the earlier story had been wrong. This story appeared without by-line the next morning in the *Commercial Appeal*. I later learned that many people in Memphis believed the first story about the "thunderous roar" and refused to believe the correction. There was even a rumor in Memphis that Sam Kahn had been so jealous of my dramatic story (and so jealous of the new afternoon paper) that he had written the second story to try to belittle my great journalistic achievement.

I was fortunate to meet a number of fine reporters who'd come South with Hoover. Few of these men had been in the Delta before, so I was busy telling them the names of people and places we encountered. Most of them did not know much about floods. They expected the "crest" of the flood to be a huge wall of water shooting down the river like a tidal wave. (In fact, the crest of the flood is simply the highest point the water reaches before it starts to recede. A real Mississippi flood is more like a glacier than a tidal wave. It may last for months, rising inch by inch, foot by foot, until it has overpowered every barrier men try to put in its path.) Before long, most of the Eastern reporters were having me check over their copy before they sent it back to their papers.

Our voyage was not all work and no play. The first night out we reporters got in a poker game. We didn't have any chips, so we used some dried beans we found in the boat's kitchen. Mr. Hoover didn't approve of gambling, but he came out of his cabin and watched our game. After a while he commented, "Whether you use a bean or a ten-dollar gold piece, they're both the same if you accept them."

In Vicksburg, some of the reporters wanted to know where to find whiskey and girls. I'd never been there before, but I'd had enough experience by then to find them what they wanted. The next night, enlivened by the jugs of moonshine I'd found for us in Vicksburg, we got into a crap game and I won a good deal of money. More important, I discovered I had won some new friends. By the time we got to New Orleans—via a special train from Vicksburg— all my new friends were saying I must come to a paper in the East and promising they'd help me get a job.

In all I spent about three weeks with Mr. Hoover on the flood trip. We got along famously from the first. He was a shy man, but he seemed to like my jokes and the way I operated. Other reporters deferred to his lofty political status, but I'd break in on him any time, amused to see the others hanging back and awaiting my reports.

I could see that Mr. Hoover liked me, but I didn't know for several years that during our trip he took time out to write a letter to Adolph Ochs, publisher of the *New York Times*, suggesting that he hire me. That might seem a strange thing for him to have done. He and I had little in common. He was a middle-aged man, a Midwesterner, a Republican, a prominent national figure, a solemn individual who didn't believe in drinking or gambling. I, in contrast, was an aggressive young Southern newspaper reporter who obviously liked to drink and play. Why should he take time out on a hectic trip to write the publisher of the *New York Times* about me?

Mr. Hoover and I never discussed his letter, in fact he never mentioned it to me, and I don't know his exact motives. But let me quote another writer on the subject. Gay Talese, in *The Kingdom and the Power*, credited me with an exceptional ability to attract the attention of older men, particularly selfmade men, and to attract help and advice from them. He added that perhaps those older men saw in me something of themselves when they were younger. I thought that a perceptive comment. I think I did have a special ability to get along with self-made men—Clayton Rand, C. P. J. Mooney and Ed Crump were all self-made. So was Herbert Hoover. I think it is quite true that men who have made it in life starting from the bottom rung tend to have a special affection, as Talese suggested, for young men who seem as ambitious and aggressive as they once were. At any rate, Mr. Hoover's letter was to be a turning-point in my career.

The *Times*, however, didn't act on Mr. Hoover's letter for more than two years, and I went to work for the Baltimore *Sun* not long after the flood. The *Sun*'s W. A. S. Douglas was the first of my new newspaper friends to follow through on his promise to help me get a new job. He was to become my close friend, and my younger daughter, Ellen Douglas Catledge, is named for him. After the flood ended, I went on a relief train to Poplar Bluff, Missouri, where a cyclone had killed more than a hundred people. Upon my return to Memphis, I had a letter from Stanley Meade Reynolds, managing editor of the *Sun*, offering me a job. I decided to accept it, although Sam Kahn, my city editor, urged me to stay. I had become one of the *Commercial Appeal*'s top reporters, with an astronomical salary of $55 a week. But I was ready to leave Memphis for $60 and I did.

I drove to Baltimore in the early summer of 1927 with five friends in an Essex car, with my little trunk strapped to the top. I had just turned twenty-six, and I was quite a different person from the young fellow who had wandered into the Memphis *Press* four years earlier, not knowing an "ad" from an "add." I had become an experienced reporter. Not a polished reporter—I would realize in Baltimore what a rough form of journalism I'd been practicing—but an experienced one. I knew I had found my life's work. I wanted to be a reporter. I wanted to see everything that happened in the world and tell it to the people who weren't so lucky as I.

I had found a calling in which energy and ambition, a talent for words and for people could compensate for the limitations of my background and education. I was young and cocky. I thought I was pretty good and other people seemed to agree. I wanted success and recognition, and I wanted to be where the action was. When Mr. Mooney was still alive, I had once told him I wanted to try for a job on a New York paper, but he'd said I wasn't ready yet, so I'd waited. Now I had an offer from one of America's great newspapers and I was anxious to make the most of it.

I was in Baltimore only two years and I'm afraid the *Sun* did more for me than I did for the *Sun*. Baltimore was to be a kind of way station for me in my journey from Memphis to New York. As such, it helped me enormously. It would have been disastrous if I had tried to move directly from the wild and woolly *Commercial Appeal* to the staid *Times*. But in two years on the *Sun* I learned to write better, to dress better, to act better—in short, to behave in a more civilized style than prevailed among Memphis newspapermen.

The *Sun*'s city editor was a gentle and meticulous man named Charles P. (Peck) Trussell, who later joined the *New York Times*.

Trussell knew good writing and knew how to get it. I had been hired as a feature writer, and this caused me some difficulty because feature writing was hard for me, but eventually I worked my way back to the straight news assignments that I preferred. I needed the discipline that my new city editor provided. On the *Commercial Appeal* the stress was on getting the news, not writing it. I'd learned a florid, folksy, rather slapdash style, with emphasis on all the gory details. Our copy was never edited, and we even wrote our own headlines. The *Sun*, more refined, was meticulously edited.

I introduced the previously unknown art of picture snatching to Baltimore, with lamentable results. The picture that I snatched, and that we printed as the likeness of a dead railroad president, turned out to be his brother, who was very much alive. At that, I gave up picture snatching. Fortunately, I found, mistakes on whether a man is dead or alive usually don't cause a great complaint. If you say a man is dead, and he is alive, he's too relieved to sue you. If you say he's alive and he's dead, he can't sue you.

Baltimore was far more concerned with cultural matters than Memphis. It was during my two years in Baltimore that I first met people with a serious interest in art and literature. One person I got to know slightly in Baltimore was H. L. Mencken. He would drop into the *Sun* office occasionally, and despite his reputation for ferocity, I always found him a gay, cheerful, and friendly man. He was a great beer drinker, and sometimes I'd see him in a speakeasy that served his favorite German beer. I got to know him better later, when I was on the *Times* and would see him every four years at the political conventions. I remember once looking over his shoulder just after Senator Borah had made a speech and seeing the memorable lead to Mencken's story: "Senator Borah is an old moo-cow."

Baltimore was a cultivated city, but it was also wide open. Prohibition was the law then, but Maryland's aristocratic governor, Albert Cabell Ritchie, wouldn't let the state police enforce it, or the Baltimore city police, over whom he had control. When federal officials would try to raid in Baltimore, the local officials would often tip off the speakeasy owners, and sometimes Governor Ritchie's men would arrest the federal officers. The governor, as you might guess, was himself a man who liked to drink. I got to know him well and I admired him for his candor. In those days he was highly regarded as a future prospect for the White House.

Thanks to the governor, the speakeasies of Baltimore thrived, and some of us thrived along with them. I was working hard—my $60 salary was the highest on the *Sun*'s local staff, and I had to earn it—but there was the time to play too. It was in Baltimore that I first learned there are better things to drink than corn whiskey.

I had my first experience as a Washington correspondent during the Presidential campaign in 1928. The *Sun* had four men in its Washington bureau and three were out following the campaign. The fourth was an outstanding newspaperman who unfortunately had let his drinking get the best of him. In 1922 he had written a feature about the burial of the Unknown Soldier, which became famous and won prizes. His inspiration had been to write the article in the form of a letter to the Unknown Soldier's mother. It was a moving piece of writing and deserved all the acclaim it received.

But now he drank too much to do his job and I had been sent to Washington not only to replace him but to tell him he was fired. It was a bad thing for the *Sun*'s editors to do, to the other reporter and to me, but they lacked the courage to break the news themselves. The reporter took my news graciously; he said he had been expecting it. But later that day his wife rushed into the office, gave me a terrible tongue lashing, and threw down on my desk a copy of his Unknown Soldier article, which had been reprinted in pamphlet form. "You'll never see the day when you can write a story like that," she shouted. I kept quiet, and all her husband said, trying to calm her, was "Now, mama, Now, mama." It was an awful experience for all of us.

The *New York Times* offered me a job in the spring of 1929. Two years had passed since Herbert Hoover wrote Adolph Ochs, the *Times*' publisher, suggesting that he hire me. I later learned that Ochs gave the letter to his acting managing editor, Frederick T. Birchall, who promptly put it in his desk drawer and forgot it. Two years later, after Hoover had become President, Ochs called on him in the White House one day and Hoover asked the publisher why he had ignored his recommendation. "You lost a good man," Hoover said. "He went to the Baltimore *Sun*."

Ochs went back to his office and chewed out Birchall and told him to hire this fellow Catledge forthwith. Had I known that, I would have held out for more than the $80 salary I eventually got from Birchall. But I knew nothing of it. I was in New Jersey covering a murder-suicide when I received a telegram from Herman Dinsmore, a friend of mine who'd recently left the *Sun* to work for the *Times*. The telegram said he had an urgent matter to discuss and I was to meet him in Philadelphia that Sunday. I thought he wanted to rent me the apartment he'd vacated in Baltimore. Instead, he informed me that Birchall wanted me to come to New York to discuss my joining the *Times*.

I told Herman I'd go to see Birchall if the *Times* wanted to pay my way, but that I really wasn't much interested in the offer. I was happy in Baltimore, I'd made a secure place for myself on the *Sun*, and I felt no urge to leave, as I had in my last year with the *Commercial Appeal*.

Yet New York was the mecca of the newspaper business and I was tempted by its challenge. One problem was that I didn't know much about the *New York Times* and wasn't very impressed by what I did know. If I'd been offered a job by Joseph Pulitzer's New York *World*—then, to all newspapermen, the greatest of papers—I'd have accepted in a minute. But the *Times* struck me as a dull, stodgy newspaper.

I sought the advice of the *Sun*'s managing editor, William E. Moore, a Missourian who had become my friend. He took me to dinner at his club that night and told me that, on behalf of the *Sun*, he would offer me a raise to $75 and would see that I was trained to assume an executive position. Then he said: "Now that I've discharged my obligation to the Baltimore *Sun*, I'll advise you as a friend—take that job. You have the makings of a great newspaper career ahead of you, but the opportunities aren't here."

I took his advice, and on August 11, 1929, I arrived in New York to start work for the *Times*.

V

Joining *The Times*

I DIDN'T know what to expect at the *Times*. During my last weeks in Baltimore I'd bought the *Times* each day and practiced writing those long, cumbersome sentences for which it was noted. The *Times'* style seemed to be never to use a period when you could insert a conjunction.

I reported to Mr. Birchall, the acting managing editor. He took me over to David Joseph, the city editor, who introduced me around the office. The city room was a big, informal place, much more like the *Commercial Appeal* than the efficient Baltimore *Sun*. I was surprised to see dozens of reporters lounging about, reading, chatting, or playing cards. The *Times* appeared to believe in hiring three men to do the work one man could do. Every year or two, some great emergency would justify this overstaffing.

I had been with the *Times* only a few days when I got my first big story. One Saturday evening word came that some Arabs had killed a group of Jewish worshipers at the Wailing Wall in Old Jerusalem. Most of the staff were at dinner or had gone home early, so I was assigned to study the clippings in our morgue and write an add on the Wailing Wall. I didn't know if the editor wanted two hundred words or two thousand. But as read the clips, and all the Biblical places I'd studied in Sunday school began coming to life, I was fascinated and let go with a long detailed article.

The next night the assistant managing editor, Joseph Tibeau, told me that Adolph Ochs, the publisher, had asked who wrote the story on the Wailing Wall, and said it was one of the most thorough pieces of writing on the subject he'd ever seen. I indicated to Tibeau that I wouldn't object if he'd mention the publisher's opinion to David Joseph, my immediate superior, and apparently he did, for I soon became the unofficial Jewish editor of the *New York Times*. There was a good deal of aftermath to the Wailing Wall incident, and Joseph told me to cover it and to ask for help if I needed it. Soon I had two or three people under me. Any news involving Jews was referred automatically to me. So it came to pass that when the Wailing Wall story began to fade, I was assigned to cover the illness, death, and burial of Louis Marshall, a famous Jewish lawyer, whose funeral was the first service ever held in the new Temple Emanu-El at Fifth Avenue and Sixty-First Street.

One morning I went to the temple trying to get some details from the temple manager, who was handling arrangements. "What do you want?" he asked me in exasperation. "I want some details on the funeral," I said. "Why do you bother me with all these damn-fool questions?" he protested. "Why don't you read the *Times*?"

I finally was taken off the Jewish beat and assigned to cover Ramsey MacDonald's visit with President Hoover. It was an easy and pleasant assignment. MacDonald arrived in New York, took a train to Washington, and accompanied Hoover to his Rapidan Camp in Virginia, where they sat on a log, puffed their pipes, and discussed the peace of the world.

When I returned to New York I was assigned to follow MacDonald on his week's visit to Canada. I decided to improve my wardrobe for this trip, so I went to the Bond clothing store on Times Square and bought a two-pants suit. I remember that I couldn't get my suit wrapped because all the salesmen and counter boys were watching the stock market reports flash across the electric news sign above Times Square. Those were the days when it seemed that everyone in New York, from bellhops to millionaires, was feverishly playing the stock market. By the time I returned from Canada two weeks later, the stock market had crashed, and although we didn't realize it, the Depression had begun. But President Hoover continued to assert that prosperity was just around the corner, and I personally was little affected by the nation's financial disaster. I was getting good assignments and rapidly securing my place on the *Times*.

On Thanksgiving night Mr. Birchall called me over and asked me if I would like to join the paper's Washington bureau. The offer was not a surprise to me, because I had had some Washington experience with the Baltimore *Sun*. Richard V. Oulahan, the *Times'* chief Washington correspondent, wanted an additional man because the New Congressional session was beginning in December, and Birchall suggested me. I think he had in mind that I would be assigned to the White House—because I knew President Hoover—but Mr. Oulahan thought differently. The best place to learn about Washington he told me, was the House of Representatives, so on December 1, 1929, I became the *Times* man in the House.

Richard Victor Oulahan was one of the finest men I ever knew. He was then about sixty-three years old, slender and handsome, rather English-looking in his dress and manner, extremely urbane. More important, he was an exceedingly kind and considerate man, never too busy to help a young reporter, whether from his own staff or a rival paper. If he saw a new reporter at the Capitol or elsewhere, he would say: "I'm Richard Oulahan of the *New York Times*. Anytime I can do anything for you, please let me know." He had said that to me when I'd come over briefly for the Baltimore *Sun*. He was without doubt the outstanding newspaper correspondent in Washington at that time and he contributed much to the respect with which the *Times* and the craft were held.

I was the ninth man in the Washington bureau and the first to have been sent from New York in a decade. Mr. Oulahan was a great reporter and a great gentleman, but he was not a great administrator, and the bureau was loosely organized, to say the least. Its members were rugged individualists, set in their ways and not to be hurried. Some days, two or three men would cover the same story, and their separate stories would be sent to New York and run in the paper. They were an indolent lot, except for a fellow named Harold McCoy, an aviation expert who'd been hired in Washington not long before I had. He was working like a Turk. He called me aside one day soon after I arrived and told me, "You and I have a great opportunity here. This is a moribund outfit, passing up more stories than they write, and all we have to do is go to it." I soon realized he was right.

I was replacing a man named John Monk, who was switching from the House to another assignment. Mr. Oulahan told me that on my first day I needn't bother about writing a story, but should start meeting people in the House. The big story that day was a Presidential message to Congress, and Mr. Oulahan would cover that himself.

But, when I returned to the office that first afternoon, Hal Smith, who was in charge of the news desk, rushed up to me and asked, "Where's your comment?"

"What comment?" I asked.

"Your comment on the President's message," Smith said.

"I have no comment on the President's message," I replied.

He explained that it was routine for the *Times* to print comment from Congressional leaders on the President's message, and I was reaching for the telephone when John Monk beckoned to me. He told me to wait until he'd finished the story he was working on, then he'd show me what to do. A few minutes later he called me over and began pounding on his typewriter. He quickly wrote out six or eight comments from the various Congressional leaders. He knew what they wanted to say and that they'd back him up.

Newspaper coverage in Washington in those days was easygoing, often slipshod. One common practice was for a correspondent to borrow the carbons—black sheets—of another correspondent's story and send it along to his office as his own. I remember once on a Presidential train trip when the celebrated correspondent of a Boston paper filed a story filled with local references not to Boston but to Newark, for he had copied the carbons of a correspondent for the Newark *News*.

Hal Smith, our desk man was a kind and considerate man, but high-strung and extremely jealous of his reputation for accuracy. He had a terrible fear of queries from the New York office. Rather than challenge New York, no matter how idiotic their questions might seem, he always replied with a story. One of Smith's mannerisms was to reply, "Good, good," to anything you told him. One day a movie theater collapsed, killing and injuring several dozen people, and that evening we were questioned by New York as to whether a particular man—Jones, I'll call him—was dead or only injured. Hal Smith grabbed the phone and called Jones' house and, as the legend had it, the conversation went like this: "Mrs. Jones, we have your husband as being dead and the wire services say he's only injured. Which is correct? He's dead? Good, good."

The Washington bureau was very bureaucratic. Most of its people resented queries and criticism from the New York office. They felt they knew Washington, and all its complexities and nuances, and the New York editors didn't. Their loyalty appeared to be to the bureau, not the paper. This kind of bureaucratic sentiment is almost incurable in the operation of a large newspaper. I think I was spared its full thrust because my first experience was in the New York office. I realized from the first that we were a New York newspaper, that my check came from New York, and that the decision-making power was and had to be in New York. When I became an executive in New York I set about deliberately to implement that view.

I hadn't been in Washington long when I realized that it was, as Harold McCoy had told me, a wide-open field for an aggressive reporter. The city was filled with stories that weren't being covered by us or anyone else. Most government officials never saw a reporter. Reporters covered the White House, the State Department, Treasury, and Congress, and that was about all. It was the quiet before the storm, the last few years when the federal government was not important or of interest to most Americans, and reporters reflected this disinterest. But I was determined to cover the House of Representatives as aggressively as I might cover the police beat in Memphis or Baltimore. It was possible, in those days, to cover the House adequately without ever talking to more than six or eight people, but I started developing dozens of sources and I soon was churning out story after story. Some days I'd have as many as five stories in the paper—none with a byline, however. No one else in our bureau was pushing that hard except Harold McCoy. There was a friendly but feverish competition between him and me—we were working hard and we loved it.

That was the situation in the bureau as the Christmas holidays arrived and everyone got a bonus except McCoy and me. I was hurt —why should the others get bonuses and we, who were doing most of the work, get none? Presumably it was because we were so new to the staff, but that didn't appease me; if I'd had an opportunity to join a newspaper union at that time I would gladly have done so. The bonuses were personal gifts from Mr. Ochs, the publisher, and reflected his paternalistic attitude toward his newspaper's staff, an attitude that I believe contributed greatly to the demand for a Newspaper Guild organization at the *Times*. In my experience with people favors distributed that way make ingrates on the one hand and enemies on the other. In publishing as well as in politics, gratitude generally consists of anticipation of favors expected rather than thanks for favors granted.

About my second or third day in Washington, I called at the White House to see Mr. Hoover. George Akerson, his press secretary, arranged the visit. George and I had become friends when he came down for the flood, and while I was with the Baltimore *Sun* I'd spent two Christmases with the Akerson family. President Hoover was most gracious with me. I'm not sure my superiors at the *Times* understood this, but Mr. Hoover and I were not close friends. I was simply a young man he'd met, been impressed by, and, as I was later to find, written a letter of recommendation for, as no doubt he had for other young men.

But we had a pleasant chat. He asked me how much money I

was making and when I told him $80 a week, he said I'd settled too cheaply. I replied that money wasn't everything, or some such banality, and he replied, "You don't want to be too idealistic where money is concerned."

He also advised me to get to know John Nance Garner, the Democratic leader in the House, and Pat Harrison, a leading Democratic Senator. He described them as able, intelligent, honest men who had been most helpful to him, despite their being in the opposition party. My impression was that Hoover admired the guile and shrewdness of professional politicians like Garner and Harrison, even though he knew he could never be like them. He was jovial and relaxed with friends but he was a stiff and unconvincing public speaker. He was far too straightforward to play Presidential politics the way an FDR or LBJ could; Hoover could never learn to flatter or cajole, to threaten or deceive. He admired the rascals in politics but he could never be one.

I accompanied Hoover on his fishing trip to Florida that first Christmas, and I sometimes covered his press conferences, but I had little personal contact with him until the 1932 campaign. I never tried to presume on our acquaintance, or on the favor he had done me; if I had I might have embarrassed us both. Hoover liked me personally, but he had little use for newspaper reporters in general, and if I had pushed too hard I might have found the door slammed in my face.

Even at best, it is hard for a reporter and a President to be friends, and when they are it will probably do the reporter more harm than good. Reporters do well to seek politicians' respect rather than their friendship, although occasionally it is possible to have both. In my experience, politicians rarely forget that they are dealing with a reporter, and a reporter is a fool if he ever forgets that he is dealing with a politician. He is a fool, too, if he ever thinks that his company or his advice is being sought because of his own charm or brilliance, rather than because of his position with a newspaper. But reporters and politicians can get along quite well, so long as both remember the realities of their relationship—that each has something the other wants. The politician wants publicity, and the reporter wants news.

Washington in the early 1930's was not as exciting a place, politically or socially, as it later became, but it was still a dazzling adventure for a young newspaperman who was fulfilling an ambition to combine his love of reporting with his fascination with politics. Besides the excitement of my career, my early months in Washington were also enlivened by the fact that I had resumed my courtship of Mildred Turpin, a young woman I'd begun dating back in Baltimore. Soon we were thinking of marriage.

There were, however, two obstacles to our marriage. One was my career; the other was my mother. Soon after I settled in Washington I sent for Mother to come live with me, as she had previously come to live with me in Memphis and Baltimore. She was by then in her sixties and it was a great pleasure for her to leave Philadelphia and come keep house for me. I was glad to have her—to please her had long been my greatest wish—and yet I was increasingly aware that I had my own life to lead. Mother believed that children were brought into the world primarily to serve their parents—as she had served hers by caring for her thirteen younger brothers and sisters. I remember someone in Philadelphia asking, when I was twenty-five or so, if I planned to be married, and my mother replying that she didn't think I needed or could afford marriage as long as she was living.

Her attitude was a very real obstacle to my marriage. Mildred often said, when we spoke of marriage, that she didn't think my mother would ever let me go or that I'd have the courage to break away from her domination. The matter was solved, however, when my Uncle Homer's wife died early in 1931 and Mother returned to Philadelphia to care for his children.

At that point we decided to be married, and we set March 19 as the date. Then the other problem, my devotion to my job, arose. On Sunday afternoon, about five days before our wedding, the White House announced that President Hoover was going on a Caribbean cruise and would take reporters along. I was in Baltimore, discussing wedding plans with Mildred, when Mr. Birchall called and asked me to go on the cruise. I instinctively accepted the assignment —I had never turned down an assignment—and then I was in a terrible spot. I had to tell my fiancée that we must postpone our wedding so I could go on a Caribbean cruise with Herbert Hoover. My fiancée was furious. She told me, in effect, to put up or shut up. She gave me twenty-four hours to work things out.

I dashed to the railroad station and caught a train for Washington. Upon arrival, I called Mr. Oulahan and told him it was urgent that I see him. He told me to come straight to his home in Georgetown, and when I arrived he led me into his study. He obviously thought I was in serious trouble, as indeed I was.

"Now, boy, tell me what's your trouble?" Mr. Oulahan asked me gravely.

I had always been rather secretive about my personal affairs, so

I had not mentioned my engagement to anyone at the *Times*. Now I explained that Mr. Birchall had asked me to go on the Presidential cruise and that the assignment would force me to postpone my wedding. As I spoke, I could see a smile sweep across Mr. Oulahan's face, but he was kind enough not to laugh. Instead he picked up the telephone and called Birchall in New York. His side of the conversation went something like this:

"Hello, FTB?" (They called each other FTB and RVO in their private conversations.) "I've just learned that President Hoover is taking a Caribbean cruise. I wonder if it would suit you if I went on that assignment? I've been working pretty hard and . . . What's that? You've already spoken to Catledge about it. Well, that complicates matters, doesn't it? But let me follow through on that. Young Catledge is a reasonable sort of fellow and he'll understand. I'll ask him if I could take the trip instead of him. All right, fine. Thank you very much."

He hung up the telephone, turned to me, smiled, bowed very graciously and said, "Go ahead, son, and get married."

And we did—in New York on March 19, 1931, at the Church of the Transfiguration, better known as the Little Church Around the Corner.

VI

Covering Congress

IN my first year in Washington, 1930, I was kept busy getting to know my way around Capitol Hill.

I've been interested in politics since I was a boy of eight or ten hanging around the courthouse in Philadelphia, but I've never been overawed by public figures. Neither am I overly cynical about them. I take them for what they are—men who are more likely to be motivated by ambition, by ego, by power hunger than by a serious desire to serve humanity, men who are generally more interested in preserving their own skins than in saving the world.

There was a comic but shrewd Congressman from Mississippi in those days named Percy Quin, who was famous for once declaring: "There often come times in a stateman's life when he must rise above principle and take a stand for his people." I was never surprised or outraged if the politicians I knew rose above principle to take a stand for their constituents, or for their own interests. That was to be expected. One of the most candid comments I ever heard on Capitol Hill was made by Congressman Martin Dies, who said of some of his colleagues: "I hear them crying about the great sacrifices they're making to be here. Personally, I'm sacrificing about $1,200 a year—that's about what I'd be making back home."

I was never much disturbed by the four-flushing and hypocrisy of politicians. If I had been, I'd have missed half the fun of my job. I was disgusted, but amused, by people like Cotton Ed Smith and Theodore Bilbo. I didn't feel that I had to accept or reject what they did. I had only to report what they did, and I got plenty of life's fun out of doing so.

Neither have I ever expected American political parties to be instruments of high purpose or ideology. The parties are groupings of state individuals and interest groups who come together periodically to elect politicians who they hope will serve their interests, political, financial, or otherwise. If high-minded public service results, it's largely a by-product, sometimes an accident. We don't have strong party discipline or ideology in America. The party platforms are compromises and are generally meaningless. The Democrats are generally a bit to the left of the Republicans, on balance, but there are liberals and conservatives in both parties, just as there are good and bad men in both parties. Both parties have in the past made great contributions to America, and both have made some horrible mistakes. Somehow the nation has struggled on, even enjoyed moments of greatness, but it is hard to say whether this is because of our politicians or despite them.

Still, I am a Democrat, both by tradition and conviction. I am a Democrat for the same reason the Pope is a Catholic—I was born one and subsequent developments persuaded me to remain one. I've scratched the Democratic ticket only once, and felt terribly unclean when I did. Part of that is tradition—in Mississippi, when I was a boy, the roots of the Democratic party went deep—but part is experience. I think the Democratic party, over the long run, will do more good for more people than the Republican party. Furthermore, Democratic rascals are more colorful.

When I first arrived in Washington I was quite comfortable politically with the Southern Democratic leaders, men who, if concerned at all, believed that social change must come slowly. But by 1933 a blind man could have seen the necessity of urgent governmental action, and I was among the millions who cheered as Roosevelt began his heroic battle against the Depression. There was much I disliked about FDR and the way he and his people operated, and I thought that some of his programs were harebrained, but I never doubted that he was moving the country in the right direction.

Nor have I, in the years since the New Deal, disagreed with the basic political philosophy of the Democratic party. This is an incredibly rich nation, the richest in history, and it is inexcusable for millions of our people to live in poverty and ignorance.

More important than my own political views, however, was my growing belief that the job of a reporter is to report, to give people facts upon which to make up their own minds, never to be a preacher or advocate. Back in my Memphis days, when the *Commercial Appeal* was battling Boss Crump, I am sure I twisted the news for political purposes, because that was what I was expected to do. But now I was older and more experienced and I saw that the great power I had as a *Times* reporter could not be abused in that manner. As a *Times* reporter my franchise was not with any political faction but with our readers. I often thought of the stories I wrote as letters to the readers, giving them facts on which to make their own decisions. As a *Times* reporter I was not closely edited or supervised, and I had plenty of freedom to play politics if I chose, but I was under the discipline of tradition, the tradition of a newspaper that had achieved greatness. It believed in full, honest reporting of the news. I found that the traditions of the *New York Times* were very compatible with my own evolving ideas, and I tried in later years to help advance those traditions.

Congress in those days was dominated by Southerners, men like Sam Rayburn, John Nance Garner, Pat Harrison, Jimmy Byrnes, Cordell Hull, Joe Robinson, and Alben Barkley. The Southerners had the powers of seniority, and also they were more closely knit than legislators from other regions. They were like a blood brotherhood. They knew they were a minority and could have strength only by unity. They differed on details, but on the great issues—race, and a generally conservative approach to social and economic issues—they usually spoke with one voice.

The Southerners had passionate dedication to their profession that was rarely matched by men from other regions. A striking number of them were, like Sam Rayburn, bachelors, and almost all of them were men with little interest in books or the arts or anything except politics. They tended to be men who had started poor, had found in politics a ladder to success, and were willing to devote their lives to it.

They were men who lived by a code, and they expected other members of Congress to live by it, and those who did not would find themselves frozen out of the Capitol's inner circle. It was a code, first, that demanded that a man's word be his bond. If Sam Rayburn or Jimmy Byrnes gave me his word on something, I would have bet my life on it. That was a feeling I never had about Franklin Roosevelt or many of his New Dealers. There was a rugged integrity among the Southerners, something like that of the newspaper business—if a man tells you something off the record, you respect the agreement, however much you might like not to.

I respected the code of Southern politicians, and many of my reservations about Franklin Roosevelt and his associates, after they took power in 1933, arose because they had a different style and a different code. It seemed to me that FDR brought to Washington politics a cynicism, a degree of double-dealing, that had not existed before. The Southerners were often old rascals, not at all attractive in modern liberal terms. Yet you had to admire their honesty.

I hasten to add that the Southerners' code allowed for a good deal of political maneuver. You didn't tell a man an out-and-out lie, but there were plenty of ways you might flatter, trick, tempt, seduce, or otherwise induce him to do your bidding. They were men who understood the weaknesses of other men and knew how to make the most of them. They were subtle men, who rarely said, "Do this" or "Do that," but could make their wishes known in ways unlikely to offend. Once President Hoover showed John Nance Garner, the Democratic leader in the House, a list of possible appointees to the board of the newly created Reconstruction Finance Corporation. The last name on the list was that of Garner's friend Jesse Jones of Texas. "That's a kangaroo list," Garner said after a moment. "What do you mean?" Hoover asked. "It's strength is in its hind legs," Garner replied. Hoover got the idea and Jones got the appointment.

Garner was one of the key people I dealt with in the House. He served in Congress for thirty years. He was Minority Leader when I arrived, but he became Speaker after the election of 1930, and of course he completed his political career by serving two terms as FDR's Vice President.

Garner was from Uvalde, Texas, and some people called him "Cactus Jack," both for his geography and his prickly temperament. He wasn't happy as Vice President—he said the office wasn't worth a "bucket of warm spit"—but he was in his glory as the leader of the House Democrats when I first knew him.

Garner was a shrewd man and a great drinker. He and Republican Speaker Longworth had a little room just off the rotunda of the Capitol which they called the "Bureau of Education." Its furnishings consisted of a table, six or eight chairs, and a large chest or bureau against one wall. The bureau was divided into numerous small cubbyholes where they and their friends stashed their liquor. We reporters knew we could usually find Garner, Longworth, Sam Rayburn, John McDuffie of Alabama, Isaac Bacharach of New Jersey, and a few other regulars there in the afternoons. Garner would say, "Gentlemen, let's go strike a blow for liberty," and they would adjourn to the Bureau of Education.

It was quite an honor to be invited to the Bureau of Education, and those who were could be sure the motive was usually political as well as social. It was the scene of much friendly persuasion. Reporters would be invited there from time to time, usually because Garner or Rayburn had some story they wanted to give us, or perhaps because they thought we knew something they wanted to know. We knew each other's interests, and while I pumped them, they pumped me. We would do our business and strike a few blows for liberty along the way.

Garner arose early each morning and ate a big breakfast. His wife served as his secretary; she would precede him to his office and have his papers ready when he arrived. He had his first drink by around noon and he was generally quite mellow by mid-afternoon. Garner contended that overeating, not overdrinking, was the great threat to a man's health. Once a Senator tried to give Garner a temperance lecture. "I'll outlive you," Garner roared at the startled Senator. "You're digging your grave with your teeth!" As it happened the Senator was dead within a year. Since Garner lived to be almost one hundred years old, he was quite a testimonial for the medicinal values of good bourbon and "branch water." But he didn't drink right through to the end. He quit at age ninety, commenting that he thought he'd had enough.

Garner lived in the Washington Hotel and he gave its management orders that he was not to be disturbed after nine in the evening. I once found out just how strictly those orders were obeyed. That was in February of 1933 when President-elect Roosevelt was shot at by a crazed would-be assassin in Miami. No shots hit Roosevelt, but his companion, Mayor Cermak of Chicago, was fatally wounded.

Early reports of the shooting did not make it clear what FDR's condition was. My first thought was to get in touch with the Vice President-elect, Garner, whose hotel was near our office. I raced to the hotel about nine-thirty and told the desk clerk I had to see Garner, and explained why. He said that was impossible. I got the night manager and told him Garner might be the next President and I had to talk to him. The manager said he wasn't interested in politics, only in following Mr. Garner's orders, come hell or high water. I asked if I could slip a note under Garner's door. He said no.

I telephoned Sam Rayburn, thinking he could help, and he asked to speak to the night manager. I could hear Rayburn swearing and shouting, but the manager never budged. Rayburn hurried to the hotel, accompanied by Congressman John McDuffie of Alabama, the Democratic whip in the House. They identified themselves to the night manager and demanded to see Garner. He refused. Rayburn said he was going on up to the room, and the night manager stepped between him and the elevator.

We didn't want a brawl, so I suggested that we send FDR a telegram in Garner's name, deploring the incident and offering any assistance needed. Our reasoning was that it might not go well for the Vice President-elect if he slept through the whole affair without showing any reaction. People might think he was hoping for the worst.

I wrote the telegram, telling Rayburn I would publish a copy in the *Times* and send copies to the wire services. The next morning I attended a press conference Garner called at his office in the Capitol. I realized then that we'd overlooked one detail. We hadn't told Garner of the telegram we'd sent for him. So at the press conference he handed out another telegram to FDR. Some reporter pointed out that his telegram had already been printed in the morning papers. Garner looked mystified but denied having sent the first telegram. Later, I am told, Roosevelt called Garner and razzed him about the two telegrams, saying he was certainly concerned about his health.

I think the smartest politician I knew in Washington was James F. Byrnes of South Carolina. Jimmy Byrnes was a fiery little man who loved both politics and bourbon, and whose intelligence and shrewdness carried him to a remarkable career in American politics.

His life began in poverty in Charleston, South Carolina. His father died before he was born, and Byrnes' mother supported him and his sister by taking in sewing. When Jimmy was a boy, his mother bought a thirty-five cent book on shorthand and taught that skill to Jimmy, his sister Leonora, and their cousin, Frank Hogan. That thirty-five cents proved to be a wise investment, for it led Jimmy to his political career, led Leonora to a secretarial job in Washington (her daughter was to become a well-known actress, Frances Farmer), and led Frank Hogan to a celebrated legal career. After Hogan won acquittal for the oilman Edward Doheny in one of the Teapot Dome cases, he asked for a check for one million dollars as his fee. He explained that as a boy back in Charleston he'd dreamed of having a check for a million dollars. He got the check, which I later saw.

Byrnes' shorthand talent led to a job in a law office, a legal career, and finally politics. In 1924, after several terms in the House, he ran for the Senate against a racist named Cole Blease and lost, mainly because he had been born a Catholic although he had given up that religion when he married. In 1930 he ran against Blease again and beat him, and despite his lack of seniority he soon became one of the most influential men in Congress.

Byrnes was strongly pro-Roosevelt in 1932. He was a major campaign strategist, and after the election he helped Raymond Moley, Rexford Tugwell, and others in the Brains Trust plan the New Deal legislative program. This meant a lot to Roosevelt, for it helped convince Congress that not everyone around FDR was a wild-eyed liberal. Byrnes was in a position of exceptional power. He was a Senate leader and also an intimate of the President.

Yet, when FDR offered him a position on the Supreme Court, Byrnes could not refuse the honor, although he was soon bored with the job. I remember calling on him in his Supreme Court chambers one day, and his greeting me, "Come on in. I get so damn lonely up here."

He jumped at the chance to leave the Court in 1942 and become Director of Economic Mobilization—a job of such importance that he was sometimes referred to as an "Assistant President." In 1944 Roosevelt told Byrnes he was his first choice for Vice President, but when organized labor objected to Byrnes, Roosevelt picked Harry Truman instead. Thus, Truman became President instead of Byrnes, and on the train returning from Roosevelt's funeral, he told Byrnes he wanted him as his Secretary of State. But the appointment did not work out well. Byrnes envied Truman his job and disdained his talents. As Truman gained confidence, he tired of Byrnes' attitude, and within a year he replaced him with General George C. Marshall.

But all these political ups and downs were far in the future when I first met Byrnes back in 1932. He and Senator Pat Harrison of Mississippi were close friends in those days. Both of them were born manipulators, and between them they could con the pants off almost anyone in Washington.

Byrnes was nervous and high-strung. All through the day he'd take detailed shorthand notes on all the conversations he had, then he'd review them at night. Byrnes liked to drink, although he rarely if ever got drunk, as Garner sometimes would. Often he and I would meet at his office or his apartment in the Shoreham Hotel at "bullbat time" for a drink. Another visitor would often be Walter Brown. The bullbat is a bird found in the South, a nighthawk, that comes out around twilight. Thus, "bullbat time" meant something like "happy hour." When he was drinking, he liked to sing hymns and old Southern ballads, and sometimes we'd sing together.

I was closer to Byrnes personally, but Pat Harrison was a better news source for me; Byrnes had a certain caginess and Harrison was

more open. The two of them served as the chief lieutenants
on the Senate floor of the Democratic leader, Joe Robinson of
Arkansas. He was an effective operator, but a rough, tough man who
brooked no interference. He would cut down his best friend to gain
some political or legislative end. Robinson was a physically powerful
man, sometimes brutal. I recall that he liked to go hunting and kill
game until it became almost slaughter—the game laws were invented to stop men like him.

Pat Harrison was far more likable. He was a tall, stoop-shouldered
giant who had been a semiprofessional baseball player earlier in life.
An easygoing, courtly man, he reminded me of Andy in *Amos and
Andy*. He was a great practical joker and also an expert golfer and
bridge player. He was a politician to the core, and when I would see
him prowling the Senate cloakroom I would wonder, "What's the old
fox up to now?"

I recall once when Harrison, as a stalling maneuver during an
anti-lynching-bill filibuster, held up proceedings for a whole day over
the chaplains prayer of the day before. He discovered that the prayer
had been omitted from the *Congressional Record* and the copy was
missing. When the chaplain submitted a substitute copy, Harrison
objected. "I want the *Record* to carry that prayer just as God heard
it," he solemnly declared.

Politics was far more a matter of personalities than issues in
those days, and one could admire the style of a Byrnes or a Harrison
without worry about the substance of what they were up to. Pat
Harrison only lied to me once, and when I caught him he admitted
it and vowed he'd never do it again. He added, with a twinkle in his
eye, "Having given you that assurance, and you having accepted it,
I now feel free to hoodwink you any time I please."

I was present during one episode that was typical of how Harrison and Byrnes worked together. It involved my friend Walter
Brown, who had been the Washington correspondent for the Greenville *News*, but had gone back to Spartanburg, Byrnes' home town, to
start a radio station. Walter and Byrnes were good friends, and some
of the Senator's friends were putting up the money for the new station, but Walter was having a hard time because none of the national networks was interested in having an outlet in Spartanburg.

At the 1940 Democratic convention, in Chicago, Byrnes and
Harrison were on the platform committee and were being bedeviled
by radio people for a freedom-of-radio plank in the platform. The
radio industry's spokesman was a CBS vice-president named Harry
Butcher. I was with the two Senators in their hotel suite one after-

noon while they were discussing the platform. The question of the freedom-of-radio plank came up. Neither of them was much interested in it, so I made a suggestion: "Why don't you tell them to take the matter up with Walter Brown?"

Senator Harrison let out a roar and in a minute had Harry Butcher, the radio man, on the phone. His comments went somethink like this: "Hello, Harry. Jim Byrnes and I have been giving that radio plank a great deal of thought. You may have a good idea, but neither of us knows much about radio, so we think we need an expert adviser. We are going to ask our friend Walter Brown, whom you know, to advise us. You talk to Walter and we'll do whatever he advises."

Perhaps it goes without saying that the pro-radio plank got full consideration and Walter Brown's radio station got a leg up on a network affiliation with CBS.

After Roosevelt took office, he was sometimes annoyed by the close relationship between Senator Byrnes and Harrison and some of us reporters. One day Roosevelt complained to Byrnes that anything he told Pat Harrison he could expect to see the next day in the *New York Times*, the Washington *Post* or the *Wall Street Journal*, because of Harrison's ties with me, Bob Albright of the *Post*, and Alfred (Mike) Flynn of the *Journal*. Byrnes passed this complaint on to Harrison, and the next time I saw Harrison he told me he might have to be more careful in what he told me because the President was angry.

Seeing one of my best sources threatened, I resorted to some of the dramatics that are part of the reporter's arsenal. "Tell me, Senator," I demanded indignantly, "are you the mouthpiece of Franklin D. Roosevelt or are you a Senator of the sovereign state of Mississippi?"

Harrison pondered this a moment, then banged his fist on his desk and roared: "By God, I'm a Senator from Mississippi and can talk to a fellow Mississippian any time I want to!"

The one time Harrison tried to deceive me was a rather silly episode involving a secret meeting he'd attended at the White House. I discovered one morning that Harrison and some other Senators had been to a meeting at the White House. Another reporter and I, putting our heads together, decided that the meeting had dealt with a financial settlement between the United States and a small European nation, perhaps Belgium.

But when I tried to call my friend Harrison he wouldn't take my calls and finally had his secretary say he hadn't been to the White

House that morning. I knew that was a lie, so I went into a great show of righteous outrage. Finally, the Senator came on the line, pleading innocence, and I declared, "I won't bother you again, ever," and hung up. He quickly called back and invited me to his office. When I got there, I insisted that I didn't need his help; I already knew all about the meeting on Belgium.

He began to chuckle. "You've got it all wrong," he said.

I asked what he meant.

"You've got the wrong country."

Now I was worried. "What country is it, Senator?"

"It begins with an 'H,' " he said.

"Hungary?" I implored. But Harrison turned in his chair and looked innocently out the window. He had promised the President not to reveal the subject of their secret meeting, and he would not. But his helpful hint—the H—was confirmation enough for me. The next morning's *Times* carried my article on a financial settlement with Hungary, and an angry President Roosevelt confirmed the story at his news conference that day, after first denying it.

There were a great many colorful characters in Congress in those days, some of them of historical importance, others now all but forgotten.

I recall a Congressman named Buchanan, who represented the Texas district which Lyndon Johnson later served. Buchanan looked like a Western gambler and reputedly always carried a couple of thousand dollars and a pearl-handled Derringer. He was immensely proud of his tiny feet—they were reputed to be about size two—and he would wear highly-polished alligator shoes and often prop his feet up on his desk on the House floor so his colleagues (and citizens in the galleries) could admire them.

Another most striking figure in the Senate in those days was Thomas Gore of Oklahoma, whose blindness did not keep him from being a colorful and outspoken politician. He once declared in a campaign speech, "My opponent has all the attributes of a dog except loyalty." Senator Gore was sometimes accompanied by his young grandson Gore Vidal, the future playwright who used the "all the attributes of a dog" line in his play *The Best Man*.

I mentioned Percy Quin, from southern Mississippi, who declared that sometimes a statesman must rise above principle to serve his people. I recall an example of Percy's political flexibility. A man in the lumber business in my home town in Mississippi came to Washington to lobby for a tariff on foreign lumber imports. I knew that

Percy was strongly anti-tariff but I took the man around to see him.

Percy told the lumber dealer: "I'm not going to vote for any tariff. I have convinced my people that the tariff is the worst evil the Republicans ever foisted on this country. Some of my people don't know what a tariff is. Some of them think it is high-toned food them Yankees eat up North. Some of them think it's poison. So I can't vote for your tariff, but I'll tell you what I'll do. I'll get you some votes."

VII

Hoover and Roosevelt

MR. OULAHAN died in the last week of 1931. He had worked himself to death. He had been covering Congressional hearings on the German reparation moratorium and, perhaps because of the bad ventilation in the hearing room and perhaps because of his chain smoking, he contracted bronchial pneumonia. He was dead within a few days.

Mr. Oulahan's death plunged our bureau into despair. If he had not been an administrator, he had been a friend, an example and an inspiration to us. We tried to get along as we were, each man continuing to do his job, but that did not work and New York sent down James A. Hagerty, a leading political writer (and father of James C. Hagerty, Eisenhower's press secretary), to run the bureau. But Hagerty didn't like Washington and requested a return to New York. He was replaced by Arthur Krock, who was then an editorial writer in New York and previously had headed the Washington bureau of the Louisville *Courier-Journal*.

Mr. Krock's coming to Washington proved to be a great boost to my career. He did not wish to stay in Washington permanently, and as soon as he arrived he began looking for someone to groom as his successor. I proved to be that someone. I won't presume to explain how I received that honor, except that as I have said, I was working harder than most people in the bureau. I do recall one

minor exchange soon after he arrived in which I made a positive
impression on him. I was covering the "Lame Duck" Amendment,
whereby the Presidential Inauguration and the opening of Congress
were to be moved up from March to January 20 and January 3,
respectively. Mr. Krock asked me why those particular dates had
been chosen. I happened to know the answer—because fewer Sundays would fall on those two dates in the following hundred years
than any other dates—and he was impressed at my response.

One night after Mr. Krock had been in Washington a few
months he invited me to his apartment for a nightcap. He poured
us champagne—my first taste of it—then got right to the point.
He said he did not want to stay in Washington—he preferred New
York—and decided I might be the one (as he put it) to "aspire" to
the position of bureau chief. He recalled in his memoirs: "I told him
I would groom him for my job if he so desired. He did, and I proceeded to give him such opportunities as I fairly could, with reference to others on the Washington staff, all of which opportunities he
grasped with the competence I had anticipated."

Krock more than kept his promise to give me opportunities for
advancement. First, he made me the *Times'* chief Capitol correspondent. I moved my base of operation to the Senate, had other
reporters working under my direction, and could assign the best
stories to myself. A few years later, he created for me the title of
Chief News Correspondent, making it quite clear that I was his heir
apparent. He also obtained several raises for me, so that by the mid-
thirties I was earning $150 a week, quite good for those Depression
days. But his master plan failed, because Mr. Krock never did return permanently to New York, and I therefore could never succeed
him as head of the Washington bureau. But that is getting a bit
ahead of my story.

Thanks to Mr. Krock's patronage my wildest dreams had come
true. At age thirty-one I was in line to be head of the *New York
Times'* Washington bureau, and I was getting choice assignments.
For the rest of the 1930's I was able to cover many of the major
political stories of the era.

The big story of 1932 was of course the Presidential election—
the decline of the Republicans, the defeat of Herbert Hoover, and the
coming of Franklin Roosevelt's New Deal. It was clear, long before
the election, that the Depression had Hoover on the political skids.
I don't know at what point he came to realize that, but in the fall
of 1931 he decided to make a trip to the Midwest to rehabilitate himself with the voters. He scheduled a speech in Des Moines and I

was assigned to go along. Hoover got a very frosty reception and ran into all sorts of distress stories. Corn could be bought in the fields then for ten cents a bushel. Many farmers were burning it for fuel. Industrial unemployment was getting worse and worse. People just would not be consoled with Hoover's vague exhortations to new efforts and with predictions that prosperity was still just around the corner.

I think Hoover really believed that prosperity was "just around the corner." I often wondered if his people told him how bad it was in the country, if messages and reports got through to him. The capacity of politicians to delude themselves to believe what they want to believe has always amazed me. They don't like to hear bad news so their friends and employees shield them from it. More important, they shield themselves; for the human animal has a limitless capacity to see only what he wants to see.

Mr. Hoover's tragedy was that, for all his decency and ability, he lacked the flexibility to take the governmental action that was needed to combat the Depression. He was the last great advocate of laissez faire. He was intellectually, politically, even morally opposed to direct participation by the federal government in human relief programs. He initiated many programs to help private enterprise fight unemployment, but he balked at direct federal involvement. He could not see that, whatever evil might attach itself to federal intervention in the economy, it was a lesser evil than the hunger, the misery, the despair of the Depression. Private enterprise was to him almost a religion.

He was sometimes accused of being cold and callous; that was unfair. In a time of the gravest crisis, Hoover lacked the imagination, the courage, or the recklessness, call it what you will, to act. Roosevelt had them all and the people sensed this and voted accordingly.

I covered the Republican convention in Chicago. It was exceedingly dull. Hoover was renominated without noticeable opposition. The only excitement I recall came when someone tried to nominate Cal Coolidge, the patron saint of prosperity. The troublemaker, a former U.S. Senator from Maryland, was thrown bodily off the rostrum.

The Democratic convention, in the same city a few weeks later, was more fun. One of its highlights was an emotional speech nominating Al Smith, the 1928 candidate, followed by a demonstration so wild and emotional that even some of FDR's sons joined in the shouting and parading. It was rather like the Stevenson demonstration at Los Angeles in 1960; the old hero aroused emotion but the new hero had the votes. In 1932 the new hero was Governor Franklin Roosevelt, who, aided by the political genius of James A. Farley, came to Chicago with the nomination all but wrapped up. His choice was finally brought about by the skillful parliamentary handling of people like Byrnes, Harrison, and, yes, Huey Long.

I was on Hoover's train during the campaign. At first he planned only a few trips, but as he began to see the public opposition to his administration, he expanded his schedule to try to avoid a disaster. I remember his trip to Detroit, then a center of unemployment. When the train arrived in the station that afternoon, an angry mob had formed across the street and was being held back by police. The security measures at the station, and at the auditorium where Hoover spoke that night, were the most extensive any of us reporters had ever seen. Hoover saw the mob and heard its boos and insults as he was hustled out of the railroad station and driven away in a closed car. He was shaken, but his faith in laissez faire was not. That night Hoover spoke in Hamtramck, a Polish section of Detroit. Once you were admitted to the auditorium, you couldn't leave. You couldn't even get up. We at the press table had to pass our copy along the line in a sort of bucket brigade. Henry Ford was on the platform and I commented in my story on his admiration for our journalistic assembly; after all, he'd invented it. It happened that, after three years with the *Times*, I got my first by-line on that Detroit story. The paper was not so generous with by-lines in those days.

On the campaign train that fall we reporters had little contact with Hoover, but he invited me in for chats once or twice. Once he spoke to me about the position of the *Times*, which had endorsed neither candidate but clearly was leaning toward Roosevelt. He probed to see if I had any idea what the *Times* might do. Finally he said, "I wish they could see the necessity of supporting the drive I am making."

In his mind his campaign was a crusade to save the country from the Democrats and whatever economic heresy they might attempt. I suppose he was somewhat encouraged by the sizable crowds he attracted in most cities. The local Republicans could always turn out the party faithful and schoolchildren to see the President. But they were rarely enthusiastic crowds. You could feel a chill in the air.

Hoover was soundly defeated, and on his last day as President I went to tell him goodbye. When his press secretary, Theodore Joslin, ushered me into the Oval Office, Hoover was standing at the window looking out at the Washington Monument. His eyes were red; it was clear he had been weeping. We sat down and he said slowly that the country was in terrible condition, that the recent wave of bank closings was disastrous, that many of the banks were crooked, that the whole economy was in jeopardy. Hoover said there was no question that a lot of bankers should be in jail, and probably would be before it was all over. Then he became caustic and somewhat profane as he spoke of his efforts to get "that man" to join him in a statement of reassurance to the country. Roosevelt had refused. He saw no point in joining hands with a discredited administration. He would wait and issue his statements when he took power. The next day, Franklin Roosevelt was inaugurated, Hoover and his wife quietly took a train to New York, and a new era began in Washington.

To me, however, the most important event of 1932 occurred about a week before the election. I was about to accompany Mr. Hoover on a trip to Indianapolis when it became clear that the birth of our first child was imminent. By then I had decided that certain personal events justified my asking for a substitute, so I stayed in Washington to greet the new arrival, a beautiful red-headed girl who was named Mildred-Lee. Four years later, in the midst of another Presidential campaign, I hurried home from a political assignment in Minnesota for the birth of our second daughter, Ellen Douglas.

I participated in our coverage of Roosevelt's Inauguration that memorable Saturday of March 4, 1933. Prior to the ceremony I had stopped by my bank to deposit my paycheck. Just after I deposited the check, I noticed a sign saying the bank would pay out no more money. I tried frantically to get my check back but it was too late. It seemed that the banks were open at one end and closed at the other.

After the Inauguration, several of us were walking from the Capitol back to our offices. I happened to spot two bright new dimes between the rails of the streetcar track. I grabbed them and shouted: "Hallelujah, the Depression's over!"

That was the feeling throughout Washington in the days and months ahead. The New Deal had begun and you could feel its electricity wherever you went. It was an intangible thing, but it is by intangibles that men are governed. I had many reservations about Roosevelt personally, but he was a great leader, and he proved his greatness in that frantic, historic Hundred Days when he gave the nation back its faith in itself.

I had never worked harder than in the Hundred Days, as one bill after another barreled from the White House up to Capitol Hill. We reporters were running around in circles trying to keep up with the new bills, much less figure out what they meant. They came on and on—the Economy Act, the CCC, the Federal Emergency Relief Act (starting the national relief program that Hoover had so feared), TVA, the Agriculture Adjustment Act, and a half-dozen others of major proportions. Reporters were not the only ones who were confused. I recall on March 9 when the Emergency Banking Act passed in a few minutes; if anyone had looked closely, he would have seen that the "bill" the sponsoring Congressman was waiving on the House floor was in truth the morning newspaper. The real bill was still being edited.

FDR sponsored some great legislation and also some legislative fiascos that are best forgotten. Washington was filled with idea peddlers in those days, and FDR bought some half-cocked plans along with the brilliant ones. Roosevelt had no master plan; he was a master of improvisation, and as the New Deal progressed he shifted .between economy and spending, between cooperation with business and trust busting.

But, however he zigged and zagged, he gave the nation a sense of action and of confidence that billions of dollars could not have bought. We didn't fully realize it at the time, but each new piece of legislation was a part of a revolution in American government. Laissez faire was dead, replaced by a belief that the federal government must concern itself with the health, the employment, the housing, the education, and the welfare of its people. No one who had criss-crossed America in the summer and fall of 1932, as I had, could doubt that some sort of revolution was at hand. Roosevelt's genius as a political leader made it a peaceful one.

Throughout 1933 I got to know—strictly professionally—most of the leading New Dealers—Raymond Moley, Rexford Tugwell, Hugh Johnson, Harry Hopkins, Tom Corcoran, Ben Cohen, Henry Wallace, Harold Ickes, and various lesser figures. I can't say that I liked all of them. I had grown accustomed to the political style of the Congressional leaders and the New Deal's style involved a different code. To many of them, the end justified the means, and you could not rely on their word as you could that of the Congressional politicians. There was an air of evangelism about them that was new to me. They had come to save America, and they had little time to waste on cynical and questioning reporters, or on Congressional traditions. It was not the substance of what they were doing I disliked but the style in which they did it.

Many of my friends among the Southern delegations felt as I did about Roosevelt and the men around him, but in the early days of the New Deal there was no question about their loyalty to him. Roosevelt was the leader of the party, the champion of the greatest Democratic victory in history, and he had no stronger supporters in Congress than Byrnes, Harrison, Robinson, Rayburn, and some of the others I have mentioned.

Still, since the Civil War, the Democratic party has been Southern-oriented, and Roosevelt's election was the first time the power of the Southerners had been challenged. So the Southern leaders in Congress viewed Roosevelt with a certain nervousness. The attitude of the Southerners was best expressed by Garner one day when some Congressional leaders complained to him that "that s. o. b. in the White House" was doing thus-and-so. "Remember," Garner said, "he's our s.o.b."

For my own part, I never fully trusted Franklin Roosevelt. I had no clear opinion of him when he became President, the slate was clean so far as I was concerned, but over the years I had many experiences which caused me to question his sincerity and his honesty where political matters were concerned. Roosevelt was a consummate manipulator, a man who misled, deceived, lied outright, when that was necessary to gain his ends. It is easy enough now, in retrospect, to say his ends justified his means, that a political leader must be indifferent to individuals in order to advance his causes, but it was not so easy to be generous or philosophical when you were one of the people being deceived.

Roosevelt was constantly playing his aides off against one another, encouraging their rivalries, keeping them in the dark about his plans (if he had any plans), and we newspapermen sometimes got caught in the middle of this puppet show. One such experience happened to me in the spring of 1934. A great issue then was whether or not Roosevelt would cut federal spending, as he'd promised when campaigning, or use federal spending to combat the Depression. A key figure in the debate was the Budget Director, Lewis Douglas, a lean, likable man, only about five years my senior, whom I'd first known as the Representative from Arizona. He was from a wealthy Arizona mining family and believed in a strictly balanced federal budget. We had always gotten along well, and one morning in 1934 he called me to his office to show me something he thought was most important. It was a White House memorandum ordering an across-the-board cutback in federal spending, to the tune of several hundred million dollars. Douglas was triumphant. As he explained it, he had been pressing this economy move on the President and now the President had accepted his policy. I was triumphant too, since he was giving me the first, exclusive story on this major decision.

My story appeared the next morning and I was admiring it at the breakfast table when I had a call from Steve Early, the President's press secretary. He was more pleasant than usual, and he said the President wanted to see me at eleven that morning.

When I entered the President's office, he threw out his hand in a welcoming gesture. "Hello, Turner," he called out happily, "where have you been so long? I said to Steve just this morning, 'What's happened to old Turner Catledge? Why doesn't he come around any more? Get him over here.' "

I was immediately skeptical of this good fellowship. I knew Roosevelt only slightly, from attending some of his press conferences, and this was our first private meeting. Not surprisingly, I saw a clipping of my story on his desk, and he was not long in getting to the point. He pointed to the clipping, patting it with his fingertips, and said he was curious how such fantastic stories got around. He said, most affably, that I needn't have swallowed such a cock-and-bull story, for all I had to do was call him and check the facts, as I was always free to do. This was news to me.

He went on to say that the final budget plans couldn't be fixed until an estimate had been made of the needs of the relief program. My story about an agreed-on cutback, he said, was made up out of whole cloth. I told him the story might be wrong but it wasn't made up out of whole cloth—I'd gotten it from what I considered a responsible source. "Exactly," he said. "But you should be more careful where you get your stories, shouldn't you?"

He then suggested that I do another story, to the effect that the budgeting process was under way but no final decision had been made. I was not to attribute this to him, but he assured me this was the "real McCoy." I later confirmed that Roosevelt had led Douglas to believe he'd accepted his budget cuts while also leading the spenders to think he was on their side.

The plot thickened when I got to my office and had a call from Secretary of the Treasury Henry Morgenthau, asking me to lunch the next day. I accepted, of course.

We had hardly placed our napkins on our laps when Morgenthau brought up my budget story—the one I'd gotten from Douglas. Morgenthau said he wanted to thank me for absolving him and his department of any part in that "leak." He said the President had called him to assure him that Catledge had given him and the

Treasury a clean bill of health. He said he was most relieved at this, because the President didn't take kindly to leaks.

I listened for a few minutes, then I told him, "Mr. Secretary, this is very interesting, but it's not true. I didn't mention you to Roosevelt and he didn't mention you to me. He didn't treat the story as a leak—he said it was made up out of whole cloth."

Morgenthau's face lapsed into a sickly grin. Morgenthau worshiped FDR and I suppose he never knew why the President would invent a fictitious conversation with me when there was no need to. But it was Roosevelt's way—perhaps that small fiction was quicker or easier than simply telling Morgenthau the truth.

Apparently Morgenthau came to understand Roosevelt better in time, for he later told of an exchange in which Roosevelt said, "Never let your left hand know what your right hand is doing." "Which hand am I, Mr. President?" Morgenthau said. "My right hand," Roosevelt replied, "but I keep my left hand under the table." Morgenthau added: "This is the most frank expression of the real FDR that I ever listened to."

Another, more serious experience I had with Roosevelt's devious ways involved my friend and mentor Arthur Krock. Mr. Krock has told the story of this story in his own memoirs, but I would like to repeat it, as seen from my point of view. But first a word about Arthur Krock.

I have never known a finer or more inspiring person. He always gave tremendous loyalty to those under his command, to the extent of being their unquestioning advocate in any dispute with the home office or the outside world. On one occasion I became angry with Senator Robert Wagner because he would not give me some advance information on a bill he was submitting to Congress. He said he was going to make a speech on the bill later in the week, when he would send me a copy. I replied, "Then I'll be in the driver's seat." The Senator, with some justification, was angered, and called Krock to say that I had threatened him. But Krock, as was his way, simply heard out the Senator's complaint and told him Catledge was too headstrong for him to handle and he'd better work his peace.

For the absolute loyalty he gave, Krock quite naturally expected absolute loyalty in return. He is a sensitive man, and quick to notice any slight. And, as often occurs with a person of such sensitivity, he could sometimes lose faith quickly in persons who had been among his closest friends. He was not always an easy man to deal with, but to those who earned his favor the rewards were great. I was particularly resentful of Roosevelt's plotting in this instance for it could have upset what was necessarily a delicate relationship between a distinguished journalist and the ambitious young reporter he had picked as his heir apparent.

The incident occurred late in 1936, after FDR's landslide re-election victory, but there had been events leading up to it. One day in July, on a train going up to the Democratic National Convention in Philadelphia, Sam Rayburn sat down beside me and we ordered drinks. Then he told me, in low, confidential tones, that he had heard I was soon to become head of the *Times* Washington bureau.

Our drinks had not yet arrived, but I was suddenly intoxicated— I felt an almost orgasmic sensation. It had been four years since Krock told me I might someday succeed him, and the possibility had never been mentioned again. Things had happened, of course, which bespoke Krock's intention more strongly than before. My excitement returned a few nights later, in the press gallery at Philadelphia's Franklin Field, where Roosevelt was speaking. Krock whispered to me that he didn't expect to return to Washington that fall, and I could look forward with some assurance to assuming his job. He was already away from Washington for the summer, and he told me to move into his office, but to say nothing, as no announcement would come until later.

But something happened between that hot July night and the cooling fall. Krock's plan to return permanently to New York did not work out. One day his secretary told me he would be returning to Washington the next Monday and I should move back to my old desk. In fact, she had already started moving my effects. Krock, to lessen my disappointment, gave me the new title "Chief News Correspondent," which made it official that I was the bureau's number-two man. I think this fact encouraged Roosevelt to try to use me to undercut Krock.

FDR called me to the White House one day and was in a bubbling good humor when I arrived. He grabbed my hand and pointed me to a chair. Then he complimented me on some stories I'd written during the campaign, particularly one in which I'd predicted he'd carry Kansas, Alf Landon's home state. "I'll bet you got that story from Arthur Capper," he said, referring to the Kansas Senator. "You win the bet," I said, and he laughed again.

Then Roosevelt shifted into a confidential mood. A "little bird" had told him, he said, that I was about to replace Arthur Krock as the *Times'* chief correspondent in Washington. I told him that was not correct—Krock was to remain the chief correspondent but I was to be his second-in-command.

Roosevelt said that he found it difficult to get along with Krock, that they had been good friends once but that for some reason, he knew not what, their friendship had soured to the point that he preferred not to deal directly with him. He then offered to help me in any way he could if we would deal directly and leave Krock out of it. He said he couldn't give me exclusive interviews but there were many ways he and his staff could be of service— as indeed there were. (Ironically, the only exclusive interview he ever gave went to Krock a few years later and won him a Pulitzer Prize, for which I was also a candidate.)

Roosevelt said I should feel free to call upon him and the White House staff at any time. Throughout his remarks, there was the clear implication that he would do all these things for me if Krock was left out of it and knew nothing about it. To me, this was a bald-faced attempt to persuade me to undercut my friend and superior. I was stunned and I said little in reply to his offer. As soon as I could I got out of there and headed straight for Krock's office to tell him what had happened.

Krock's reaction was hard to fathom. He showed neither surprise nor anger. I don't recall that he said a word, just nodded and sent me on my way. It was almost twenty years later that I learned I had not made myself clear to Krock that day. He thought I had indeed been tempted by Roosevelt's offer to be disloyal to him. I found this out in 1955 when Mr. Krock wrote a short private memoir called "My Life with Turner Catledge." I will quote from his essay at some length, for in addition to the FDR episode it gives Krock's memories of our relationship over a number of years.

For various causes the Washington Bureau at the opening of 1932 was a dis-organized operation. The first thing I did, with the invaluable assistance of the Managing Editor's office, was to build the smoothest and most efficient news machine within my capabilities. When that was done I began my other task.

Among the several talented men whom I found in the bureau, one in particular made an instant and powerful impression on me. To explain how great was this effect I may say that, even if he had not been a Southerner like myself, I should have picked him. . . .

Some months after I began to observe Mr. Catledge closely came a night when the staff of the Bureau worked late on an eruption of big stories. At closing time I asked Mr. Catledge if he would come to my apartment in the Wardman Park Hotel for a nightcap. He did. I told him then that I intended to train him to succeed me as The Washington Correspondent, that I was convinced I could, though the obligation I had assumed and the mounting tensions in the news might defer, perhaps for ten or fifteen years, the day when I would recommend him for succession.

I sketched what kind of training I had in mind for him—in a letter I wrote to him in 1947 I remarked that he was now in the midst of acquiring "the global education which for years I have been anxious for you to have." Mr. Catledge has described what I said to him that night as "a blueprint of the major happenings of my life since."

Thereafter his work and his personality increasingly confirmed me in my choice. In 1936, in recognition of his abilities and to allay any heart-sickness he might be experiencing from hope deferred (for I could not yet set a date for recommending to the Publisher his succession) I publicly gave Mr. Catledge the new title of "Chief News Correspondent" of the Bureau.

(Typically, President F. D. Roosevelt, who had grown unfond of my reporting, saw in this a chance to get rid of me in Washington—he had tried and failed once before in a direct approach to Mr. Ochs. What the President said to Mr. Catledge and what was his reply is a story for him to tell. But at any rate the President proposed such news favoritism for Mr. Catledge as to discredit the head of the Bureau, myself. If Mr. Catledge was dazzled for a time [and he did, I think, consult a friend or two], let only those blame him who were never taken to the mountain top.)

Delighted as I was to have this memoir, I was sorry to learn, so belatedly, that Mr. Krock thought I had been "dazzled" by Roosevelt's offer, or that I had consulted with friends before making my decision. I quickly wrote to Mr. Krock saying that was not the case, and he wrote back saying, "I suppose the insinuation of undermining was so slight and subtle, knowing the gentleman, that you had to think it over before you realized what he was proposing. That is why I assumed that you were 'dazzled' for a time, as certainly I should have been."

VIII

The Court-Packing Bill

ON the night of February 4, 1937, President and Mrs. Roosevelt entertained a group of Washington reporters and their wives and several members of the White House staff, about thirty persons in all, at an informal dinner in their personal quarters in the White House. My wife and I were among those attending. I recall that we arrived a little late owing to slow traffic caused by a snowstorm. FDR was in a jovial mood that evening, and Mrs. Roosevelt was her usual charming, talkative, flutter-about self.

After dessert, the President invited the men into his oval study for brandy. He rolled his wheelchair around behind his big desk and we took seats in the chairs and sofas scattered about the room. A waiter passed around liqueurs and cigars, and FDR fastened a cigarette in his long ivory holder and lit up. And, when I say he lit up, I mean more than his cigarette. He gave a raucous guffaw, as if laughing at a particularly funny joke, and between chuckles he told us we had better be at the White House press conference that next morning, and be there on time, because he was going to release the biggest story since his Inauguration.

A dozen questions were about to be asked, but he held up his hand, palm forward, to ward them off. He said he wouldn't elaborate. He laughed some more, and, looking at his watch, said it was too late for us to check other sources, and that wouldn't help anyway because no one else knew what he was going to do. Roosevelt loved a secret, and he continued to torment us for several minutes before he changed the subject. But just as our session broke up, and Roosevelt was wheeling his chair out of the room, he again held up his hand, laughed joyously, and warned us to be on time the next morning.

Needless to say, we reporters were dizzy with curiosity and frustration. As we left, we stopped on the White House portico to take stock. We speculated on the possibilities—war debts, pending appointments, new legislation—but one topic that never entered our minds was the Supreme Court. The conflict between Roosevelt and the Court was old hat, part of the local scenery. If we had thought of the Court, we would have recalled that Roosevelt had entertained the Justices at a pleasant White House dinner only two nights before, an annual event in that era.

Some of us, when we got home, called and woke our most reliable sources, but all we learned was that leaders of Congress had been summoned to the White House the next morning, with no idea why.

His secret was, of course, the famous Court-enlargement or "Court-packing" bill, a proposal to allow the President to appoint a new Justice, up to a total of fifteen, for every Justice who refused to retire at full pay within six months of reaching the age of seventy.

The ages of the nine Justices at that time were Brandeis, 80; Van Devanter, 77; McReynolds, 75; Sutherland, 74; Hughes, 74; Butler, 70; Cardozo, 66; Stone, 65; and Roberts, 61. By the start of 1937, they had struck down nine of eleven major New Deal programs; the only two to pass were the Tennessee Valley Authority and the devaluation of gold.

Thus, there was no doubt about the intent of the Court-enlargement bill—Roosevelt would get around its conservative majority by expanding the court and appointing men who thought as he did on social issues. As he saw it, the Court, in outlawing his New Deal programs, was thwarting the national will.

The Court-packing drama's prologue had been privately played in the President's office on May 31, 1935, four days after the Supreme Court had unanimously invalidated the National Recovery Act. Some of us thought the Court had done Roosevelt a favor, since NRA was both unpopular and unworkable. But Roosevelt did not agree, and on May 31 he told Felix Frankfurter and General Hugh Johnson, the NRA's first administrator, that he wouldn't take this defeat lying down, that the country was with him and he would bring the Court into line, even if he had to "pack it."

During the next year, members of the President's inner circle knew that he planned to challenge the Court if the 1936 election went well. The election went very well, too well perhaps, for it convinced him he was invincible and thus led him into the greatest political defeat of his career—the Court-packing battle of 1937 and its outgrowth, the attempt to purge conservative Democrats in 1938.

My coverage of the Court bill, from FDR's sending it to Congress on February 5 to its death 168 days later, was a high spot of my reporting career. I followed the story seven days a week, writing every *Times* story on it except one, one day when I was sick. I had been building my contacts in Congress, and especially among the Southern leaders, for seven years, and on this story my contacts paid off. The center stage of the action was the Senate, and there was little that happened on the Court bill in the Senate that I did not know, often before the President and his advisers knew it.

The secret part of the drama took place in the winter of 1936-37 as Roosevelt studied several anti-Court proposals submitted to him by Attorney General Homer Cummings and decided that the plan to "pack"—or enlarge—the Court was the best.

There was much reason for Roosevelt to think he could win Congressional approval of a Court-expansion bill. Congress was angry at the Court, too. When the Court struck down New Deal legislation, it was striking down acts of Congress. Early in January, 1937, when a triumphant Roosevelt delivered his State of the Union Message, he received wild ovations that indicated he was in complete control of Congress. His speech included a number of remarks critical of the Court, and these were cheered especially loudly. The members of the Supreme Court broke tradition by not attending the State of the Union Message. They knew they'd be in the line of fire and they didn't intend to sit there and hear Congress cheer while Roosevelt denounced them.

The plan became public on February 5 when Roosevelt unveiled it first to Congress leaders, then to reporters. He was very casual with the Congressional leaders. His secretary handed them copies of the bill, which they had no time to read, then FDR made a few general comments. The meeting lasted only a few minutes, for the President had to hurry on to his press conference. Most of the Congressional leaders were stunned. Roosevelt did not ask for their comments and they did not volunteer any.

But one Congressman, Hatton Sumners, chairman of the House Judiciary Committee, had a comment as he and the others rode back to the Capitol.

"Boys," he said, "here's where I cash in my chips."

Dexter Library
Northland College
Ashland, Wisconsin 54806

He thus became the first Democrat to defect on the Court bill, the first of many. It was largely because of Sumners' opposition that the administration decided to seek passage for the bill first in the Senate.

Roosevelt was probably surprised by the violent opposition his bill aroused, opposition among some of his most devout admirers, like Felix Frankfurter. The President had logic on his side. He had an overwhelming popular mandate for reform, yet five old men on the Court were thwarting his reforms. What could be more logical than to expand the Court, by a perfectly valid piece of legislation, so he could appoint to it men who believed as he did?

But politics is not always logical. Roosevelt had once dismissed the Court as an appendage of the Republican party, but to millions of Americans it is an almost religious institution, a great temple in which solemn, incorruptible men in black robes make great decisions that protect the Constitution and thus the national honor. Roosevelt's view of the Court may have been the more realistic, but the popular view was to prevail.

Another, more personal point about the bill outraged many liberals, its implication that old age equaled judicial inability. This seemed an insult to the eighty-year-old Justice Brandeis, who was perhaps the only man in America whom liberals admired more than Roosevelt himself, and it also insulted the still-fresh memory of Justice Holmes. Roosevelt of course brushed these objections aside, saying that the principle involved in the Court bill was more important than personal feelings. But personal feelings cannot be ignored in politics—Brandeis hated the bill, as did Justices Cardozo and Stone, two other New Deal stalwarts, and they let their friends know how they felt.

Roosevelt was supremely confident. By mid-February, the Democratic leaders in the House reported he could count on a one-hundred-vote majority there, and Joe Robinson, the Senate Majority Leader, reported fifty-four sure votes. When Vice President Garner, sensing the trouble ahead, suggested a compromise bill, Roosevelt laughed loudly.

But, while Roosevelt laughed, his opposition made two great gains in those early weeks. First, the Republican leaders in Congress shrewdly agreed to a "conspiracy of silence" against the bill. They decided that if they attacked the bill the Democrats might unite, but that if they kept quiet the rival Democratic factions would be encouraged to fight among themselves. It was a wise strategy.

The other gain for the opposition came when Tom Corcoran

(who didn't like the Court-packing scheme, but fought for it vigorously) had lunch with Senator Burton K. Wheeler. They had worked together effectively on FDR's Holding Company Bill, and Corcoran hinted that the Senator could name two or three of the new Justices if he backed the Court-expansion bill. Wheeler declined, and the hot-tempered Corcoran pounded the table.

"It's going to pass," he declared.

"I tell you it isn't going to pass," Wheeler replied. "And, what's more, I'm going to fight it with everything I've got."

Thus the opposition acquired its leader, a man whose record of untiring effort for liberal causes and against the monied interests made it impossible to impute reactionary motives to him. Wheeler simply felt that meddling with the Supreme Court, for however worthy a purpose, was wrong. He soon emerged as the leader of a well-organized, and ever-growing band of Democratic oppositionists.

The jockeying for public opinion had begun. Roosevelt banked heavily on his golden voice. On March 4, in a nationally broadcast speech delivered at a Democratic party dinner, he made a plea for party loyalty. Five days later, in one of his "fireside chats," he asked the nation to trust him, to have faith in him and his motives. Before that talk, many of Roosevelt's advisers were urging him to compromise, to say he would accept a constitutional amendment as a substitute for his bill, but he refused, and in retrospect we see what a mistake that was.

The oppositionists were also busy. They managed one coup when they obtained a letter from Chief Justice Hughes denying that new Justices were needed so the Court could keep up with its work. The administration thus had to abandon one of its key arguments.

FDR's defeat was assured on March 29, when the Court upheld the Railway Labor Act and the Farm Mortgage Moratorium Act, both by unanimous decisions, and by a five-to-four decision reversed its stand of a few months earlier on the New York Minimum Wage Law. Justice Roberts had moved over to form a liberal majority. Two weeks later, the Court upheld the Wagner Labor Relations Act —and in a supreme political paradox Roosevelt had won and he had also lost.

The Court had decided to save itself by reversing itself, to defeat Roosevelt by giving him what he wanted. Two months before he had taken a radical move to get a liberal Court. Now he had a liberal Court and he had to decide what to do about it. He could have announced that, since the Court had liberalized itself, he would abandon his Court plan. Instead, he declared that the Court's move was only political expediency, that the national welfare was still at the whim of a few old men, and that he still wanted and needed his Court bill.

After the Court upheld the Wagner Act, Roosevelt told his Congressional leaders he was pressing ahead with the bill. He did not ask their advice, just as he had not asked it about the Court scheme in the first place. The Democratic leaders were deeply concerned about the split the bill was creating in the party, but when they tried to advise the President he ignored them. They were offended, and they resolved to offer no more advice until it was called for, come what may.

Yet many of them believed it sheer folly to push the bill after the Court had reversed itself. As Jimmy Byrnes put it, "Why run for a train after you've caught it?" But Roosevelt kept running.

One reason Roosevelt kept running was overconfidence, the overconfidence of a man who had enjoyed a decade of success in great political matters. Another reason was both personal and political. It involved a complicated equation between him, his Majority Leader, Joe Robinson of Arkansas, and one of the ultra-conservatives on the Court, Justice Van Devanter.

Roosevelt had made a promise, some two years earlier, that Robinson would have the next appointment to the Supreme Court. It was well known, too, that Robinson wanted that appointment, to crown his political career. Deep inside, Robinson must have had misgivings about the Court bill, for he was a traditionalist by nature, but he had to fight for it, because he was the Democratic Leader and also because he could hardly expect his appointment unless he gave his all for the bill.

It happened that one leading Republican oppositionist, Senator Borah of Idaho, was a close friend of Justice Van Devanter and knew he was anxious to retire. Borah discussed this fact with Senator Wheeler, and they agreed that Van Devanter's retirement might resolve the entire dispute—Roosevelt could replace him with Joe Robinson and thus get his desired majority without the Court-expansion plan. In theory FDR could appoint Robinson and drop the controversial bill.

Van Devanter did retire, on May 18, but Roosevelt refused to drop the bill. The reason was one that created even further division among the Democrats—Roosevelt and many of the men around him did not trust Robinson. He had fought hard for the New Deal, but he was a Southerner and therefore suspect. The President's advisers, men like Corcoran and Hopkins, and to an extent Roosevelt himself, thought of the Southerners as a pack of dust-stained politicians, adequate to lead Congress, but lacking in the New Deal brand of realism. They feared that Robinson might revert to conservatism if given the security of the Supreme Court.

Thus, to appoint Robinson was not good enough—they might just face another hostile five-to-four majority. If Robinson was to get an appointment, as he must, the Court must be expanded so a liberal majority would be assured.

After Van Devanter retired, the President proceeded to treat Joe Robinson shabbily. Robinson should have been called in and given some assurance of his status. Instead, he was ignored, and he was too proud to call the President first and seem to be begging. Finally, after two weeks of silence, Robinson was summoned to the White House. The President's talk with Robinson on June 3 marked a turning point in the Court fight. Roosevelt finally agreed he would have to compromise. The President asked for advice, and Robinson suggested that he be allowed to settle matters the best he could. Robinson was smiling when he left the White House. But forty-one days later he would be dead and so would Roosevelt's hopes even for a face-saving compromise.

Robinson, given full command of a fight, and assured that he was slated for the Supreme Court, threw himself into the battle with the single-mindedness of a man whose life's ambition is about to be fulfilled. He shrewdly seized upon a compromise proposal that would allow the President to appoint an extra Justice for each Justice who passed age seventy-five, but forbade more than one such appointment per year. Then, in a long series of personal interviews, he persuaded fifty-two Senators to support this compromise. Most agreed out of loyalty to Robinson, not out of enthusiasm for the bill, but he got his votes.

Robinson's next duty was to lead the Senate loyalists in the floor debate. A great red-faced, heavy-bodied man with a roaring voice, he stood in the crowded chamber, sawing the air with his right arm, bellowing his challenges and threats to the opposition. Robinson was essentially an ordinary partisan politician, without remarkable intellectual equipment, but he had a solidity and vitality which made him a leader. He compelled respect.

As Robinson led the debate, he was angry and bellicose, and the opposition replied in kind. From the press gallery, we could see him grow angry and red-faced at the heckling. Senator Royal Copeland of New York, a physician, hurried over to Robinson and told him to take it easy, that he was endangering his life. That only made Robinson madder. The debate dragged on for a week and Robinson grew depressed, both by the attacks on the Senate floor and by the news that some of the President's intimates were saying that if he didn't get the bill he'd never get the Supreme Court appointment.

On July 12 Robinson left the Senate floor with a pain in his chest. On the morning of the 13th he felt too weak to go to the Capitol, and remained in his small apartment nearby to rest. The next morning he was found dead there, sprawled on the floor in his pajamas. His glasses were on the bed and beside his right hand was a copy of the *Congressional Record.* This last fact intensified a bitter belief among his friends that he had worked himself to death, fighting a lost cause for an ungrateful President.

When Robinson died, the Court bill died with him, although another nine days were required to bury it. Senators who had pledged their vote to Robinson felt that his death ended their commitments. Roosevelt did not help matters any when he declined to make the trip to Arkansas for Robinson's funeral.

Funeral trains in those days were great political institutions, and this was one of the greatest of them all. I upset some Senators by describing it in one of my dispatches as "a political convention on wheels." On that train, speeding through the flatlands of middle America, a political caucus was going on from the baggage car behind the engine to the door of the flower-banked office car carrying Robinson's body at the rear.

Thirty-odd Senators, assorted Representatives, a dozen or so reporters, and three top political agents for the administration—Jim Farley, Charles West, and Joe Keenan—were aboard. The administration's men were still trying to find a compromise solution to the Court bill, but the Senators were much more interested in who would succeed Robinson as Senate Majority Leader. The two contenders were Alben Barkley of Kentucky, an all-out supporter of Roosevelt, and Pat Harrison of Mississippi, who wanted the Senate Democrats to maintain a degree of independence from the White House.

The politicking was so intense that I commented in one story that the main business of the trip—burying Joe Robinson—was all but overlooked. When a copy of my article reached the train, as it headed back to Washington, I was summoned to see Senators Harrison and Byrnes in their drawing room. Two other reporters, who had made similar observations, were also summoned, and Senator Harrison proceeded to upbraid us for "irreverent" reporting.

"You newspaper boys should be ashamed of yourselves," he said, "for writing that we've turned this train into a political convention on wheels. We've been to Little Rock to bury our good old friend, that distinguished American, Joe Robinson, and you are describing us as a bunch of callous politicians."

Senator Byrnes chimed in, pounding the table and shouting with outrage at our cynicism.

Harrison added, "Why, you say here in one place that we've been buttonholing Senators for their votes on the leadership contest." He paused, looked at Senator Byrnes, and added with his slyest chuckle, "Jim, is there anyone we've overlooked?"

One example of their buttonholing Senators on that train ride involved Senator Claude Pepper of Florida. Pepper usually went down the line with FDR, but he was supporting Harrison for Senate Leader instead of Roosevelt's candidate, Barkley. Pepper told Byrnes and Harrison of a freshman Senator, a former judge, whose vote they might win with some subtle persuasion. So Byrnes and Harrison called the Senator in for a friendly chat and proceeded to woo him. They said they understood he'd once been a distinguished judge and commented that he surely should serve on the Judiciary Committee someday. The implication was clear that they'd be deciding who served on the Judiciary Committee. They never asked for the ex-judge's vote for Harrison, but they got it anyway, although I don't recall that the man ever got on Judiciary.

When the train had arrived in Little Rock, Vice President Garner had been on the platform to greet it. The old Uvalde fox was in a self-declared exile from Washington, as a result of his disgust with Roosevelt's handling of the labor situation and his failure to balance the budget. Nonetheless, he was disturbed by the split in the party that the Court fight was causing, and he joined the return trip of the funeral train in hopes he could patch up the dispute.

As the return trip began, Garner held a series of conferences with leaders on both sides of the fight. Garner was occupying the office car in which Robinson's body had made the trip to Arkansas and that was where his conferences were held. By the end of the first day, he saw that no compromise was possible. The administration faced total defeat.

On July 20, Garner visited the White House. The President greeted him with a great show of cordiality. Garner said he had come to talk about the Court fight. Roosevelt nodded.

"Boss, do you want it with the bark on or the bark off?" Garner asked.

The President said he didn't understand that phrase. Garner explained that in his part of Texas people asked for opinions "with

the bark off" if they wanted the naked truth, but if they wanted their
feelings spared they asked for advice "with the bark on." Roosevelt
laughed heartily at this, and said Garner should speak "with the bark
off." Somehow this exchange sums up much of the trouble he had
with his Southern allies on the Court fight and on many other matters. Figuratively, sometimes literally, they didn't speak the same
language.

Garner gave him the facts, and Roosevelt agreed that the bill
would have to be withdrawn, as it was, on July 29, ending the 168-
day struggle. A brief obituary for the bill was spoken on the Senate
floor. Members of the Judiciary Committee, to spare the President
further embarrassment, had agreed that the bill could be recom-
mitted without ever mentioning the words "Supreme Court." But,
as Senator Logan of Kentucky made the motion for recommittal, old
Hiram Johnson of California, who was not a party to the agreement,
had a question.

"The Supreme Court is out of it?" he demanded.

"The Supreme Court is out of it," Logan replied solemnly.

"Glory be to God!" shouted Johnson and the galleries broke into
wild applause.

Only a few seconds later, the Logan motion to recommit passed
by 70 to 21. The Court fight was over, but the battle within the
Democratic party had just begun.

Joe Alsop and I started collaborating on magazine articles early
in 1936. He was working as a Capitol Hill correspondent for the
New York *Herald Tribune*, and we hit it off well as friendly competitors. Joe was then a jolly fat lad, 25 years old and weighing about
260 pounds. One day he asked if I'd like to collaborate with him on
an article for the *Saturday Evening Post* on Joe Robinson. I said
I'd be glad to—magazine writing meant extra money, a boost for
my standing as a writer, and an opportunity to write in more depth
and detail than I could in daily newspaper articles.

Joe suggested the article to the *Post* editors and they were delighted at the idea of a collaboration by two rival reporters. The
Robinson article pleased the *Post,* and we wrote six or eight more
articles for it in the next couple of years. We were paid about $1,250
to $1,500 for each article. Even split two ways, that was good money
in those days.

In writing the articles, one of us would sit at the typewriter and
the other would pace the floor. We would toss ideas and phrases
back and forth until we'd decided what to say, then the one at the

typewriter would type it out. We had plenty of arguments, and sometimes I'd catch Joe writing things his way despite my objections. Joe was an exceedingly well-educated young man and a wonderful stylist. The references to Shakespeare and the classics in our articles were usually his, while the more homely phrases tended to be mine. The collaboration produced, I think, a richer, fuller style than either of us could have managed alone.

From April to August, while the Court fight was in progress, Joe was in the Johns Hopkins Hospital in Baltimore shedding eighty-odd pounds, but we continued with our writing. I would go to Baltimore a couple of nights a week and by dodging nurses and violating visiting hours I was able to continue our partnership. Joe hated missing the Court fight and was thrilled by my descriptions of it. We'd been discussing the idea of writing a book on the Senate and we agreed that the Court fight should be one chapter in it. When a *Post* editor called to complain that we hadn't written for him lately, Joe told him of our projected book, and the editor proposed that we go ahead with the chapter on the Court fight and the *Post* would publish it.

The result was a three-part series in the *Post,* appearing in September and October, for which we were paid $6,000. We wrote the series on Saturdays and Sundays in a room in the Carlton Hotel, using my *Times* articles as a starting point, but adding more research and elaboration. We found the actors in the drama, both from the Senate and the administration, anxious to put forth their versions of the events. The only exception was the President, with whom we did not speak, although he and Joe were cousins. I must confess that I was often shocked to discover through our additional research the imperfections and inaccuracies of the newspaper reporting of the episode, my own included, and in many instances we were able to set the record straight.

Once the articles appeared in the *Post,* a number of publishers said they'd like to issue our version of the Court fight as a book. Some were anxious to publish the *Post* articles as they were, but Joe and I thought the story should be further expanded and refined for book publication. We settled on Doubleday, Doran as our publisher, largely because another of Joe's cousins, Theodore Roosevelt, Jr., was an editor there. We received a flat payment of $1,800 with no royalties later. Theodore Roosevelt, Jr., was quite confident that the book would win the next year's $2,500 prize for the Theodore Roosevelt Memorial Book Award, but although the book, called *The 168 Days,* was favorably reviewed and became a best seller, we didn't win the award.

With my money from the *Post* articles and the book, my wife and I made our first trip to Europe. While I was away Joe and I were approached about writing a syndicated political column for the North American Newspaper Alliance. Joe was very much annoyed that I didn't warm to this offer. I felt, as I told him, that we got along together very well so long as we could tell each other to go to hell, as we sometimes did, but we shouldn't be too dependent on one another. Joe thought I was too dazzled by the *New York Times,* too reluctant to strike out on my own. Perhaps he was right. But devotion to the *Times* was not the only reason I passed up that opportunity. I didn't want to get into political punditry. I wanted to stick to reporting, where I was more confident and where I thought I could do my best work.

IX

FDR's Purge

THE defeat of the Court-enlargement bill left President Roosevelt with quite a long son-of-a-bitch list. The full extent of his anger and bitterness became apparent in the spring of 1938, when he began his campaign to "purge" conservative Democrats in the party primaries that year.

Roosevelt was frustrated by the fact that, despite his great victory in 1936, his legislative program had bogged down in Congress in 1937. He felt that many moderate and conservative Democrats had ridden to victory on his coat tails, then had stabbed him in the back once they got to Capitol Hill. The purge was a bold attempt to defeat key conservative Democrats and in so doing to intimidate others. To achieve it, Roosevelt had to reverse his policy of never intervening in party primary elections, and this reversal outraged traditional politicians like Jim Farley. A crude grab for power, the purge turned out to be an almost total disaster for Roosevelt, one that might have been his political undoing had not the coming of the war assured his re-election.

I was able to observe much of the 1938 purge struggle, both from my outpost on Capitol Hill and as a roving political correspondent. Rumors of a possible purge had been spreading in Congress throughout the early spring. Despite Roosevelt's love of secrecy, it was hard to keep such a sensational plan secret, particularly when some administration figures, like Farley, opposed the plan and confided in the conservative Democratic Senators.

The first tangible evidence of the purge campaign came on May 25 when Harry Hopkins went out of his way to tell a reporter that if he were voting in his native Iowa that year, he would vote for Representative O. D. Wearin against incumbent Senator Guy Gillette in the Democratic primary.

Harry Hopkins was, of course, the WPA (Works Progress Administration) administrator, an intimate of the President, and one of the shrewdest men in Washington. It was inconceivable that his slap at Gillette was a casual or accidental remark. When news of his remarks reached Capitol Hill, the conservative Democrats knew the battle had begun. Several Senators told me that day that Hopkins' support of Wearin was only the curtain raiser in a campaign to rid the party of less-than-one-hundred-percent New Dealers. They told me that the administration's political agents were already lining up candidates to run against Senators George in Georgia, Smith in South Carolina, McCarran in Nevada, and Tydings in Maryland. They were entirely right in their predictions.

Roosevelt deserves full credit—or blame—for the purge campaign, but undoubtedly several advisers did all they could to encourage it, including Hopkins, Tom Corcoran, Harold Ickes, and the President's son James Roosevelt. Hopkins was believed to be the strongest proponent of the purge. Many of us believed that Hopkins hoped to be the Democratic candidate for President in 1940, if Roosevelt did not seek a third term, and saw the purge as a means of eliminating conservative opposition within the party.

Soon after Hopkins kicked off the purge in Iowa, I journeyed out to that state to see how the President's scheme was working. I found the state's Democrats in open rebellion against the President. The state's Governor, its other Senator, and virtually every political leader down to the precinct level, had come out strong for Gillette. On June 7 he defeated the administration's candidate by a two-to-one margin. The first purge attempt had suffered a stinging defeat, but Roosevelt pushed ahead with the plan.

In July Roosevelt made a zigzag train trip across the nation, stopping off in a half-dozen states to give his blessing to candidates he favored. In Kentucky, he sang the praises of the loyal Alben Barkley, and noted that it would take many years for his opponent, Governor A. B. (Happy) Chandler to equal Barkley's experience and seniority. In Oklahoma he praised his "old friend" Senator Elmer Thomas and in Texas he had warm words for Congressmen Lyndon

Johnson and Maury Maverick and a pointed snub for Senator Tom Connally. Passing through Arizona he did his best to ignore Senator Pat McCarran, and in California he found another "old friend" in Senator William McAdoo.

Roosevelt then began a long sea cruise from California through the Panama Canal and back to Florida. While he was on the high seas, he received some good political news. Senators Barkley and Thomas, aided by his blessing, had won their primaries. This was encouraging to Roosevelt, so as he moved back to Washington by train he decided to launch his purge in earnest against a major opponent, Senator Walter George of Georgia.

I did not know Senator George intimately, but I held him in great respect. He was not a member of the Bureau of Education, nor was he one who induced close relationships. He was from a poor family in Vienna (pronounced Vy-anna), Georgia, had studied law and become a judge at an early age. He always retained the dignified manner of a judge. His bearing is suggested by the fact that his wife always called him "Mr. George." He was an excellent orator. He may have been the only man in the Senate whom Huey Long was afraid of; once, after George had cut him to ribbons with a few scornful remarks, Long said, "Boy, I'll never tangle with that porcupine again."

With his dignity and reserve, George had never been viewed as a demagogue, or even as a politician with much mass appeal. The Georgia Power Company was one of the great forces in that state's politics, and George was considered its candidate. At least he was of the essence of Southern conservatism. However, in the purge campaign, Franklin Roosevelt achieved the considerable feat of making Walter George into a man of the people.

Their clash began with a remarkable confrontation in a football stadium in Barnesville, Georgia, on August 11. In theory, FDR was there to throw the switch for a new federal electrification project. In fact, he forgot to throw the switch, but he nonetheless jolted his audience by urging them not to return Walter George to the Senate. With Senator George on the platform with him, the President said of him, "On most public questions, he and I do not speak the same language."

When Roosevelt finished, Senator George shook his hand and said: "Mr. President, I want you to know that I accept the challenge."

I was present when George began his counterattack four days later in the little town of Waycross. He spoke to a sweltering crowd of fifteen hundred who had come to see him fight for his political life. It was a dramatic moment, and George made the most of it.

"I was born in South Georgia," he began, "the son of a tenant farmer. I have known how it feels to want things I cannot have. Back there in the days when, as a boy, I plowed the white soil of . . ." Here his voice broke. A tear trickled down the side of his face. You could have heard a pin drop. The audience was his.

George then proceeded to deliver a brilliant political speech. One of his themes was that he was a true Democrat—but an independent Georgia Democrat.

"Don't you want to choose your own representatives?" he shouted, throwing his head forward so a lock of hair shot across his brow like the crack of a whip.

"Yes," the crowd roared.

"Don't you want him to use his own sincere, God-given independent judgment?"

"Yes," they roared again.

George's basic problem was that FDR was immensely popular in Georgia—the President had attacked him, but he dared not attack the President. So, in the classic political style, he attacked the people around the President. "I know, like all other human beings, the President is often supplied with misinformation."

George then proceeded to denounce Tom Corcoran; "Benny" Cohen; James Ford, the Negro Vice Presidential nominee of the Communist party; and "the Communist group of John L. Lewis."

It was anti-Negro, anti-Semitic, anti-labor, anti-Yankee—and the crowd loved it. Soon they were on their feet, cheering wildly. Shouts of "Go to 'em, Walter," and "Let 'em have it," were punctuated by rebel yells.

As I watched this scene, I was both amused and startled. It was amusing to see this angry crowd screaming, "Go to 'em, Walter," for he was the last man in America most of them would have called Walter in normal circumstances. This dignified, tall man in a blue suit and starched collar was everything his audience was not—but in this hour he had become their champion. Yet it saddened me, too, to hear a racist speech come out of Walter George's mouth, for I knew from the Senate what reasoned, eloquent speeches he could deliver. But in political terms his speech was brilliant. Four weeks later he was re-elected by a wide margin, and FDR's candidate finished a poor third. George had done what he had to do. It reminded me of what Pat Harrison used to say—that he could be a statesman for five years, but on the sixth—election year—he went back home to "sling the shit."

The Georgia, South Carolina, and Maryland primaries all took place in late August and early September. I shuttled among the

three states reporting on them. In South Carolina, Roosevelt backed
Governor Olin Johnson against Senator Ellison D. ("Cotton Ed")
Smith, and in Maryland the New Dealers were pushing Representative David J. Lewis, a dedicated liberal who once had worked as a
coal miner, against Senator Millard Tydings.

I saw the same factors at work in all three states. Southerners
are easily offended by "outsiders." The President was "meddling,"
"interfering in local affairs." Moreover, many people were becoming
disenchanted with the New Deal programs, if not with Roosevelt
himself. Perhaps the trouble with the purge was that it was too
logical, more logical than American politics is. If FDR was immensely popular, as he unquestionably was, it seemed logical that
he should use his popularity to elect Democrats who would support
him. But the fact is that the majority of the voters are entirely
willing to vote for a liberal President and a conservative Senator, and
see nothing inconsistent in their actions. To a great extent, this
illogic is a result of our system of checks and balances.

One of the unpleasant by-products of the purge campaign was a
revival of racism in Southern politics. There was no justice in
Southern race relations in the 1930s, but at least there was a measure of restraint. It was not a time of violence, and some small progress had been made. But some of the targets of Roosevelt's purge
found it useful to picture themselves as defenders of white supremacy and their New Deal opponents as race mixers and to stir up the
fears of white Southerners that the federal government was out to
give Negroes the vote. The bitterness of the "Reconstruction Era" was
easily re-aroused.

As I wrote in a dispatch on August 27: "It cannot be said
definitely now that the new management of the Democratic party
has any definite designs toward re-enfranchising Southern Negroes
or interfering in the South's segregation laws. It can be reported,
however, that the politicians seeking to defend themselves against
the 'purge' are shouting the possibilities and citing evidence which,
apparently, is carrying conviction to many that white supremacy has
returned as a political issue in the South."

The worst offender was Ellison DuRant (Cotton Ed) Smith of
South Carolina.

Cotton Ed was a racist of the first order, yet he was no illiterate
redneck, as were some of his fellow demagogues. He could read
Latin and Greek and could quote endlessly from the classics. When
he was ungrammatical, it was deliberate and for a purpose. He was
not much of a statesman, but he was a great showman. I remember
saying to him once, "Senator, somebody told me you'd shoot a duck

on water." Cotton Ed thought about it a moment, then replied, "Depends how bad I wanted a duck."

He was a rumpled thick-set man with a salt-and-pepper mustache, who loved hunting and fishing. There was a famous picture of him surrounded by a couple of dozen of his hunting dogs. He autographed a copy for my (and his) friend Walter Brown: "For Walter, who is as faithful as one of these." Cotton Ed had the reputation of being notoriously slow to pay his bills; his friends used to say they had to keep running him for the Senate so he'd collect enough campaign funds to pay his debts. If so, it was a successful strategy—he was running for his sixth term in the Senate when Roosevelt set out to defeat him.

Smith was almost omitted from the purge. On the way up from Georgia, when he had declared war on Walter George, Roosevelt stopped briefly in Greenville, South Carolina. Jimmy Byrnes was still very friendly with Roosevelt, and some of his political allies boarded Roosevelt's train to try to persuade Roosevelt not to intervene in South Carolina. They thought they had persuaded Harry Hopkins, who in turn thought he had persuaded Roosevelt, but then Roosevelt impulsively went after Smith anyway.

Smith had once made a remark during debate on a minimum-wage bill that could be interpreted as justifying a wage of fifty cents a day in sunny South Carolina. So Roosevelt, just as his train was pulling out of Greenville, declared, "I don't believe any family or man can live on fifty cents a day."

He didn't mention Smith by name, but the challenge was clear. No one doubted that Cotton Ed thought plenty of people could and should live on fifty cents a day. But Senator Byrnes and my friend Walter Brown, one of Cotton Ed's strategists, checked the *Congressional Record* and found that what the Senator had said was quite ambiguous. It could be read to say the opposite—that no man could live on fifty cents a day in South Carolina. Within twenty-four hours, the Smith organization was blanketing the state with copies of the *Congressional Record* page, with Smith's remarks circled in red. The caption said, "This page of the *Congressional Record* is reproduced and circulated by friends of Senator Smith who resent the efforts of Olin Johnson and his henchmen to try to trick President Roosevelt into telling a lie." Here again, the purge victims were walking a narrow line. They didn't dare call FDR a liar. But they were happy to suggest that someone else had tricked the popular President into telling a lie.

The purgees were drawn together in common defense. They exchanged ideas and plans. One night late in the South Carolina primary I went to see Cotton Ed at the house he had taken over in Columbia. He was chomping away on a big cud of tobacco, spitting at and frequently missing a tomato can. He and I and Walter Brown were talking when a call came for the Senator from Senator George over in Georgia, who wanted to know how things were looking. In the course of the conversation Senator George said: "Well, Ed, I guess we'll have to agree with Jim Farley that Roosevelt is his own worst enemy."

"Not so long as I live," Cotton Ed shouted.

I won't try to describe Ed Smith's campaign in detail. Suffice to say that he won handsomely. But there is one aspect of Smith's campaign, involving his racism, that I'll describe because it had an amusing aftermath that involved me.

Cotton Ed, as I've said, was using the race issue as a weapon in his fight against Roosevelt. Ed used to say that his platform had only four planks—tariff for revenue only, high prices for cotton, states' rights, and white supremacy. He said that any man who couldn't be elected in South Carolina on that platform must have serious personality problems.

But by 1938 three of his planks were sagging. The tariff issue had been taken away by Cordell Hull's reciprocal trade policies; cotton marketing had largely been taken over by government; and states' rights was a dying concern because the states had so willingly accepted the New Deal welfare programs. This left only white supremacy for Cotton Ed to run on, and run on it he did.

Unwittingly, Smith had laid the groundwork for his 1938 campaign in 1936 when he walked out of the Democratic National Convention, in Philadelphia, because a Negro minister was called on to offer the prayer at one of the sessions. (The minister later commented: "Brother Smith needs more prayer.")

Ordinarily, for a South Carolina Democrat to walk out of the Democratic convention would have hurt him politically back home—it would be like an archbishop walking out of the Vatican. But, given the new racial fears of 1938, Smith was able to use his walkout to good advantage. He made a famous speech one hot sultry evening in Gaffney, South Carolina, when someone in the audience asked him if it was true he'd walked out of the Democratic convention. I'm sure Smith or his aides had planted that question, for he was ready with an impassioned reply. The gist of Cotton Ed's long and flamboyant declaration was that, yes, it was true, he had walked out of the Democratic convention rather than suffer the indignity of being led in prayer by a black man—and he was proud of it!

The audience in Gaffney loved that declaration and Smith repeated the speech all over South Carolina. I heard it many times and, to my outsider's ears, it was a hilariously funny performance. (One might say, too, that it was sad, even tragic, that the voters of South Carolina responded to such an appeal, but the speech was nonetheless funny.) When I returned to Washington I would repeat the speech to my friends, sometimes embellishing it a bit in the process. I told it to George Holmes, then President of the Gridiron Club, and he insisted that I deliver my Cotton Ed speech at the annual Gridiron Dinner that year. I did, and the audience enjoyed it, and my rendition became an annual event for a number of years.

The first time I delivered the speech as part of a skit at a Gridiron Dinner, Cotton Ed was present and I hadn't any idea what his reaction would be. I'd tipped off Jimmy Byrnes to be prepared to subdue Senator Smith if he became violent. But Cotton Ed loved the attention. He stood up and laughed and applauded after I finished, and after that he always called me Senator Smith. But eventually the speech became a casualty of the maturing national understanding of civil rights, for by the early 1950s racial humor no longer was funny—even when the target of the humor was not the Negroes but the demagogue.

X

Rogues and Statesmen

AS a Washington correspondent, and as a national correspondent who made political scouting tours across America every two years, I got to know most of the politicians who flourished in the decade and a half beginning in 1930. For the most part, these were professional, not personal, relationships but they were usually quite cordial. We reporters interviewed the politicians in Washington, rode with them on campaign trains, drank and commiserated with them at the national conventions, and a good deal of affection and understanding often arose on both sides.

Most of the politicians I knew are well-known American figures, and have been the subjects of exhaustive biographical studies. Without attempting to compete with the historians, I would like to add a few recollections of my own.

One of the politicians I liked best was Fiorello La Guardia. Almost everyone in Washington liked La Guardia. He was fiery and independent, and he could be cruel and ruthless politically, but personally he was a warm, delightful man. At least that was true when I knew him as Congressman; later, as Mayor of New York, he became more difficult to deal with. But in Washington he was a great favorite of newspapermen. Some of us who were especially close to him would sometimes be invited to his apartment for Sunday-night dinner. He and his wife, his second wife, lived in an apartment in Foggy Bottom, near the present location of the State Department.

Both the food and drink were excellent at La Guardia's dinners. He hated Prohibition and delighted in flouting it. But the real attraction was his Italian dinners. His wife would sit with the guests while La Guardia did the cooking, dancing in and out of the kitchen with his pots and pans, stirring the spaghetti and sauces, always talking a blue streak. Then, after the meal, came the pièce de résistance. Those were the days of the Ford Symphony Hour on the radio, and when it came on La Guardia would change from his chef's outfit to tails and white tie, bring out a podium and music rack, seize his baton and "conduct" the symphony. It was truly a virtuoso performance.

One thing that made La Guardia such a fine news contact was his own curiosity, and his own need to know. Being a loner, he had to get his own information. He didn't get much from other politicians, but he considered reporters one of his best sources. In my case, of course, he wanted a close contact on the *New York Times,* which served his constituency, but we moved beyond our professional relationship to a personal fondness that lasted as long as he lived. He loved children, and when my wife was expecting our first child in 1932 he asked about her every time I saw him. Soon after the child was born, he was defeated and returned to New York, but he sent the baby a gift—a picture of himself. A year or so later, after he had been elected mayor, he and his wife came to Washington on a visit and spent an afternoon at my house, with the mayor down on the floor most of the time giving my little girl a "horsy" ride on his back.

Most of the Southern Congressmen, who often weren't fond of their Eastern colleagues, nonetheless liked La Guardia. Garner was fond of him in his gruff way; he called La Guardia "Frijole," the name of a small Mexican bean. The Southerners liked him because he fought hard for the causes he believed in and because he could be a team player when necessary. Also, he shared the Southerners' fascination with parliamentary procedure. And he was a wonderful orator, one who could say more in five minutes than most men could in thirty. Sometimes La Guardia would jump up and make a speech for the sheer joy or devilment involved. When La Guardia made enemies, it was because his belief in his own righteousness sometimes led him to abuse and humiliate his adversaries. He lacked the Southerners' talent for getting his way in a quiet manner. But La Guardia had guts; everyone agreed to that.

Huey Long was as colorful as La Guardia but far less likable. I first heard of Long in 1927 when the Baltimore *Sun* sent me on a political scouting trip through the South. Long was then Louisiana's public-service commissioner and was running for governor. The reporters and politicians I talked to didn't think he had a chance, but he won and went on to gain absolute control over Louisiana politics.

When Long came to the Senate in the early thirties, he arrived in Washington with a large retinue of hangers-on and a lot of fanfare. He didn't intend to be a quiet first-term Senator, and he wasn't. His popular appeal was spreading beyond Louisiana and other Senators grudgingly recognized him as a force to be reckoned with. Long had supported FDR in 1932, but after Roosevelt became President the two became bitter enemies. Long envied Roosevelt's power and popularity, and Roosevelt feared Long's growing political following. Long never bothered to hide his hate for Roosevelt. He used to say that two men were running the country—Franklin Roosevelt and the last man he'd talked to. The men Long hated most always seemed to be the few who got more attention than he did—I'm thinking particularly of Roosevelt and of Hugh Johnson, the flamboyant director of the National Recovery Administration.

Huey Long loved attention—he even dressed to get attention. His suits were always expensive and flashy. "Never dress down to your constituents," he would say. "Always dress so that a woman can point to you and say, 'Someday my boy may be able to wear clothes like that.'" Long had several new suits made for the 1932 Democratic convention in Chicago. He knew Senator James Hamilton Lewis of Illinois, who was famous for his red beard and natty attire, would be there, and he declared: "I'm gonna outdress that pink-whiskered son of a bitch in his own town."

His fellow Senators feared both his sharp tongue and his political strength—for by the mid-thirties he had proved that his support could elect political candidates, both in Louisiana and in other Southern states. He was known in the Senate as a brilliant and totally reckless debater. He would attack anyone and say anything, and few Senators wanted to risk an exchange with him. Long had a talent for bringing out the worst in people. One Senator he loved to needle was Carter Glass of Virginia, a courtly little man who'd served in Woodrow Wilson's Cabinet. Senator Glass ignored Long as long as he could, but one day he exploded and called Huey a "Goddamned son of a bitch." Long was delighted, and Glass deeply regretted having lost his temper. He said he'd never before in his life used language like that. He remained bitter about Long, and he once told me, "I'd vote to expel him from the Senate and never ask the charges."

One man who didn't mind trading insults with Long was General

Hugh Johnson. A famous clash between the two came in March of 1935, after Johnson had left the NRA to write a newspaper column. On March 4, in a speech carried on national radio, he launched a merciless attack on Long and Father Coughlin, the demagogic priest. "You can laugh at Father Coughlin, you can snort at Huey Long," Johnson declared, "but this country was never under a greater menace." He said Long was "a dictator by force of arms and Adolf Hitler has nothing on him any way you care to look at it."

This attack was the talk of the nation for several days. In political circles, it was widely assumed that Hugh Johnson's intent was to undercut Long's emergence as a Presidential possibility in 1936—for his share-the-wealth proposals were gaining national attention, and had already prompted Roosevelt to propose an ill-considered share-the-wealth tax scheme.

The morning after Johnson's speech, Krock sent me to see Long for his reply. Long was virtually frothing at the mouth, ranting about the revenge he would wreak on General Johnson. He was flabbergasted when I delivered Krock's message that the *Times* would print whatever reply he wanted to make—he knew we opposed him and he couldn't believe we'd treat him fairly in our news columns. He brought his statement to our office that afternoon and he was friendly but very loud. At times he behaved like a wild man. He made one dash through our offices to Krock's room during which he knocked over several chairs. A bystander might have thought him drunk, but I think he was simply overcome with rage and frustration at having been painfully attacked and being unable to get revenge.

He intended to get revenge, however. In a speech in the Senate that day, Long attacked not only Hugh Johnson but all the men he thought were behind him: Roosevelt, Jim Farley, and the Majority Leader, Joe Robinson.

"Beware! Beware!" Long warned Robinson. "If things go on as they have been going, you will not be here next year."

Long, swaggering about in a bright pink shirt, was clearly threatening Robinson—oppose me and I'll come to Arkansas and turn the voters against you.

Robinson had had enough. He rose in bitter anger. "Egotism, arrogance, and ignorance," he said, "are seldom displayed in the Senate of the United States. They require a measure of talent possessed only by the Senator from Louisiana." He went on to denounce Long's comments as "the ravings of a madman." Other Senators joined in the attack. But Long just listened and smiled.

Three days later, Long addressed the nation on the radio. Most

people expected a wild counterattack on Hugh Johnson, but instead
Huey was the soul of sweet reasonableness. "It will serve no useful
purpose," he said, "for me to call my opponents more bitter names
than they called me." He then proceeded to outline his share-the-
wealth program to the largest audience he would ever address.

It was a brilliant performance. As much as one might have
enjoyed Johnson's attack on Long, there was little doubt that Long
had come out ahead on the exchange. My reports in the *Times* that
Sunday warned that Johnson's attack had "probably transformed
Huey Long from a clown into a real political menace." Whether or
not I was right we'll never know, for six months later, on September
8, Huey Long was gunned down at the State Capitol in Louisiana.

In June of 1935, a few months after his exchange with Johnson,
Huey talked his way through what was then the longest one-man
filibuster in Senate history. The filibuster was itself an indirect
attack on Hugh Johnson, for it was intended to prevent the con-
tinuation of Johnson's beloved NRA. The NRA Act was three days
away from expiration and Long hoped to speak the full three days.
He failed because he overestimated his stamina and because he
underestimated the willingness of his opponents to apply Senate
rules against him.

One rule, rarely enforced, said that a speaker could yield to
another speaker only once and still regain the floor; after that he
needed unanimous consent of the Senators present to resume speaking. Thus, strict enforcement of the rules would allow Long only one
break in his filibuster—for rest, for food, or to go to the bathroom.
And Vice President Garner intended to apply the rules, and to keep
the Senate in continuous session until he wore Long down. Thus,
after Long had spoken for six or eight hours, he yielded to a friend
and dashed out to the bathroom. After that, he couldn't get unanimous consent to yield without losing the floor.

Nonetheless, Long's marathon lasted most of the night, and we
reporters in the press gallery were pulling for him—it was the best
show of the year. There was no rule in the Senate, as in the House,
that a speaker's remarks be germane to the legislation, so he told
all sorts of stories. Those of us who knew Long were sending him
notes suggesting which of his famous tales to tell next.

At our suggestion he gave the recipes for dozens of exotic drinks
they mix down in Louisiana, and then we got him started on a di-
gression on health, and on how oysters and fish, cooked Louisiana
style, could promote longevity. Sometime after midnight, the Senate
sergeant-at-arms came up to the press gallery and said Vice Presi-

dent Garner had requested that the press not give Senator Long any more suggestions. Sometime in the early morning Huey suddenly stopped talking, bolted out the door and to the bathroom, and his filibuster ended after fifteen and a half hours.

I was not surprised when I was called to the office that night in 1935 and told Huey had been shot. He had used violence and strong-arm tactics to repress his political enemies in Louisiana, and violence was used to bring him down. But Huey Long was one of the great might-have-beens of American politics. We will never know whether he could have built a national political movement, or what he might have accomplished if all his brilliance and energy had been focused on constructive goals.

Hugh Johnson was famous for a lot besides standing up to Huey Long. He was one of the most fantastic figures on the Washington scene in the 1930s, and one of the most capable.

Johnson was in his early fifties when the New Deal began. He'd spent his boyhood in the Oklahoma Territory, before it was a state, and been educated at West Point. He was a tornado of a man and he blazed into the New Deal with the same energy he'd shown as a young cavalry officer serving with General Pershing in Mexico in 1916. During the First World War he was assigned to the War Industries Board and there he caught the eye of Bernard Baruch. Johnson had a plan for organizing American industry into a system of groupings to obtain maximum effectiveness during the war. The Armistice came before his plan could be put into effect, but a dozen to fifteen years later, as FDR was searching for a way to cope with the Depression, Baruch and Johnson persuaded the President-elect that this sort of business-government cooperation, with a measure of government control, was the answer. Johnson's plan finally crystallized into the National Recovery Act, which I covered on its journey through Congress. My introduction to Johnson came through Baruch, whom I'd gotten to know through Arthur Krock and Senators Harrison and Byrnes. With Baruch, Harrison, and Byrnes behind it, the NRA didn't have much trouble getting through Congress, and to no one's surprise Hugh Johnson became its administrator.

Soon after Johnson took over at NRA, I wrote a magazine piece on him. He liked the article, although some parts of it were critical. Thereafter he called me "babyface," and in his book, *The Blue Eagle: From Egg to Earth*, he wrote: "Turner Catledge has a baby face that masks a keen intelligence. He can ask the deadliest questions with an expression like the Age of Innocence."

The job of the NRA, which was symbolized by its Blue Eagle seal, was to persuade businessmen to draw up codes of fair competition. These codes were supposed to bring about more orderly pricing and selling policies, end wasteful competition, and bring higher wages and shorter hours for workers. To a great extent, Hugh Johnson's Blue Eagle hatched the five-day week and opened the gates for widespread unionization in this country. To these ends, Johnson rushed endlessly around America in an army plane, making speeches, making promises, coaxing businessmen into cooperation. NRA sponsored a mammoth "recovery parade" on Fifth Avenue, and as Johnson stood there for hours, grinning and waving at thousands of marchers, he seemed to confirm the New Deal's promise that prosperity was, indeed, coming around the corner.

Johnson worked hard and he relaxed hard. In his travels around the country he would go days without sleep. He was a heavy drinker and sometimes he'd unwind with drinking sprees. Other times, when he was near the breaking point, he would fly out to Oklahoma to visit his mother. All he wanted was to lie a few hours on a couch with his head in his mother's lap.

He was an erudite man, who could quote at great length from the great poets and from the Bible. He could also make use of the picturesque language of the Southwest. I remember his once telling me about encountering two of his bureaucratic rivals, Harold Ickes and Frances Perkins, coming out of President Roosevelt's office. "I could tell by the expression on their faces," Johnson told me, "that they'd been skinning a neighbor's cow."

Hugh Johnson's clashes with Ickes, Miss Perkins, and others helped speed his exit from the government. He was a man of extremes: he worked hard, played hard, fought hard; he was too assertive, too independent, perhaps too brilliant, for a bureaucratic career. He was burnt out before long, broke with Roosevelt, and left government to write a newspaper column that often attacked his old New Deal colleagues. I recall one of the last times I saw him, in the late thirties. He called and asked me to come to his suite in the Carlton Hotel. He greeted me at the door like a long-lost brother. I'd rarely seen such a mess of a man. He had become terribly fat, his face was red as a strawberry, and he had a stubble of several days' growth of beard on his face. His eyes were glazed and he was barely articulate—for a moment I thought he was drunk. Then, inside the suite, I saw three secretaries rattling away on typewriters. It developed that Johnson had contracted to write a book and had forgotten about it. Three days earlier, the publisher had called to ask about the manuscript. The deadline had been a challenge to Johnson, so he'd gone to bed for twenty-four hours, awakened refreshed, and dictated the book in one sitting. I thought perhaps he wanted my help on the book, but that was not the case. He wanted to know if I'd go to New York and help his friend Baruch with a book.

I got to know Alf Landon during his ill-fated candidacy for President in 1936. Landon was Governor of Kansas, a lawyer who'd made a fortune in the oil business, then turned his attention to politics. He was a shrewd politician—his success as a college politician won him the nickname "Fox"—but he was a warm, unpretentious, thoroughly likable man, one of the most genuinely lovable public men I've known.

Landon's defeat in 1936 was inevitable—everyone saw this but Landon—but he won the respect of many of us for the devotion and courage he put into his hopeless cause. It's hard to believe he thought he could win, but on election night his wife organized a small "victory" party for their family and a few friends. They listened tearfully as Landon was buried in the Democratic landslide, left only with Maine, Vermont—and an uncut victory cake on the table.

During the 1936 campaign Russell Wiggins and I toured the country by car, talking to hundreds of people, trying to take the political pulse of America. Russ was then Washington correspondent for the St. Paul *Pioneer Press*, later worked for a short time on the *New York Times*, then became editor of the Washington *Post*, then U.S. Ambassador to the United Nations. He was a delightful traveling companion—we drove six or seven thousand miles and I was never once bored or irritated. I even liked his singing—he rendered "Londonderry Air" at least twenty times. Furthermore, our trip was a professional success—we made very few errors as we predicted the election results in the states we visited.

We stopped in Topeka and were deluged by the euphoria at Landon's headquarters. His people were so sure of victory that we began to wonder about the contrary findings we'd made in our travels. Then we had a confidential chat with Senator Arthur Capper, a canny, ninety-pound political wizard, a man I once described as able to put both ears to the ground at the same time, and he left us with no doubt that we were right and Landon's people wrong.

I made only one election bet that year. I told Bob Sherrod of *Time* Magazine that Landon would lose his own state, Kansas, and Bob wouldn't believe me. So we put $25 on it and I won. When I talked to Landon, however, I couldn't muster the courage to tell him

I thought he'd lose his own state. When men in politics say, "Tell me the truth," they rarely mean it.

After 1936, whenever I was on political scouting trips in the Midwest, I always arranged a visit with Landon in Topeka, often for Sunday dinner. Those Sunday dinners with the Landons were a highlight for me and other political writers who often accompanied me—Bernard Kilgore of the *Wall Street Journal*, Dewey Fleming of the Baltimore *Sun*, Roscoe Drummond of the *Christian Science Monitor*, Alvin McCoy of the Kansas City *Star*, and others. Landon used to say that come mid-October he'd tell Mrs. Landon to fatten up some chickens, because pretty soon Turner Catledge and his gang would be around with their ears stuck out for information and their tongues hanging out for roast chicken.

One of those Sunday dinners, in the summer of 1940, turned into quite a political story. After dinner, Landon took us into his study and said he needed our help. His problem was political. President Roosevelt had invited him to the White House the following Wednesday. This was just weeks before the Republican convention, and there was talk in Washington (encouraged by Roosevelt) that the President would appoint several Republicans to form a "coalition" Cabinet. At one level, this was to unify the country against the increasing dangers of war. At another level, coalition government would undercut Republican opposition to Roosevelt in the coming election.

The speculation was that Roosevelt intended to appoint both Landon and his 1936 running mate, Colonel Frank Knox, to the Cabinet. One Republican who opposed this coalition was Senator Robert Taft, himself a contender for the nomination, who feared any actions that might blur the Republican vs. Democrat issues by focusing all attention on the war, which we had not yet joined. Taft had been to see Landon shortly before our visit, urging him to refuse any appointment.

Thus Landon's problem: he was afraid that once he got to the White House the President would persuade him to accept an appointment, yet he feared seeming rude if he turned the appointment down in advance. So he asked us reporters for advice: how could he turn down the offer in advance? Or, more precisely, how could we turn it down for him? We canvassed various ways in which we could write a "knowing" story without quoting him.

Finally one reporter said: "Governor, why don't you just say you won't accept any appointment? It's been in all the papers that you'll be offered one. If you want to turn it down, do it."

This challenged Alf, so he said he'd do it—turn down the offer that hadn't been made. Kilgore, Drummond, and I helped him write his statement, then we filed it to be carried in the next morning's papers. There then took place some fancy political maneuvering.

Landon departed by train late that day for Washington. When he stopped to change trains in Chicago next morning, he had a message from the White House. One of Roosevelt's aides said his invitation to the White House had been canceled, in light of his statement that he'd accept no appointment, and the aide suggested that Landon say he had a bad cold and return to Topeka. Landon agreed to call off his trip, but he wouldn't say it was because he had a cold. He had taken notes on his talk with the White House representative and he told reporters exactly what had happened.

But, before we could get that story into print, Landon got another call. This time it was Roosevelt, saying, "Alf, there's been a misunderstanding. You come on to Washington." So Landon had to tell the newsmen to ignore his story of why the trip was canceled. The White House put out a story that it had all been a misunderstanding—there had never been any intent to disinvite Landon, only to postpone the visit by one day. So Landon had his visit with Roosevelt, but no Cabinet offer was made to him. I think it was unfortunate that Landon didn't join the Cabinet, for he could have made a great contribution during the war.

In covering the 1940 Republican primaries I got to know all the party's leading contenders—Thomas Dewey, Wendell Willkie, Arthur Vandenberg and Robert Taft—and the one I cared for the most, personally, was Taft. He was not a warm or genial man—he was cold, and could be extremely harsh and righteous—but there was a tremendous honesty about him that commanded respect, and beneath his frigid exterior he was a shy, pleasant sort of man. Sometimes his stubborn honesty made him seem awkward in the context of the Senate—it was the very opposite of the "to get along, go along" philosophy that prevails in Congress. Bob Taft would not "go along" with anything he was not convinced of after his long and tortuous process of reasoning.

I remember an encounter with Taft on a train during the Kansas visit of 1940 when we'd both seen Alf Landon. The Kansas political leaders had been telling him that he needed to moderate his position on the war, that he was remaining too isolationist at a time when public sentiment was moving against Nazi Germany. I visited Taft in his Pullman car at a time when he was mulling over the issue. His glasses had slipped down, halfway off his face, and he kept

repeating, in a distant voice, "I'm just not going to do it." He couldn't
shift his views for political expedience, and that was one reason he
never captured the Republican nomination, even though he was a
contender from the 1940 convention to the one in 1952.

Taft was a poor speaker. I recall one evening when Franklin
Roosevelt demolished him in a joint speaking appearance. The occasion was the Gridiron Dinner following the 1938 elections. Taft
spoke first, representing the Republicans, followed by Roosevelt,
representing his party. Taft laid an egg—his speech was dull and
his attempts at humor were not successful. Then Roosevelt came on.
The President had every reason to be angry at Taft, for Taft had
launched harsh partisan attacks against the Democrats in the campaign.

So, when Roosevelt began to speak, he addressed himself to Taft.
He recalled that Taft had lived in the White House in 1909-13, when
his father was President. Roosevelt, his eyes sparkling, went on to
describe the White House as it was back in those days, back in the
horse-and-buggy era. He described the coming of the first automobile
to the White House and the excitement it created. He went on, in a
quietly devastating way, to paint Taft as a man who was still living
in the horse-and-buggy era, who had never progressed past 1913,
who would spend all his life living in the political past. It was a
savage but beautiful performance, and when I saw Taft the next day
all he could say was "He really tore me apart, didn't he?"

Wendell Willkie was more of a match for Roosevelt, for he was
similarly equipped with charm, sophistication and daring. Taft and
Tom Dewey were cold men, men who projected no mass appeal, but
Willkie had what was later called charisma and that was one reason
the Republicans nominated him in 1940.

Willkie was a political freak, a man who dashed in from the
political badland of Wall Street to win the prize that some politicians
seek for a lifetime. His political career in retrospect seems almost unbelievable. He first won national attention by championing the public-
utility holding companies when the New Deal, riding a wave of
popular support, set out to abolish them. Willkie was president of
one of the holding companies, the Commonwealth Southern Company, which owned utilities firms in the South and Midwest. These
"holding" companies—as distinguished from "operating" companies
—seemed to the New Dealers to be more interested in making profits
for Eastern financial interests than in producing cheap electric
power for consumers.

Roosevelt once told a Georgia audience that when he first came to Warm Springs he was shocked to find the rates for electricity about four times what he paid in Hyde Park, and this discovery had spurred his determination to provide cheap electric power throughout America. As President, he pursued this goal by creating the Tennessee Valley Authority and by his bill to outlaw the holding companies. It was the latter fight that made Willkie into a national figure.

Willkie was often in Washington in the mid-thirties, lobbying against the holding-company bill. That was how he learned about politics—as an anti-New Deal lobbyist. He was an impressive man, big and bold, bluff and brilliant, endlessly energetic. I generally talked to Willkie when he was in Washington and sometimes I wrote stories about what he had to say. I did this despite the fact that it won me criticism from some other reporters. The press corps, I'm sorry to report, was dividing too much along party lines in those days, and some Democratic reporters resented anyone who gave aid and comfort to the Republican "enemy."

I found Willkie an excellent source of political intelligence. For one thing, he kept extremely well informed on the fights within the administration over TVA.

Willkie was a most disorganized person. If you visited his hotel room you'd likely see his clothes scattered everywhere—shirt under the bed, socks on the chandelier. His campaign train in 1940 was in such a state of chaos that one reporter described it as resembling a bawdy house when the madam was away and the girls were running the joint. In the fall of 1941, when I was about to go to work for Marshall Field's Chicago *Sun*, I had a personal experience with Willkie's lack of organization. He drew up my contractual agreement with the *Sun*, involving salary, insurance, job security, and the like. The contract he wrote was three pages long and I couldn't understand it. I took it to another lawyer and he didn't understand it either. One of Willkie's provisions was that Marshall Field put my salary for five years in escrow, so I would be guaranteed getting it. The other lawyer said, "Do you want to ask Marshall Field, one of the richest men in America to put your salary in escrow? If that's all the confidence you have in him, why would you work for him?" This lawyer wrote me a new contract, about three paragraphs long, which was more than adequate.

For all his disorganization, Willkie captured the 1940 nomination that both Taft and Dewey wanted. The main reason for his coup was that throughout the summer a group of clever political operators had quietly been lining up delegate support, making it possible for

Willkie to charge in and capture the nomination with the kind of flamboyant flourish he excelled at.

Arthur Krock and I had an amazing talk with Willkie in the early hours of June 24, 1940, soon after we arrived in Philadelphia to cover the Republican convention. At about midnight we took a cab to the Benjamin Franklin Hotel to see Alf Landon, but upon arrival we encountered Willkie and his wife. He insisted that we come to his hotel to talk and have a drink. We did, and after we arrived Mrs. Willkie retired to the bedroom and we sent the bellhop out for a bottle of Scotch and settled back to talk politics.

Willkie was optimistic about his chances for the nomination, but when Krock asked him who his floor leader was for the convention, we were astounded to hear him say he didn't know what a floor leader was. We explained to him the duties of a floor leader, and also the need for him to have a strategy committee.

Willkie well understood that he could only be nominated after Dewey and Taft had made their "runs" for the nomination and fallen short. But he did not seem to understand that he needed a close-knit organization to make sure that the delegates turned to him after the others had failed. The point is that Willkie, as a corporation executive and lobbyist, understood the broad issues of political power, but he was not versed in mechanical matters like a party convention.

Once he was nominated, Willkie was sure he could win. He hit hard on the "sacrilege" of Roosevelt's seeking a third term. He also played on the nation's war fears. The Low Countries and France had fallen, the latter in the week Willkie was nominated. He took full advantage of fears that Roosevelt was itching to get into the war, but the election proved that more people trusted Roosevelt than Willkie. It turned out that the country was more war-minded than either thought.

I boarded Willkie's campaign train in Indiana in mid-October and found him supremely confident. I thought he was mistaken; my own soundings had convinced me Roosevelt would win again. Most people were more afraid of losing their New Deal benefits if the Republicans took over than of war if the Democrats stayed in. Willkie asked me to tell him frankly what I thought his chances were, and I did, because he was one of those rare persons who meant it when they said, "Tell me the truth." My opinion didn't bother Willkie a bit. He said I was probably right at the time of my inquiries but public opinion was rapidly moving his way. Willkie was without guile and I don't doubt that he fully believed this. He was a man of vast self-confidence. He was a fighter, one who never quit swinging, but he had the misfortune, like Adlai Stevenson in the next decade, to run against a man who was unbeatable.

After his defeat in 1940, Willkie sincerely wished the winner well. He became one of Roosevelt's greatest supporters in the conduct of the war and in preparations for peace. He didn't live to see the peace. He died of a heart attack on October 8, 1944, after having failed on the comeback trail in the Wisconsin primary.

He was only fifty-two when he died, and he might have had a great political future ahead of him. As early as July 14, 1943, I reported in the *Times* that some Democrats believed Roosevelt would offer to make Willkie his running-mate in 1944 if the Republicans failed to nominate him for President. The playwright Robert Sherwood, who was a speechwriter for Roosevelt, later wrote: "It was my belief in 1943 and early in 1944 that if Willkie were to win the Republican nomination in 1944 Roosevelt would not run for a fourth term."

There were even some secret negotiations in 1944 between Willkie and Roosevelt about starting a new political party that would unite the liberal wings of both the Republican and the Democratic parties. Clearly, had he lived, Willkie would have remained a contender for the Presidential nomination of one or another of the parties. His strength as a political candidate was that he had a leg in both camps. Republicans respected his Wall Street ties, his businessman's mind, and his anti-New Deal leadership. Yet Willkie had been a lifelong Democrat and on most issues his thinking was far more progressive than that of the Republican party.

Back in 1940, just after Willkie's nomination, he sent me a note saying he'd like to see me when I was next in New York. It turned out that he wanted to talk about my future, not his. We met for breakfast at his apartment on Fifth Avenue, and we talked for a few minutes about his nomination, which he said was still almost unbelievable to him. He said he thought he'd have trouble with some Old Guard Republicans, because of the issues he proposed to raise in the campaign. He added, with his characteristic little giggle, that the first thing he had to do was change his voter registration from Democrat to Republican.

But then he got to the point of our meeting. He said that Mrs. Helen Reid, whose family owned the New York *Herald Tribune*, and was vice president of it, wanted very much to talk to me about my joining her newspaper's staff. Would I be interested enough to talk to her? I said I would, and he immediately picked up the phone, called Mrs. Reid, and arranged for me to see her that morning.

Mrs. Reid was most gracious when I met with her, as she always was, but she soon got to business. She said that Willkie was going to be the next President and she wanted to strengthen her Washington bureau in preparation for the Republican administration. She said that, since I was well acquainted with Willkie, the combination of the *Herald Tribune*, President Willkie, and me would be unbeatable. She added that I could aspire to higher things, perhaps someday becoming managing editor.

Strangely enough, I was not much interested, although the salary Mrs. Reid mentioned was more than I was drawing from the *Times*. I told her I would consider the offer, for I felt in fairness to myself I should take inventory of my prospects at the *Times*. I felt that way especially since Arthur Krock evidently had decided to stay in Washington. Arthur knew I was restless and he tried in various ways to accommodate me, but his plan to return to New York, as outlined to me back in 1932, was further than ever in the future.

I spoke to Jimmy James, the managing editor of the *Times*, and he sent me immediately to see the publisher, Arthur Hays Sulzberger. Jimmy apparently called Sulzberger as I was on my way to his office, for the publisher greeted me with a smile and in his delightful, offhand style he said, "I'm not going to let you leave the *New York Times*." I replied frankly that I didn't want to leave but I had my future to consider. He shoved a pad of paper across the desk to me. "Write your own ticket," he said.

Apparently he wanted me to write on the pad the amount of money I wanted to stay. I couldn't imagine doing that, so I laughed and pushed the pad back, saying that I'd better not write my own ticket lest I shortchange myself. He then wrote an amount on the pad and shoved it at me again. He didn't want to discuss my future assignments, saying only, "You have everything to gain on this paper."

He turned out to be right, although before his prophecy was realized I had left the *Times* briefly and found I was not happy at another newspaper.

XI

Chicago Sabbatical

I SPENT nineteen months, from October 1, 1941, until May 1, 1943, working for Marshall Field's new Chicago *Sun,* most of that time as the *Sun's* editor. I gained a million dollars' worth of experience at the *Sun*—and I wouldn't go through it again for ten million dollars.

The Chicago *Sun,* during the period I was with it, was a case study in how not to run a newspaper. This seemed strange to outsiders, for the *Sun* had much going for it. It had a liberal and enlightened founder, Marshall Field III, and it had access to his vast fortune—he set aside $5 million to bankroll its first five years. It had an aggressive, experienced publisher, Silliman Evans. It had, for better or worse, my services first as correspondent and then as editor. It had some outstanding editorial writers and reporters. And it served a city that needed the type of honest, liberal newspaper Field was determined to produce.

Yet, the *Sun's* early years were chaotic. The paper was not an outstanding one, and this fact was reflected in its sales, which hovered around 250,000 when Field had hoped for two or three times that number.

The first thing wrong with the *Sun* was that it was started largely for a negative reason—to fight Colonel Robert Rutherford McCormick and his reactionary Chicago *Tribune.* To fight the *Tribune* may have been a noble cause, but it was too narrow a philosophical base on which to build a newspaper. From this inadequate philosophy followed the *Sun*'s first problem in practice—it was rushed too hurriedly into existence. Perhaps never again in journalism has the saying "haste makes waste" been so expensively proved.

It was early in 1941 that Field resolved to start a newspaper. The international situation gave him a sense of urgency. Roosevelt was trying to move the nation toward support of England's lonely stand against Hitler, and Colonel McCormick was fighting him tooth and nail. To McCormick, who hated the English, Roosevelt was a warmonger who was trying to rush the United States into European disputes that were none of our concern. The *Tribune*'s influence on the American heartland was great, and to Field and others who thought the United States must fight Nazism, McCormick's daily tirades were agonizing. All this contributed to the haste with which the *Sun* was started.

Field's first job was to find a publisher to run the paper for him, since he lacked adequate experience and wanted to remain in the background. His choice, in mid-1941, was Silliman Evans, the publisher of the Nashville *Tennessean*. Evans had begun his newspaper career in Texas as a reporter for the Fort Worth *Star-Telegram,* and a protégé of its publisher, Amon Carter. He came to Washington as a lobbyist for an airline company, and I knew him primarily as one of John Nance Garner's closest political advisers. In the mid-thirties, with financial help from wealthy New Dealers, he acquired the then-bankrupt Nashville *Tennessean,* which he soon built into one of the South's leading pro–New Deal newspapers. Evans was a tough, aggressive, two-fisted newspaper publisher. He liked a good political fight and he believed that a newspaper should never shy away from self-promotion. To Marshall Field and some of his advisers, Evans seemed an ideal man to head up a liberal paper in the most rough-and-tumble newspaper city in America.

I often disagreed with Evans. Our basic approach to the newspaper business differed in many ways. Yet I don't blame him for the *Sun*'s troubles. He did what he was asked to do—he started a newspaper from scratch in six months. He acted with the full backing of the owner, Marshall Field, who rarely challenged Evans' decisions. He had been brought, as I had, into a strange, confusing situation, and he was trying to make the best of it. Field's biographer, Stephen Becker, wrote that Field should have fired Evans and let me run the paper. I appreciate the compliment, but I don't think that my running the paper would have solved the *Sun*'s problems. Its basic problem was that it was started too fast, with inadequate planning and staffing, and with too many non-Chicagoans (myself included) in top editorial jobs. Nothing Evans or I could have done could have overcome those problems in the *Sun*'s first few years. Only time and growth could have solved them.

My first inkling that I was being considered for a position with the *Sun* came one evening in the fall of 1941 as I was dining with Senator Walter George in his apartment at the Mayflower Hotel. I received a call from Arthur Krock, who said Jesse Jones had told him that Evans was considering me for editor of the new paper. I was immediately interested. I had concluded, after ten years as Krock's heir apparent, that I was permanently boxed in as number-two man in the Washington bureau. Moreover, my requests for foreign experience had been repeatedly rejected, with my superiors always saying I was needed in Washington. Krock, knowing of my interest, urged me to "take a fling at it," although he predicted that I'd soon want to return to the *Times*.

On the positive side, I knew that a substantial salary increase would be involved, and I was fascinated by what might be done with a paper in a great, vibrant city like Chicago. I was attracted too by reports that Evans intended to assemble an "all-star" staff of proven newspapermen.

My first disappointment came in my initial meeting with Evans. He informed me that he had hired Rex Smith of *Newsweek* to be the *Sun*'s editor. He had another job to offer me: chief political writer and roving correspondent, based in Washington but with the world as my beat. After a talk with Field I accepted the offer. My salary was $25,000 a year.

My excitement began to lessen a bit when I made my first visit to Chicago, in the weeks before the *Sun*'s first edition on December 4. Evans was a great believer in hoopla and promotion. The new paper's name was chosen by a $10,000 prize contest which drew 220,000 entries. (*Sun* was the most often suggested name; the prize went to a gentleman whose accompanying essay explained that "When morning comes you look for two things to make your world right: you look for the sun and sunlight, and you look for your morning paper. . . ." Instead of hiring one advertising agency to promote the new paper, Evans hired three or four, and the result was wasteful and unproductive. He gave endless parties at his suite in the Ambassador East. I recall one lavish party Evans gave celebrating the *Sun*'s forthcoming book-review supplement; it was a fine party but the supplement was never begun.

Nor was an outstanding staff being assembled—except for a few "stars" at the top. A Hearst paper had recently folded in Chicago, and nearly half the *Sun*'s staff was these ex-Hearstmen, few of whom were outstanding or had any sympathy for Field's liberal politics. I remember the sinking feeling I had on my first visit to the *Sun*'s Chicago office, when it seemed to me that Evans and his top editors were more concerned about which comic strips they would carry than what reporters they would hire or what policies they would follow. To try to compensate for the general mediocrity of the staff, Evans hired a number of high-salaried, well-known newspapermen, of whom I was one. But our reputations could not compensate for the paper's too-hurried, jerry-built framework, or for our ignorance about Chicago.

At the outset, all this was not my worry. I had a dream assignment, and I set out to make the most of it.

My most memorable experience as roving correspondent came in late December, when I covered Winston Churchill's visit to the United States and Canada, only weeks after Pearl Harbor. He discussed war policy with Roosevelt in Washington, then went by train to Ottawa, and I was among the reporters accompanying him. We left Washington on the Sunday after Christmas and proceeded northward in bitter cold weather. But it was warm and cozy inside the train, for the Canadians were rolling out the red carpet for Churchill and we reporters shared in the festivities. The highlight of his visit to Canada was a speech to Parliament, which he delivered first in English and then again in French, winning the hearts of the French Canadians.

His train started back to Washington on New Year's Eve. As midnight neared, a page went through the train shouting that the "PM" wanted all of us to join him in the dining car. We had hardly assembled when the great man came in, calling for drinks all around. When everyone had a whiskey-and-soda, Churchill raised his glass and drank to the Americans, then we Americans drank to the British, then everyone drank to Churchill. He responded by leading the singing of "Auld Lang Syne." When he had finished the first verse, he launched into a jazzed-up version, grabbed a hand on either side, and led in a ring-around-the-rosy jig.

A few weeks later, I was in Rio de Janeiro for an inter-American conference when I saw an article in *Time* magazine, titled "The Setting Sun," that detailed all the *Sun*'s difficulties. *Time*'s account agreed with reports I'd been hearing, and at my earliest opportunity I returned to Chicago to have a look at the situation. Upon my arrival, I learned that Rex Smith, the editor, was entering the army—

taking the easy way out, I thought. Evans named me to replace him as acting editor, and a few weeks later the "acting" was dropped and I was editor of the *Sun*.

My first assignment was to do some dirty work for Evans. He had decided that some of the people Rex Smith had hired should now be fired, and I was instructed to fire them. I did, although I felt terribly guilty about it. One man, an editorial writer who was a friend of mine, I transferred to Washington instead of firing, and later I had sharp words with Evans about this decision.

We soon clashed again over another matter. The *Sun* had been carrying each Sunday a "Publisher's Column," in which Evans stated his views. I found this column extremely corny, both in conception and in execution. Evans wasn't even using the column to advance his political views. The column was largely Evans' attempt to introduce himself to the Chicago business community and also to try to stir up some advertising. One day I threw it out. Evans quickly appeared to inform me that he was running the paper. I reminded him that I was the editor, and told him the Sunday column had to go. He stormed off, but returned a few minutes later and suggested we go out for a drink. And he dropped on my desk the little metal dingbat, picturing a quill and scroll, that was used at the top of his column. That was his way of saying he agreed to drop the column.

The confusion I found at the *Sun* was incredible. The paper was operating virtually without a business department, or even an auditor. Circulation procedures were chaotic. The *Sun's* first edition had been 900,000 copies, but circulation soon dropped below 250,000. Marshall Field, however, still thought his paper was selling some 700,000 copies a day. No one had told him differently. Circulation was not helped, of course, by the pressure that Colonel McCormick's *Tribune* was bringing on news dealers not to sell the *Sun*, and by the fact that his veto had kept us from getting the Associated Press wire service. By 1943, the *Sun* was losing between $125,000 and $150,000 a week.

Obviously, the key figure in the situation was Marshall Field. My own belief was that he should have become an active, deeply involved publisher. His lack of newspaper experience could have been overcome by his good instincts, his intelligence, and his intimate knowledge of Chicago. But deep involvement was not Field's style. He was a shy, modest, self-effacing man. My impression was that he had a deep feeling of guilt about his vast inherited fortune. This was reflected in his liberal politics, in his philanthropy, and in his horror of seeming to throw his weight around. However, he didn't mind throwing his money around, and he lived lavishly.

When I was editor of the *Sun,* I had a daily editorial conference. Once Field rather shyly asked me if he could sit in on the conference. I said, "Mr. Field, for what you're paying for your ticket, you can have any seat in the house."

He attended a few conferences, but he rarely voiced opinions, and the paper continued to do without the contribution he might have made. I liked and respected Field, but he lacked the temperament to be a great newspaper publisher. In my mind's eye, he was always a chicken being plucked, a helpless dupe being taken for a crazy, $100,000-a-week joyride.

As editor, I continued to have differences with Evans. Both with the Baltimore *Sun* and the *New York Times,* I had come to prefer a conservative style of make-up. Evans, however, liked big, blaring headlines, and his preference was in line with Chicago tradition, although at sharp variance with his practices in Nashville. I tried to cut down on the size of headlines, unless we had a story that merited them, but I ran into opposition not only from Evans but from our circulation department, which wanted big headlines to attract street sales.

Evans liked to use gimmicks, self-promotion, and sob-sister stories. At one point, despite many objections, he insisted on carrying an astrology column on the editorial page. Once during the war we carried an incredibly corny feature about a local boy who was the first American GI to arrive in Ireland and about the girl friend he had waiting back in Chicago. All this was against my instincts, but I did not have full editorial control.

For me the most painful part of my Chicago experience was that I could not respect the paper I was trying to serve. In Memphis, in Baltimore, and in New York, I had felt I was working for a great newspaper. I did not feel that way about the *Sun,* and no doubt my feelings affected my work. I recall when I would try to recruit reporters from other papers, and they would say, "I'll come to the *Sun* if you're going to stay as editor," I could give them no such assurance.

The *Sun* lacked tradition. Too much tradition can hold a paper back, but too little—or none—can leave a paper circling about in confusion, like a rudderless ship. The *Sun* also lacked cohesion. Evans flew off most weekends to Nashville, where he continued as publisher of the *Tennessean.* Field's liberal intentions were diluted by the lack of liberalism in some of his reporters and editorialists.

The paper's focus was blurred by differences among me, Evans, and others.

Worst of all, the paper lacked roots in Chicago. A great lesson I learned there was that a newspaper cannot be imported into a city from without, no matter how high-priced its editors, how rich its publisher, how noble its politics. It must have roots deep in the city's culture, needs, hopes, dreams, even its prejudices. Those roots take time to go down; no amount of cash can fertilize them. That lesson was confirmed for me later in the *New York Times'* failure in its West Coast venture.

The Chicago *Tribune* was outrageously right-wing, and often unforgivably vicious toward its political antagonists. But most people do not care much about politics. They ignored Colonel McCormick's tirades against the twentieth century and enjoyed the *Tribune's* excellent coverage of local news, sports and women's news, and its dozens of comic strips. The *Tribune*, right or wrong, was undeniably a Chicago newspaper. It was what Chicago wanted and, I sometimes thought, what Chicago deserved.

The absolute low point of my Chicago experience came one day when I was called before a local grand jury. This came about when, after a series of unsolved sex crimes, one of our editors wrote an editorial suggesting that someone had bribed the district attorney's office. The district attorney quickly summoned me before a grand jury. He was hopping mad and he asked who had written the editorial. I said I would not answer that, but as editor I took full responsibility for everything that appeared in the paper. He asked what was the source of the editorial. I said it was based on the news stories we'd carried on the sex crimes.

He then got out the clippings and began to question me about them. He soon saw that I didn't know where any of the streets involved were, and he made the most of it, forcing me to confess my ignorance over and over. It was a humiliating experience, but it underscored the lesson I had finally learned—a man who didn't even know the streets in a city had no business being editor of a newspaper there.

There was one important aftermath to my grand-jury appearance. The district attorney called the city editor of the *Tribune*, Don Maxwell, and told him of my testimony, hoping the *Tribune* would complete my humiliation by carrying an article on it. The district attorney had misjudged the code of the journalism fraternity, for Maxwell told him off, and we became good friends. In later years, when I was managing editor of the *Times* and Don was editor of the

Tribune, our two publishers would sometimes feud and we'd be called on to mediate. Usually, the *Tribune* would carry some editorial attacking the *Times* for its "left-wing" politics. My publisher, Arthur Hays Sulzberger, would threaten to break off the profitable relationship whereby the *Tribune* distributed our news service west of the Mississippi. Twice, during such crises, I flew to Chicago, had delightful visits with Don, then he and I would solemnly inform our publishers that all had been solved. By that time, both publishers had forgotten the issues.

By early 1943 I realized I would not be happy until I got back to the *Times*. Fortunately, Sulzberger and Krock had given me a standing invitation to return. When through Krock I signaled that I was ready to come, he wired back that "the red carpet is out."

For me, returning to the *Times* was like waking from a nightmare. I went back to my job as number-two man in the Washington bureau, although I was given a new title. Before leaving, I had been Chief News Correspondent. Now I was called National Correspondent, a title invented by Krock which no one else had ever held. I did not get an increase in salary, although I could have had one for the asking. When I left the *Sun*, I was making $26,500. But I told Sulzberger I wanted to return to the *Times* at the salary I'd had when I left, $12,000. Perhaps it was a foolish gesture on my part, but my emotional state at the time was akin to that of the Prodigal Son returning home.

XII

To Burma and Back

WHEN I returned to the *Times* Washington bureau in the spring of 1943, I became a member of a small group of Washington newspapermen whom General George Marshall and Admiral Ernest J. King called in from time to time for candid briefings on war plans and policy. We followed blow by blow the controversy over the European invasion route and we knew within days of the decision for a cross-Channel invasion. These briefings gave us a high-level look at war policy (and an intimate glimpse of two fascinating but very different men—Marshall, the magnificent soldier-statesman; King, the resolute, single-purpose military man)—but they were no substitute for the overseas war correspondent experience I wanted. The publisher and the managing editor of the *Times* rebuffed all my pleas, saying I was needed in Washington.

Then I got a chance. The publisher, Arthur Hays Sulzberger, was a member of the national board of the American Red Cross, and he believed that the wartime activities of the Red Cross deserved more coverage. He mentioned this to Arthur Krock, who suggested me for the assignment. I was not entirely overjoyed with the task, for I knew that covering the Red Cross would not be the same as covering military combat. Nonetheless, it was a way to get overseas. Moreover, in the newspaper business, you don't loosely snub your publisher's pet projects.

133

Sulzberger mentioned my assignment to General Marshall, who called me aside after his next press briefing and promised me every assistance in transportation, clearance, and the like. He also said he would like to broaden my commission. Would I undertake for him a study of troop morale wherever I went? He wanted a third-party view of troop discipline and the effect of the indoctrinations the men were receiving. A particular concern, he said, was the performance and standing of Negro troops. He said he was under great pressure from "over there"—and he gestured toward the White House—to push them along. The Army was still segregated, with Negro soldiers getting only the most menial duties. Mrs. Roosevelt was pushing for better assignments for Negroes, but military commanders were resisting, and Marshall was caught in the middle. He said he would appreciate a frank, informal briefing when I returned. Naturally I promised to provide it, and I did bring back some observations which General Marshall said were helpful, if not always to his liking.

Thus commissioned, I set out from Washington, two days before Thanksgiving of 1943, on a four-month tour of the Western war zone. I had waited two weeks for formal orders to come through, and then the head of the Army Air Transport Command advised me to forget the orders. He noted that I knew many of the Air Force commanders along my route and he predicted that they would speed me along from one stop to the next. He started the process by getting me a ride to Miami, where the ATC commander, whom I knew, got me another hop to the base at Recife, Brazil, from which planes were being shuttled across to North Africa. The commanding officer in Brazil was an acquaintance of mine from Washington, the son-in-law of the president of the bank where I kept my few dollars, and he shot me on to Algiers in record time.

As we alighted from the plane in Algiers, the first person I saw was a young Air Force general who, as a captain, had been a close friend of mine in Washington. This kind of luck—being at the right place at the right time, and knowing the right people—stayed with me throughout the trip, as indeed it has throughout my life.

While I was in Algiers, I got word from General Carl (Tooey, to his friends) Spaatz that I was to report to his headquarters in Tunis. Spaatz was an old friend of mine from Washington. He had just learned that he was to be transferred to London to help plan and execute the invasion of Europe, particularly the bombing that would precede the sea and ground assault, and he had invited members of his North African Bomber Command to meet with him for final discussions and also for some relaxation. I was to participate in the latter.

Spaatz and his staff had taken over a villa outside Tunis, but his personal quarters were in a trailer parked in a remote corner of one of the villa's gardens. His headquarters was called the Spaatzwaffe. At lunch that day quite a lot of Air Force brass was present; one of the distinguished figures was General Jimmy Doolittle. Also present was Brigadier General Elliot Roosevelt, who, I was told, was doing a fine job directing photo-reconnaissance for the Bomber Command. After lunch, I visited Tooey Spaatz in his trailer. We talked about the Air Force some, but mostly we sang some of the songs we'd sung together at many parties in Washington, songs like "We Never Miss Aunt Clara" and "There's a Hole in the Old Oaken Bucket" and "Bellbottom Trousers," plus some parodies I'd written for Gridiron Club shows. Tooey played the accompaniment on his guitar, at which he was quite expert. I remember wondering what Eisenhower would have thought if he'd walked in to find one of his top generals singing parodies with a newspaperman.

After a while, I asked: "Tooey, I'm afraid I'm taking up too much of your time. Don't you have something else to do?"

"If I had anything else to do," he said, "I wouldn't be doing my job."

General Spaatz, like most American officers I met on my trip, was extremely frank with me and other newspapermen. He was, of course, an unabashed booster of the Air Force—which then was beginning to agitate for an identity separate from the Army—but during the war I rarely felt that he or other officers were trying to use me or the other reporters to further their service's goals. During the war, at least at the top levels I was dealing with, the interservice rivalries were played down; of course they surfaced again after the war when Truman set out to unite the services within a Department of Defense.

The Red Cross in Naples arranged for me to accompany some of its people who were helping staff an experimental hospital near the front where the army was trying to treat the growing number of cases of "battle fatigue." The sad fact was that many U.S. soldiers had not been prepared to withstand battle conditions, and consequently were going to pieces in combat. Thus, the Army Medical Corps had started experimental hospitals, seeking medical solutions for the broken and demoralized soldiers. I spent Christmas Eve in one of these hospitals. It was a grim scene. About three hundred men were lying on cots under a dark tent. Some of the men were asleep, or awake but immobilized by shock or drugs. Others were moaning, weeping, or even screaming. The Red Cross man, a St.

Louis real-estate man in civilian life, and I went among the cots to talk to the men. Many of them revealed a terrible sense of shame that they had broken and left their buddies to fight without them. Many wept as they talked to us. My companion hit upon a means of quieting the men—one that was quickly noted by the doctors. He would ask each man what his home town was, and because he was widely traveled, he knew some item about almost every home town. If he didn't, he would ask, and thus start a conversation. As he talked to one GI, often another in a nearby cot would join in the conversation to tell about his town. Once he had half a dozen GIs sitting on the edge of their cots arguing the merits of their home towns. Perhaps it wasn't very scientific, but that talk of home seemed to help some of those pitiful lads on that lonely Christmas Eve. I soon got into the act myself, and put to good use some of the scraps of local color I'd collected on my political tours.

On Christmas Day I proceeded up to the front with some other correspondents. The heaviest fighting was going on before the town of Cassino, where the Germans had taken a stand to try to stop the Fifth Army from crossing the Rapido River. We watched the fighting from an olive grove on a mountainside behind the little town of Santa Vittoria, later the scene of a popular novel. We stayed in the olive grove until some American tanks moved in and drew German artillery fire from across the valley. All of us then scattered, the tanks included, except one correspondent with a passion for accuracy and the affliction of stammering, who wouldn't leave until he'd gotten the correct spelling of the name of the Minneapolis lawyer who was commanding the tanks. His stammer grew worse as the shelling increased.

I was continually impressed with the bravery of the Red Cross personnel. Unarmed, they pushed right up to the fighting lines. That Christmas Day I observed a pretty Red Cross girl take a tray of doughnuts into a foxhole in easy gunshot range of the Germans. This seemed to me quite a risk for a relatively minor mission, but the unit commander said it was of immeasurable value in terms of troop morale.

I wrote a feature story about the Red Cross worker in the foxhole on Christmas Day—she was Isabella Hughes of Baltimore—and I later got to know a good many of the other Red Cross girls. Without exception, they were attractive, wholesome American girls, and no one who wasn't there can fully understand what it meant to the front-line GI to have a glimpse of and perhaps a few words with an American girl. Once, with the guns booming all around us, I watched a girl named Bunny Currie, of Greenwich, Connecticut, serve coffee and doughnuts to some gun crews. One GI asked the girl if he could hold her hand for a moment. Bunny walked over and took his muddy paw. The other soldiers guffawed for a moment, then most of them lined up to touch her hand too.

Soon after Christmas I resumed my flight eastward. I flew to Algiers and from there on to Cairo. On the flight to Cairo we had engine trouble and the pilot landed in Tripoli for repairs. We passengers were taken by truck to a most unusual British officers' club for a drink. The officers' club was in a tent out on the desert. It featured a bar, a kitchen, and a number of overstuffed chairs, all arranged on a handsome Oriental rug that had been laid directly on the sand.

Despite the unusual surroundings, it was every inch a British gentlemen's club. When one of my American companions walked up to the bar for a drink, with his cap cocked down over his eye, a British officer rose from his overstuffed chair and coolly asked him to remove his headpiece.

It was past midnight when we got to Cairo. The *New York Times* had a news bureau in the Continental Hotel but I was unable to rouse anyone there. The bedroom was occupied by Marina Sulzberger, the wife of Cy Sulzberger, whom I'd left back in Italy. She was so sound asleep that she didn't hear me pounding on the door, so I spent the rest of the night downstairs on the tile floor of the hotel's men's room. The next morning I met Marina, a lovely, delightful little Greek girl. When I introduced myself she grabbed my hand and exclaimed, "Did you know I'm going to have a baby?"

Marina's apartment was the rallying point for many Greeks who'd fled the Italian and German occupation of their country. She had been ordered by her doctor to spend most of her time in bed until her child was born, and at most hours of day and night there was a Greek council of war in progress around her bed. Her friends were especially concerned about relatives who'd been captured in Greece, charged with espionage, and sometimes sentenced to death. One so sentenced was Marina's own brother, but about the time I arrived news came that he and several others had escaped. So I spent some pleasant hours with some very happy Greeks.

I hitchhiked from Cairo to Iran, where I observed the brilliant trucking operation whereby our lend-lease materials were delivered to the Russians. From Iran I flew to New Delhi, then on to Burma in a B-24 piloted by a Texan named Kelly who happened to be drunk on the flight but got us there without incident, except for a collision with a buzzard.

In Burma I spent a day and a night with my friend from the 1927 flood, Colonel Lewis Pick. Back in the flood days he had been a dark-haired, outspoken captain in charge of the Corps of Engineers office in New Orleans. I always remembered the advice he gave Herbert Hoover on how to deal with the flood: "First find out what the ole Mississippi wants to do, then he'p him do it." At this second meeting, Pick was a rugged, white-haired colonel (later major general) who had recently become a legend through his spectacular work in building the Ledo section of the Burma Road. Directing the labor of 45,000 soldiers and 42,000 natives, he drove 483 miles of road through the mountains and jungles from India to China. It was estimated that he averaged a mile of road a day, at a cost of a million dollars a mile. The Ledo Road was widely known as Pick's Pike, and its construction won him the Distinguished Service Medal.

Pick arranged for me to be flown farther to the northeast of Burma, to the headquarters of General Joseph "Vinegar Joe" Stilwell, who had recently led a mixture of U.S. and Chinese troops on a famous retreat along the Burma Road. His little camp was a far cry from the plush headquarters facilities I'd stayed in elsewhere. We lived in tents, and the camp was heavily guarded against the possibility of a Japanese raid. I spent two days and a night there, and on one occasion Stilwell and I talked at length about the situation in China. He had high praise for the Chinese soldier, but he was highly critical of their commanders. He cited their corruption and questioned their essential patriotism. He was bitterly satirical of Generalissimo Chiang Kai-shek, whom he called the Gee-Mo, as well as of Madame Chiang, whom he had dubbed Snow White.

I had hoped to get across the Hump into China, but after several days of trying to hitch a flight, and running into overloaded planes and bad weather, I gave up and headed back west with London as my goal.

My tour had been interesting, and had taken me places I might not otherwise have seen, but I remained unsatisfied. I wanted to cover the war itself. Several times I wired New York asking permission to broaden my assignment, but I was always told to stick to the Red Cross. I had to push hard to write stories about Red Cross activities that could compete for attention with dispatches from our war correspondents. But of course my Red Cross stories really didn't have to compete for space in the paper, given Sulzberger's wish that the organization be publicized. That was part of my discontent. To a large extent I had been on a phony assignment, publicizing the

Red Cross beyond what it merited, to please our publisher and to help the organization's fund-raising efforts back home.

Obviously, I saw many fine people doing fine work in the Red Cross, but I saw many snafus too. There was the constant problem of duplicating services. It was wonderful, for example, that the Red Cross girls took coffee and doughnuts to the soldiers at the front on Christmas—but the army had already served them a hot turkey dinner that day. There was, too, the problem of creeping bureaucracy. A Red Cross program might be doing a fine job, but the war would pass it by, and the program would have become self-perpetuating. These were questions I left out of my dispatches but later reported to Marshall and Sulzberger. I also made a report to the national board of the Red Cross, telling them the bad with the good, but I don't know that it ever caused any changes.

It took me a week's hitchhiking to get to London, by way of Calcutta, New Delhi, Karachi, Algiers, Casablanca, and Prestwick, Scotland. Space in London was at a premium, but my VIP status rated me a room at the Grosvenor House, which was being used by American officers. After a few days, General Spaatz invited me to move in with him at Park House, and I turned my room in Grosvenor House over to Spaatz's daughter Katherine, a Red Cross trainee there, and some of her co-workers. Sulzberger's daughter Ruth, incidentally, was also a Red Cross worker in England, as was Ambassador Joe Kennedy's daughter Kathleen.

Scotty Reston was acting head of the *Times* London bureau while I was there, and one day he invited me to join him and his wife, Sally, on a weekend visit with Lord and Lady Astor at Cliveden, the Astors' splendid country estate on the Thames in Buckinghamshire.

Cliveden, with Nancy Astor reigning supreme as its hostess, had been a famous mingling place for politicians and journalists for a decade—it was sometimes called the "second Foreign Office." Lord Astor's brother controlled the *Times* of London and his son, David, edited the *Observer,* which put the family at the apex of establishment politics.

Nancy Astor was herself something of an institution. She was then around sixty years old, and she had been a famous and formidable character since girlhood. She was a Virginia-born beauty, one of the famous Langhorne sisters—another sister had married the artist Charles Dana Gibson and become the original Gibson girl. Nancy's marriage to Lord Astor had led her into politics. When her husband succeeded to his title, and thus to the House of Lords, she stood for his seat in Commons, becoming the first woman member of the House. She was an incorrigible do-gooder, with a particular interest in temperance and women's rights.

The Restons briefed me on Lady Astor as we rode the train out to Cliveden on Saturday afternoon, and told me they had already briefed her on the fact that I was a Mississippian. This was important, as Nancy Astor was something of a professional Southerner, and prided herself on the hospitality she extended to Southerners who came to London.

We were met at the station by the Astors' combination chauffeur-butler—a combination forced by the wartime shortage of servants. It was a raw, cold winter day, and we were glad when we arrived at Cliveden, where the chauffeur turned butler and led us through a great hall into a library with a roaring fire at one end. A man and woman were sitting before the fire. The man proved to be Lord Astor, a small, gentle man whose warm greeting put me immediately at ease. The woman was his sister, who lived nearby. He said that Nancy—Lady Astor—was visiting a neighbor and would be back soon.

We were shown to our rooms, where Scotty and I fortified ourselves with a couple of slugs of bourbon. This was a necessary precaution, because Lady Astor ordinarily allowed no liquor to be served at Cliveden. She was a rabid prohibitionist, with her natural instincts to temperance compounded by her devout adherence to Christian Science. A few minutes after we returned to the drawing room, there was a commotion in the hallway.

"That's Nancy," Lord Astor said with a grin, and indeed it was. She burst into the drawing room with her little hat slanted over one eye.

"Where is that Southern white trash?" she shouted, just for openers, and then she began circling around me like a strange animal confronting another of its kind. When she had milked this act for all it was worth, she rushed at me with outstretched hand. "Shake," she said. "I'm Southern white trash too."

Lady Astor was quite a show-off. She was outspoken and sometimes outrageous. An act was expected of her, and she generally provided it. I found her fun but exhausting—you never knew what she would say or do next. She was not a woman I'd have wanted to spend any extended period with. But we had many laughs together that weekend, for she always seated me beside her at meals. I was fascinated by her habit of chewing gum between courses.

On Sunday evening, General Jimmy Doolittle, then at the peak of his grace and ebullience, came for dinner with members of his staff. Before dinner, when the butler asked him if he'd like some tea, Doolittle said he'd rather have whiskey and soda. The butler's mouth dropped and there was a moment of stunned silence. Then Lord Astor whispered to the butler and handed him a small key which he fished from his vest pocket. The butler left and returned in a few minutes bearing a bottle of Scotch and a siphon of soda on a tray. He arrived just as Lady Astor made her entrance. I was expecting the worst, but Lord Astor said a few words to his wife and she made no objection—only a look of some disdain as the drinks were passed around. The Restons and I took advantage of Doolittle's prestige to have our first public drinks of the weekend.

A minute later, two of the Astors' sons, Bill and David, came down the stairs. "David," exclaimed Bill, "do you smell what I smell?" They too made a beeline for the bottle of Scotch. The incident gave me the impression that, although Lady Astor got most of the attention around Cliveden, Lord Astor was the boss whenever he chose to be.

After dinner that evening, Lady Astor got out her Bible and her copy of Mary Baker Eddy's "Science and Health," as, I was told, was her custom. She sat on the floor beside the couch where she had seated Doolittle, and between her reading of the Bible and the Eddy materials, she led the general through a full telling of the story of his daring bombing raid over Tokyo.

Just before we left Monday morning, Nancy invited us to the family's private apartment. She wanted to show us some letters she had received from George Bernard Shaw. This prompted Lord Astor to tell of the time when he and his wife had accompanied Shaw to Moscow, where they had an interview with Stalin. Nancy, he said, had been instructed to keep her mouth shut, and she tried her best, but it was evident that she was suffering. Finally Stalin, seeing her discomfort, asked if she had anything to say. "Yes," she blurted out, "how much longer are you going to continue to shoot people and send people to Siberia?" Lord Astor said he was about to go through the floor when he saw that Stalin was smiling. "As long as it's to the interest of the state," the dictator said.

I returned to New York aboard the *Queen Mary*, along with the Restons. The voyage was most pleasant. The *Queen Mary* had been converted into a troop ship. It had just delivered a U.S. Army division to Scotland and was on its way back with four thousand hospitalized soldiers, three hundred civilians, and the Archbishop of York. All passengers were given some duty in keeping with their talents.

The Restons and I were assigned to help get out the ship's news-paper, and the archbishop was assigned to the business of preaching and praying. There was plenty to pray about, as German submarines still patrolled those waters, and we moved in a zigzag course in hopes of avoiding them. Either the zigzagging or the praying worked, for we made it to New York unharmed, although there were reports of U-boats in our path.

When I finally got back to New York and reached my hotel, I had a message saying the publisher, Arthur Hays Sulzberger, wanted to see me the next day. It was during that conversation that I learned that one of his reasons for sending me abroad on the Red Cross tour was to give me foreign experience that would help qualify me for an editorial job in New York. Sulzberger told me he had been talking to James about me, that the *Times* was looking for editorial talent, and he reminded me that he'd said when I returned from Chicago that there was always room at the top on the *Times*. He said he wanted me to consider coming to New York in an executive capacity. He spoke of Jimmy James, the managing editor, saying that he didn't know what he would do if anything happened to him. He quickly added that the managing editor's job was James' as long as he wanted it, but he seemed to be hinting that I might aspire to it someday. But the job he held out to me was that of day foreign news editor. That opening existed because Charles Lincoln had re-signed after a row with Bruce Rae, the sometimes irascible assistant managing editor.

After talking with Sulzberger, I talked with James, and I gath-ered that, although he liked me, he was none too anxious to see me in the foreign-news slot. The problem was that James was a former foreign correspondent, and he was quite happy for the job to be vacant so he could make the foreign news decisions himself. James said he wanted me to cover the forthcoming Presidential campaign —and I wanted to cover it—so we finally agreed that, if neither I nor James nor Sulzberger changed his mind, I could come to New York after the November election.

XIII

The 1944 Campaign

I RETURNED to Washington in mid-March and after a few days of rest I resumed my role as the *Times'* national correspondent. On a trip around the country to see what the national mood was in that election year, it was soon apparent to me that FDR would be renominated and almost certainly re-elected. The war was on in full fury and the third term was no longer an issue. It was clear, too, that Thomas E. Dewey had the inside track for the Republican nomination. About the only interesting question left was whether Roosevelt would ditch Henry A. Wallace, his controversial Vice President, and if so, whom he would choose to replace him. Roosevelt's health was the subject of much speculation in those days. He often looked haggard and drawn, and it seemed impossible that he could survive four more trying years as President. But those close to him knew his remarkable ability to bounce back from illness or exhaustion with a few days' rest, and I think in many minds was growing a belief that FDR was indestructible. I think FDR himself believed that.

When I returned to Washington, Jimmy Byrnes, then director of the Office of War Mobilization, told me the President wanted to see me. He said Roosevelt wanted to talk to me about what I had seen in Europe and the Near East, and also that he imagined Roosevelt wanted to sound me out on the results of my political scouting trip. The main question Roosevelt was interested in, I imagined, was how people were responding to the idea of a fourth term. I was prepared to give him good news on that one, for my observation had been that, once the no-third-term tradition had been broken in 1940, people had ceased to care much about a fourth term. They weren't going to defeat Roosevelt in the middle of a war.

Soon after I spoke to Byrnes, I had a call from the White House saying the President wanted to see me, and the next morning I went there to talk to him.

When I entered the President's office, and had my first glimpse of him in several months, I was shocked and horrified—so much so that my impulse was to turn around and leave. I felt I was seeing something I shouldn't see. He had lost a great deal of weight. His shirt collar hung so loose on his neck that you could have put your hand inside it. He was sitting there with a vague, glassy-eyed expression on his face and his mouth hanging open.

Reluctantly, I sat down and we started talking. I expected him to ask me about the political situation, but he never did. He would start talking about something, then in midsentence he would stop and his mouth would drop open and he'd sit staring at me in silence. I knew I was looking at a terribly sick man. I had seen a good friend of mine, Senator Pat Harrison, in almost the same condition. A doctor had explained to me that it was a case of a man's heart not pumping enough blood to his brain, so that at times he simply could not speak or think to his full capacity.

We sat in silence for some time. Finally I mentioned the Teheran Conference, and that I had been in Teheran on my recent trip. Either the subject of Teheran or something else stimulated him, for he started talking about that city. He asked if I'd noticed the water system there. I certainly had, for the water flowed in open ditches down both sides of the main streets.

"You know, they use that for everything," Roosevelt told me. "They wash in it; they wash their clothes in it; they pee in it—and twenty feet down the street you'll see somebody drinking from it."

He laughed uproariously at that. And I might say in passing that this was quite typical of Roosevelt's humor as I had known it over the years. Roosevelt was a subtle man politically, but his humor was not subtle. The stories he told were invariably very blunt. Not dirty stories, but stories with humor that was extremely broad and blunt. Roosevelt's humor consisted largely of his own laughter. He would tell a story that he thought funny and he would laugh, and of course everyone else had to laugh too, since he was President. His position enabled him to tease other people a great deal, par-

Above, Lee and Willie Catledge, the author's parents, after their wedding in 1898. At right, the author at the age of three, with his sister Bessie.

The author's birthplace, the farmhouse of his paternal grandfather in New Prospect, Miss. From left: the author's Uncle John Catledge; his mother, holding his sister Bessie; and his grandmother, Sarah Johnston Catledge.

The building at right housed the *Neshoba* (Miss.) *Democrat,* the paper that gave the author the job that started his career.

The colorful Memphis newspaper editor C. P. J. Mooney, whom the author calls "one of the great influences on my professional life."

Boss Crump, the autocrat of Memphis, rejoiced when his men thrashed young Catledge for prying into voting irregularities.
Associated Press Photo

The author, an eager young Washington reporter for the *New York Times*, as he interviewed one of his favorite politicians, Senator Pat Harrison of Mississippi.

Senator "Cotton Ed" Smith of South Carolina was another Catledge favorite—not for his racist politics but for the flamboyance of his demagoguery. *UPI*

Catledge was just a face in the crowd (far right in top photo) at Franklin Roosevelt's first press conference as President. But when Catledge rose in the *Times'* Washington bureau, FDR tried to use him to undercut bureau chief Arthur Krock (shown here with another rising young Timesman, James Reston).

1944: To size Catledge up before offering him an editor's job, *Times* publisher Arthur Hays Sulzberger (right) took Catledge on a tour of Pacific battlefronts, preceded by a drinking bout in San Francisco.

Above: A daily news conference was one of the author's first innovations when he became an editor. Clifton Daniel (sitting to Catledge's left) and Theodore Bernstein (to his right) were among those who helped Catledge rejuvenate the once-dull paper. In recognition of their success, *The New Yorker* printed the cartoon at left. *Drawing by Chon Day.* © *1962 The New Yorker Magazine, Inc.*

Catledge (second from left) was an usher in Daniel's wedding to Margaret Truman in 1956. Catledge assisted Daniel's career, but Daniel's temperament worked against his succeeding Catledge as the top editor.

The managing editor of the *New York Times* is almost automatically on close terms with the highest public figures. Below, Catledge with Vice President Nixon in 1960. *Wide World*

President Kennedy speaks somberly with Catledge on the day of the Bay of Pigs disaster.

One of the major crises of the author's career was the 114-day strike of the *Times* in 1962-63. Catledge used opera glasses to observe the picket lines.

Another crisis involved correspondent Herbert Matthews, here with Fidel Castro. When Matthews was accused of over-enthusiasm for Castro, the *Times* failed to give him full support.

The author had frequent encounters with Adolph Ochs' descendants, the principal owners of the *Times*. Above, Arthur Hays Sulzberger and the redoubtable General Julius Ochs Adler. Below, foreign correspondent C. L. Sulzberger, with whom Catledge had recurrent differences. *Wide World*

Iphigene Sulzberger, matriarch of the family, often sent Catledge notes praising or criticizing items in the paper.

Arthur "Punch" Sulzberger, Jr., and his wife, Carol, with the author and his wife, Abby, as they sailed for Europe together in 1964. When Punch became publisher, Catledge stood by him during the famous battle with the Washington bureau, then stepped down as executive editor at Punch's request.

ticularly those who worked for him, but this amounted more to a sense of fun than to a sense of humor.

Stimulated perhaps by his own laughter at the Teheran water system, Roosevelt began telling me about the Teheran Conference he'd attended a few months earlier. He spoke at length about a dinner he, Churchill, and Stalin attended, along with a few of their aides, at the end of the conference. There were much drinking and laughter, and many toasts, but as Roosevelt told me the story, two of the toasts resulted in unpleasant scenes.

The first incident came about because Stalin was irritated at the British for diverting some airplanes—fifty, I believe, was the number —that the United States had sent overseas, intended for Russia. The British thought they needed the planes worse than the Russians, so they took them. Stalin was angry, and throughout the dinner he kept coming back to those fifty planes, needling Churchill. Finally, Roosevelt said, Stalin walked over and stuck his glass of vodka right under Churchill's nose, and declared, "Here's a toast to the fifty airplanes that were stolen from Russia." Whereupon Churchill became quite angry.

But that was only a curtain raiser. Some time later, Stalin proposed a toast: "Here's to fifty thousand Germans who will have to be executed at the end of the war in order to insure the continuing peace of the world." At that, Churchill jumped up and said he would not drink to any such proposition and he wouldn't remain in a room where it was being discussed. The situation was very tense, Roosevelt said, adding that he blamed it on Churchill for losing his sense of humor. To lighten the tension, Roosevelt intervened by raising his glass and saying: "In that case, I propose an amendment to that toast. Here's to the 49,000 Germans who will have to be killed."

Whereupon Stalin jumped up and said, "Mr. President, you certainly have a sense of humor," and said he would accept the amendment and started dancing around the room, at which point everyone broke into laughter, except Churchill.

I didn't know what to make of that story, first because of the condition Roosevelt was in that day, and second because I suspected that his jealousy of Churchill might color anything he said about him. So I was surprised to learn, some years later, that the story was true, or at least substantially so.

When the *Times* published the Yalta Papers in March of 1955, a sentence in Ambassador Bohlen's minutes said, referring to Roosevelt: "And he hoped that Marshal Stalin would again propose a toast to the execution of 50,000 officers of the German Army." In context, the "again" referred to the Teheran Conference the previous year.

And later, in Churchill's memoirs, I read his more detailed account of the incident. Churchill relates that Stalin "entered in a genial manner upon a serious and even deadly aspect of the punishment to be inflicted upon the Germans." Fifty thousand officers and technicians should be shot at the end of the war, Stalin said, whereupon Churchill declared that his government would never be a party to such an action. "Fifty thousand must be shot," Stalin persisted, and Churchill replied, "I would rather be taken out into the garden here and now and be shot myself than sully my own and my country's honour by such infamy."

At this point, Churchill wrote, Roosevelt intervened with his "compromise" proposal that not fifty thousand Germans, but only forty-nine thousand, should be shot. Churchill took this as an attempt to make a joke of the matter, but at that point the President's son, Elliott Roosevelt, stood up and said "how cordially he agreed with Marshal Stalin's plan and how sure he was that the United States Army would support it." At that, Churchill left the room, but Stalin and Molotov followed him and assured him the whole thing was a joke. Churchill then returned to the party, although he was not convinced that Stalin was entirely joking.

In any event, Roosevelt told me his version of the story, and my talk with him lasted more than an hour. His appointments secretary, General Edwin M. (Pa) Watson, came to the door several times but Roosevelt would raise his hand (a hand so thin you could almost see through it) and tell me to stay. I had the impression of a man who very badly wanted someone to talk to. And so we talked on, although he never brought up politics. Repeatedly he would lose his train of thought, stop, and stare blankly at me. It was an agonizing experience for me. Finally, a waiter brought his lunch, and Watson said his luncheon guest was waiting, and I was able to make my escape.

The only issue for the Democrats that year was who would be Roosevelt's running mate. Roosevelt had gotten Henry Wallace in 1940 by saying that he wouldn't run without him, but now a good deal of opposition to Wallace had developed and I think Roosevelt himself was somewhat disillusioned with him. Wallace was an ultraliberal, in the context of that era, and he was also something of a mystic—a difficult character for most politicians to understand. There was a story around the political gossip circuit in 1944 that Wallace was somehow involved with a woman in New York. Indeed, some interested persons tried to sell such a story to both the *Herald Tribune* and the *New York Times*. As I was told the story, when FDR heard the news he was delighted—if Wallace was having an affair with a woman, that was at least something he could understand. Roosevelt also quietly subscribed to the theory that an involvement with a woman was not always disadvantageous to a politician, as witness the case of Grover Cleveland and his siring of an illegitimate child. But later reports indicated that Wallace's involvement with the woman was not physical but metaphysical— they were involved together in a quest to discover the true Buddha. At that, I was told, Roosevelt threw up his hands in dismay, saying in effect, "We can handle sex but we can't handle religion."

I covered several state Democratic conventions that summer, and in all there was strong anti-Wallace feeling. As this sentiment spread, the word back in Washington was that Jimmy Byrnes was Roosevelt's choice to replace Wallace. Roosevelt had personally indicated to Byrnes that he was his choice (according to the Byrnes camp), although he couldn't say so publicly because Wallace had insisted on staying in the race. However, when the convention arrived, Roosevelt ditched Byrnes because of opposition from organized labor and from Ed Flynn, the New York City Democratic leader, and turned instead to Harry Truman, whose greatest qualification was that no one had anything against him.

A great deal of wheeling and dealing went on in the days preceding the Vice Presidential nomination, but probably two events were crucial. One was Ed Flynn's telling Roosevelt that Byrne's nomination would cost the ticket two hundred thousand votes in Harlem. The second was FDR's famous "Clear it with Sidney" declaration.

The "Clear it with Sidney" line was spoken just a few days before the nomination. Roosevelt met with Chicago Mayor Ed Kelly and with Bob Hannegan, chairman of the Democratic National Committee, at the Chicago train depot, and while ostensibly expressing his support for Byrnes, he added, "Clear it with Sidney." Sidney was Sidney Hillman, the powerful president of the Amalgamated Clothing Workers union, who opposed Byrnes because of his "hold-the-line"-on-wages policy as war mobilization chief. So, for all Roosevelt's apparent support for Byrnes, "Clear it with Sidney" was a death sentence for Byrnes' candidacy. This was typical of the ambiguous way Roosevelt did business.

Mayor Ed Kelly told me about the "Clear it with Sidney" line, but it could not be attributed to him. Nor did I think it should appear under my by-line, since my friendship with Byrnes and Kelly was well known. Thus it was arranged that Arthur Krock would use it in a story under his by-line, and Krock therefore became the target of the many outraged denials from Democrats. The Republicans quickly made the phrase the most famous political slogan of the campaign, declaring that the Democrats were clearing "everything" with the union bosses.

My impression, from talking to most of the politicians involved, was that Byrnes could have had the Vice Presidential nomination if he had been willing to make a fight of it on the convention floor. But Byrnes would not do this, largely because he feared the religious issue would be raised and would embarrass his wife. So he left the convention and returned to South Carolina, deeply embittered by Roosevelt's treatment of him, and Harry Truman became the Vice Presidential nominee and, a few months later, the President. Despite my personal affection for Byrnes, I think things worked out for the best. I fear that Byrnes was too committed to the South, emotionally and politically, to have succeeded as President.

Byrnes, of course, went on to be Truman's first Secretary of State, and in August of 1945 I had a terrible time convincing him I couldn't go to work for him as the State Department's public-affairs chief. I told him I wanted to be an observer of politics, not a participant. What I couldn't tell him was that I knew our long-standing friendship would alter considerably if he became the boss and I was the press agent. He renewed the offer one day that August in his office, and when I pleaded that I couldn't live on the $9,000 or so the government would pay me, he said something like "Don't worry, Baruch can take care of that." That completely put me off, for although I was an admirer of Baruch, I didn't want him slipping me any money under the table.

During this conversation with Byrnes, there was a great deal of confusion. People were running in and out. He finally explained to me that the Japanese had sent an offer of surrender, but somehow the message had been lost somewhere between the War Department message center and the State Department. A military officer came in and Byrnes gave him a furious dressing-down. Finally the message was located, and Byrnes called Truman to tell him. He also told Truman I was with him, and handed me the phone. "Why don't you quit stalling and take that job?" Truman demanded, and I stammered some reply. When I finally got back to my office I called my publisher, Arthur Hays Sulzberger, and told him he'd have to save me. Sulzberger was very good about that sort of thing, and he called Byrnes and convinced him the *Times* couldn't possibly spare me.

I returned to Chicago on a Sunday in mid-October of 1944, when Mayor La Guardia was there making a speech on Roosevelt's behalf. I called him at his hotel and he asked me to come to see him. When I arrived, Mayor Kelly was with him, and they were about to leave for the Coliseum, where La Guardia was speaking. They asked me to accompany them, and once we were in Kelly's car, he asked me, "What do you think about Roosevelt coming out here to make a big speech at Soldier Field?"

The speech was Kelly's idea, but La Guardia was all for it. "We've just got to get him to come out here," La Guardia said. "A tremendous crowd out here will cinch it." "I can certainly guarantee you a crowd," Kelly promised.

The problem was Roosevelt had made few, if any, campaign speeches. His ploy that year was to make "inspection tours" of defense plants and address the workers, but not to admit he was campaigning. But Kelly and La Guardia wanted him to come make a rousing political speech in Chicago, and I think they were less interested in my opinion than in my writing an article that might help persuade Roosevelt to come.

So, after we had discussed the local political situation a few minutes, I said, "Okay, gentlemen, do I have a story or not?" Kelly said, "Yes, you have a story, that we are setting things up for a big speech in Chicago. But be careful because we haven't got his consent yet. The story is that we are urging him to come out here for a big speech and the likelihood is that he will."

My story appeared the next morning, Monday, and early Tuesday morning, when I was back home in Washington, I had a call saying that the President wanted to see me. So I started for the White House, but with an unhappy, squeamish feeling, remembering how he had been the last time I'd seen him.

But, when I walked into his office, a new man was sitting there beaming at me. He was still thin and emaciated, but he had life and spirit in his face, and I remember thinking, "It's the campaign that's revived him—politics is this man's life's blood."

He immediately began talking about the campaign. He wanted to compare the information he was getting with what I had seen in my travels. Most of what I told him was encouraging, for I had no doubt he would win again. But he wasn't claiming everything, and his predictions on some regions were less optimisitc than mine. Like all successful politicians, he was running scared.

Finally he said, "Now this story you had yesterday morning from Chicago. I haven't decided on that yet. Do you think I'm in trouble in Illinois? Do you think it would be good for me to go out there?"

I said, "Mr. President, you shouldn't ask my advice. You don't even know whether I'm for or against you."

He tilted his head about and had a good laugh at that. "Don't ask my opinion as to what you should do," I continued, "but I can tell you this. Mayor Kelly thinks you ought to go. He thinks the Chicago *Tribune*'s attacks on you have had some impact, but if you'll make an appearance, it'll clinch the state for you. And I don't have to tell you that the Illinois electoral votes are important to you."

"Why don't we make a little deal?" Roosevelt said. "You write a story that says I'll go, but you say it on your own. Don't tell Fiorello or Ed Kelly I said I was going, because I'll tell them later. But go ahead and say it's going to be done."

I wrote my story as he suggested, and he didn't let me down. On the evening of October 29 he gave a fighting political speech to 110,000 persons in Soldier Field, while at least another 110,000 stood outside in the stadium's parking lots. It was one of the greatest political rallies in American history, and it climaxed a whirlwind tour in which Roosevelt was seen by more than a million voters in six states in only two days. Needless to say, Roosevelt won easily that year, and he carried Illinois by a landslide.

But the real point I want to make is what a different man he was in October from the man I had talked with in May. I don't think the real state of his health had changed much but I think Roosevelt was stimulated by the challenge of the political campaign. His blood was flowing that day, and his mind was right on the beam. It was the last time I saw him.

XIV

Travels with the Publisher

IT was on a cold, wind-blown night of October 18, 1944, in Fargo, North Dakota, that I got the unexpected word that I was to accompany our publisher, Arthur Hays Sulzberger, on a five-week tour of the Pacific war theaters.

I was on a political scouting trip and was on my way to catch a train for Minneapolis when I stopped by the Western Union office to see if I might have any telegrams. There was one, and I tore it open, suspecting it was from Sunday Editor Lester Markel regarding a *Magazine* piece I'd just filed the day before. But the telegram was from Sulzberger and it said: "I am going to the Pacific immediately after election for Red Cross. Would you care to go along not only as a companion but also to write articles similar to those you did from Europe and Asia. Postscript: Do you play gin rummy?"

I promptly wired back that I would be happy to accompany him. Breaking the news to my family, however, was not easy. We had just moved to New York and I was expected home after my campaign travels ended. I was back in New York to write the lead election-night story, on Roosevelt's win over Dewey, but that Saturday I left for San Francisco, where I was to meet Sulzberger. He'd gone on ahead to visit his son Punch, then a Marine trainee at Camp Pendleton, California. My trip began by air, but my flight was grounded in Salt Lake City and I continued by train. I arrived in

San Francisco on November 13 and the publisher and I then engaged in what we later called the Battle of the Top of the Mark. Before relating the encounter, however, perhaps I should say a few words about my relationship then with Sulzberger.

He was fifty-three years old and had been publisher of the *Times* for nine years. He was extremely urbane, self-confident, and intelligent, one of the easiest men to deal with I've ever known. We had known each other for a decade and, as I've related, he had often extended kindnesses to me and assured me I had a fine future with the *Times*. However, until then ours was largely a professional relationship; we were friendly but by no means intimate. It was on this trip that we began to move toward personal friendship and intimacy.

His Pacific tour had a dual purpose. Officially, he was traveling as a member of the central board of the Red Cross to observe Red Cross operations and discuss them with military commanders. His second, unofficial purpose was to see the war, so that the *New York Times* could give readers a better understanding of it. But the official Red Cross capacity was needed to overcome the government's refusal to let newspaper publishers travel in war areas.

Certainly one reason I was chosen to accompany him was that, on the basis of my previous trip to Europe and the Near East, I was well acquainted with the operations of the Red Cross. But I can see in retrospect that Sulzberger had another reason for taking me. He wanted to look me over. I had known for some months that I was slated for an editor's job in New York, and I thought it would be assistant foreign editor—these trips were helping establish my "foreign" credentials. But Sulzberger knew something I did not—that he had me in mind for assistant managing editor. Perhaps he was already thinking ahead to the time when he would have to pick a successor to Jimmy James as managing editor; I don't know. I do know that he wanted editors whom he found personally compatible as well as professionally capable.

The Battle of the Top of the Mark was my first big test.

Both of us arrived in San Francisco about noon on the 13th and we spent the afternoon checking in with the Red Cross and with military officials. It was almost sundown when we finished all the red tape—sundown on a beautiful autumn evening in the most beautiful of American cities. AHS suggested that we proceed to our hotel, the Mark Hopkins.

At the elevator there, Sulzberger asked me: "Do you think we should go to our rooms first, or proceed directly to the Top of the Mark?"

"Mr. Sulzberger," I replied, "that's a serious question to which I've already given considerable thought. I think we should go directly to the Top of the Mark."

"That makes sense to me," he said, and we took the elevator to the beautiful penthouse lounge, where we were seated on a comfortable divan, with a table before it, and glorious view of the north side of San Francisco, the bay, and the Golden Gate Bridge.

We proceeded rapidly to the business at hand. We ordered two Scotches, then two more. On the third round AHS proposed that we have doubles. We had two doubles and we talked. We had two more doubles and we talked some more. We talked about everything —the beauty of San Francisco, his ambitions for the *Times*, even some of his personal difficulties. His father-in-law, Adolph Ochs, had been the classic case of the father who thinks no man is good enough for his daughter, and he had not exhibited great tact or affection in his dealings with his son-in-law and heir apparent. I remember Sulzberger telling me, "You can go home at night and tell your wife what an S.O.B. your boss is, but I could never do that."

We ordered two more double Scotches and, as we were both obviously quite sober and rational, AHS asked the waiter, "Are you sure these are doubles?"

The waiter laughed. "Am I sure?" he said. "You've drunk practically a bottle already."

By that time, we were too pleasantly disposed to argue, so we kept on talking and ordering "just one more before dinner." We had entered the Top of the Mark about five, and about nine Sulzberger unexpectedly stuck out his hand, shook mine, and said, "Well, you pass."

I wanted to know what he meant, but he insisted that we go down for dinner, and it was only after we had ordered that he explained.

Sulzberger had made a trip to Russia the previous year, accompanied by Scotty Reston, and Scotty had repeatedly been stumped by the publisher's heavy schedule of eating and drinking. Scotty, in addition to his usual moderation, had been suffering from undulant fever and he simply couldn't drink very much. He had told Sulzberger that on his next trip he should have someone who could keep up with him. Scotty and I had made a few political reporting trips together, and when Sulzberger told him he was taking me to the Pacific, Scotty said, "That's good—now you'll have someone who will drink and carouse with you." So, Sulzberger explained, he had decided to test my capacities at the outset of our Pacific odyssey.

Fortunately, I passed the test.

We left San Francisco on November 14 and returned to New York on December 9, after traveling some twenty-five thousand miles in the Pacific. We carried with us a letter of introduction from Secretary of the Navy James V. Forrestal, and everywhere we went we met with top-ranking military commanders and (with rare exceptions) were treated with the utmost courtesy. Ours was a VIP trip, yet there were frequent opportunities to talk with the GIs, to slog about in the mud, to see the wounded and the refugees, and on one occasion to be shot at.

The shooting incident occurred late in November on the little island of Peleliu, which is about midway between New Guinea and the Philippines. We were taken on a jeep tour of Peleliu by Marine General Campbell and Navy Captain Oates. The sections of the island we saw had been contested by the Japanese until only two days earlier, and pockets of resistance still existed. They took us up a mountain ridge where the fighting had been especially heavy. We parked the jeep and got out.

Captain Oates was relieving himself beside the road and General Campbell stood in front of the jeep, waving his hand toward the ridge and saying, "We wiped out all organized resistance here two days ago."

Just then, Sulzberger and I heard a "Zing! Smack!" as a sniper's bullet whizzed between our heads. It hit a rock and ricocheted into a stump, setting it on fire. Only Sulzberger and I had heard the bullet, and he said to the general: "Well, I don't believe all resistance has stopped."

"What do you mean?" General Campbell asked.

"This just arrived," Sulzberger said, pointing to the smoking stump.

"We'd better get the hell out of here," the general declared.

I was in total agreement, but we had to wait for Captain Oates to finish relieving himself, which seemed to take hours. Hoping to appear calm, I walked around so the jeep was between me and the sniper. Then, for added safety, I bent down and tied my shoe until everyone was ready to depart.

As we bounced down the hillside, General Campbell tried to reassure us. "The Nips can't hit anything," he said. "They always miss." Still, it seemed to me that one might shoot at Sulzberger, miss him, and hit me by accident.

We completed our mission in Peleliu without further incident and flew on to Leyte and General MacArthur. Needless to say, MacArthur's house was the largest, most elegant, and driest in Leyte. It was a square stucco structure, with the main floor raised above a ground-floor basement. It had been an officers club during the Japanese occupation, and the Japanese must have known MacArthur was living in it, for it was a principal target for air raids. It had been strafed repeatedly and was pockmarked inside and out with machine-gun bullet holes. My room had a gaping hole through the wall made the week before by a 20-mm. shell.

MacArthur lived there with his staff, headed by General Richard K. Sutherland, Chief of Staff of the Southwest Pacific Command, and General Kenney, the short, burly commander of the Southwest Pacific Army Air Forces. Other generals on MacArthur's staff lived nearby, and all partook of his mess, over which he presided regally.

At MacArthur's house, Colonel Lloyd (Larry) Lehrbas, an old friend of mine from the Associated Press staff in Washington, now serving as MacArthur's personal aide, met us at the door. He said Sulzberger would share a room with General Kenney and I would quarter with him, Lehrbas. MacArthur came out to greet us just before lunch. He was overflowing with cordiality. I thought this was not a show but the man's natural manner.

Ten generals joined us for lunch. MacArthur, with AHS seated on his right, easily dominated the conversation. After lunch, Mac-Arthur had General Sutherland brief us on the plans to recapture the Philippines. Sutherland told us everything about the still-secret plans. When we left we knew a strike was coming at Ormoc and preparations were under way for it at Tacloban and Hollandia. We knew the date set for the invasion of Mindoro and the forces to be employed. We knew, in short, a great deal more than we wanted to know, since we were traveling in battle zones and it was not impossible that we might be captured by the Japanese. Both Sulzberger and I felt very uncomfortable about that briefing, but apparently MacArthur had told Sutherland to tell us the whole story, and he'd done so. This disposition to take American newspapermen into full confidence was typical throughout the armed forces during the war, from General Marshall and Admiral King in Washington down to the lowliest GI.

After the briefing, we joined MacArthur on his porch for one of the most fascinating talks with a public figure that either of us had ever experienced. The general went through his whole story. He told how Roosevelt had ordered him to leave Bataan, how he got to Australia, how he came to realize that his enemies in the War Department wanted to undercut him. He spoke of his conflicts with the Navy, how his name had been mentioned for the Republican nomination for President, and the problems this created between him and Roosevelt. He spoke with pride of his military success in "island hopping" from New Guinea to Leyte. He spoke of the war in strictly personal terms—my infantry, my artillery, my men, my strategy, and so on. As he spoke, he was variously the military expert, the political figure, the man of destiny. Sulzberger and I later agreed we had never met a more egotistical man, nor one more aware of his egotism and more able and determined to back it up with his deeds.

We returned to dine with MacArthur at 6 P.M. Larry Lehrbas had warned us of the general's famous punctuality, so we arrived early, as did the various generals who shared MacArthur's mess. But 6 P.M. came and went with no sign of MacArthur. From the direction of his room, however, we heard a voice making what sounded to me like a political speech, so well modulated, well rehearsed and self-assured was it. I thought perhaps it was a radio broadcast from the United States, but my comment to that effect only drew blank stares from the generals. Then Larry Lehrbas motioned to me and I followed him to a small office near MacArthur's room. From there, without MacArthur's knowing it, AHS and I listened as MacArthur angrily dressed down the U.S. Navy, in the person of Vice Admiral Tom Kinkaid.

The timing of MacArthur's plans to invade Mindoro and Luzon had been questioned by the Navy's high command in Washington. MacArthur was boss of both the Army and Navy in this area, but not over their general staffs. Word had come to Admiral Kinkaid, MacArthur's naval commander, from Admiral Nimitz in Honolulu that the Navy high command thought it would be suicide for the Navy to run the Japanese gauntlet up to Mindoro until the Army Air Force could provide more air protection from Japanese suicide raids.

So Admiral Kinkaid had come ashore from his flagship in Tacloban Bay to break this news, and MacArthur had exploded. He was impatient to get on to Mindoro and then to Luzon, for he dreamed of marching in triumph down the streets of Manila early the next spring.

MacArthur proceeded to let the Navy have it with both barrels. "What do they have ships for?" he demanded. Ships, he declared, were just as expendable as "my" tanks, and the sailors could run their risks the same as "my" soldiers. The Navy, he said, "has a moth-eaten tradition that an officer who loses his ship is disgraced," and naval commanders therefore were afraid to take chances. "What do the American people expect you to do with all that hardware if not to throw it at the enemy?" he demanded of Kinkaid.

We could hear perfectly and we could even see the two commanders through a crack in the door. Kinkaid seemed to be used to these outbursts, for he leaned against the foot of the bed and said little in reply. MacArthur paced the room like a trial lawyer shouting at a witness. He flung his arms in the air, thrust his finger under the admiral's nose, and sometimes stopped and stared incredulously at him with his hands on his hips and his chin extended.

Finally, at the height of his performance, MacArthur stopped, burst into a smile, put both hands on Kinkaid's shoulders, and said, "But, Tommy, I love you just the same. Let's go to dinner and then send them a cable."

The next day MacArthur told us that he and the Navy had reached a compromise whereby the invasion was postponed for ten days. Not knowing we had overheard his speech to Kinkaid, he told us the entire story. He delivered to Sulzberger at breakfast the same speech he had made to Kinkaid, stressing the Navy's "reluctance to meet the enemy."

The following day, December 1, we left MacArthur for a visit to the front. On this trip we saw one of the most moving sights of our journey, the old San Salvador Cathedral at Palo, which had been converted into a hospital for wounded American soldiers. The huge cathedral stood opposite the town square, a twelve-foot statue of Jesus before it, jeeps and U.S. Army tents beside it, its twin spires rising with timeless dignity above the war-created devastation of Palo. Inside, the pews had been replaced by long rows of hospital cots, perhaps two hundred in all. There were operating tables on both sides of the vestibule. One operation was in progress when we arrived, and the bloody gauze on the floor indicated that others had recently been completed.

Men in all stages of injury sat or lay on the cots. Some stared up toward the huge, ornate altar, backed by statues of the saints. Others were drugged with morphine to ease their pain, and yet others had arms or legs stretched out with ropes and pulleys to mend their broken bones.

There was no attempt to keep native worshipers out of the cathedral. On the contrary, the doctors believed the presence of worshipers helped the wounded men. Candles burned on the high altar and native women, their heads covered with black shawls, knelt at the holy stations, counting their rosary beads and chanting prayers. We were told that on Sundays hundreds of Filipinos crowded the church, kneeling among the wounded Americans to pray. If ever there was a place where prayer was in order, that was it.

We returned to Leyte for a final day with MacArthur before moving on to Hollandia, in New Guinea.

During the last night of our stay, we were sitting just outside the general's bedroom-office, listening to General Kenney tell of the techniques the Air Force had developed for skip-bombing Japanese ships, when MacArthur strolled majestically into the room. He walked to a map, pointed to it with his forefinger, and said to Kenney: "George, it just occurred to me that Jap suicide flyers are coming from some spot right in here. What do you say to the proposition of detaching a squadron from my old Fifth Air Force and sending them up there to work over that point a bit?"

"General, you read my mind," Kenney replied. "I gave that exact order this morning and we're flying two dozen sorties against that point tomorrow."

MacArthur turned to AHS with a flourish and at the same time put his hand on Kenney's head. "There, you see," he declared with pleasure. "What did I tell you about my boys?"

Then, turning to General Kenney, who looked like a schoolboy being praised by his teacher, MacArthur added, "Georgie, you are the joy of my life."

With that, he popped his corncob pipe back into his mouth, thrust his chin forward, and followed it out the door. It was an exit that a Lunt or a Barrymore could hardly have duplicated.

Sulzberger and I arrived at La Guardia Airport early in the morning of December 19. To me the most important thing about our Pacific trip was the new intimacy it created between me and Sulzberger. For more than a month, we ate and drank together, often slept and bathed together, were even shot at together. These experiences taught us more about each other than we could have learned in a decade of formal office dealings. We finished the trip with countless common memories, starting with our drinking bout at the Mark Hopkins, which enabled us to joke for years about our respective drinking capacities. Another joke grew up between us because a general who entertained us somehow got the idea my name was Leiter, and kept calling me Mr. Leiter despite numerous corrections. Sulzberger found this highly amusing, and thereafter he would often call me Mr. Leiter. I have a memo from him dated May 17, 1965, more than twenty years after our trip, in which he said that he'd seen me on a television show and he joked that "it didn't sound like the Mr. Leiter I knew!"

If we had been unable to get along together, we would certainly have found it out during that trip. As it was, we found that we got along extremely well. I respected his intelligence, his sophistication, his ready humor, and his great desire to make the *New York Times* a better newspaper. I think that he, in turn, respected my developing professional competence, and my equal concern for the *Times'* future excellence. And a month at close quarters showed us we could work together. At the time I didn't fully realize how important it was to Sulzberger to have editors he could work with pleasantly. I later realized that one of his problems in those days was that his managing editor, Jimmy James, often regarded him rather scornfully and made no secret of it. Sulzberger found that my attitude toward him was not one of scorn toward a fellow who'd become a publisher by marrying the boss's daughter, but of respect for a man who, although not technically a newspaperman, shared my concern for excellence in the paper.

It was early in our Pacific trip, the day we arrived in Honolulu, that I first learned I was to go to New York not as foreign news editor but as assistant managing editor. Bruce Rae, who met us in Honolulu, had been assistant managing editor, but he had had trouble getting along with James and some others on the staff, so he had been sent to the Pacific to oversee war coverage in that area. Bruce had been one of the greatest reporters in the history of the *Times*, but he was temperamentally ill-suited to be an executive. So one of Sulzberger's missions on this trip was to tell Bruce that when he returned to New York it would not be as assistant managing editor, that I would be moving into that slot.

My appointment as assistant managing editor suggested that I was being put in the line of succession to become managing editor. However, that possibility seemed very distant. Sulzberger had told me that Jimmy James would be managing editor as long as he wanted the job, and he was many years from retirement age. I had spent twelve years waiting vainly to succeed Arthur Krock in Washington, so I didn't get my hopes up about succeeding James any time soon.

XV

Assistant Managing Editor

JANUARY 2, 1945, was my first day as assistant managing editor of the *Times*, a post I held for six years. It was a time of valuable training and experience for me, yet often a frustrating time as well. I had not been in the New York office long before I began to feel the *Times* was in a contradictory and deceptive situation. On the one hand, the paper was financially successful and enjoyed national and international prestige. Yet it seemed to me also to suffer both from mounting internal problems and from an unnecessary stodginess in the way the news was reported and written, in comparison to other New York papers. These problems seemed to me so serious that I doubted the paper's continued pre-eminence unless they were corrected.

My frustrations arose from the fact that as assistant managing editor I was in an excellent position to observe the *Times'* problems but in a poor position to do anything about them. I believed that most of these problems existed because the managing editor, Edwin L. (Jimmy) James, who was both my friend and my boss, was not providing the aggressive leadership demanded of his position. When now and then I would suggest improvements to James, his attitude would be, "Why change? We're doing all right, aren't we?" Success is a hard argument to counter, particularly in as tradition-minded an institution as the *Times*. I had neither the authority nor the desire to make changes that James didn't want made. I had to consider, too, the possibility that he was right. So in large part my years as assistant managing editor became a time of watching and waiting.

Perhaps the paper's most serious internal problem was the deep division between the "day side" and the "night side" editors. We had two shifts of editors, one that worked during the day, when most news is gathered and written, and another that worked at night when the paper was actually put together and printed. The problem was in maintaining cooperation and continuity between the two shifts.

I had received advance warning of the *Times'* day-night problem in the summer of 1944 when I shared a hotel room in Chicago, during the Democratic Convention, with Neil MacNeil, the assistant night managing editor. At the time, I knew I was headed for an executive job in New York, but MacNeil did not, so I rather shamelessly pumped him for information on how things operated. He quite bluntly told me that Jimmy James, the titular boss of the paper, was in fact a figurehead who had little to do with running the paper, and that he and the night managing editor, Raymond McCaw, were actually making the key decisions. When I asked about the job of foreign news editor, which I thought I would be filling, MacNeil shrugged and said, "Oh, that's on the day side." As far as he was concerned, no day-side editor was of any great significance.

I was not in New York long before I saw that MacNeil had not exaggerated. A seemingly unbridgeable split existed between the day and night editors, with the night editors—the "bullpen" as we called them—quite indifferent to the day editors' views and instructions. The night editors' autonomy existed because Jimmy James didn't want a fight, didn't want any trouble, only wanted to enjoy the prerogatives of the managing editor's job and to be out of the office by early evening. Let the paper and everyone on it enjoy its success, James felt. I had long since learned, back in Memphis and Baltimore, that you can't leave the office at six and run a morning newspaper. Key decisions on what stories get into the paper, how much space they receive, where they are placed, and how they are written and edited are going to be made at night. If the top editor isn't on the scene, or at least represented by an alter ego, an editor who *is* there will soon be running the paper.

Each of the decisions involved may be small in itself, and not seem worth a fight, but the sum of the decisions, night after night, will determine the character of the newspaper.

There was hardly any effective planning on the day side. James would leave at six or seven, McCaw wouldn't come in until nine, and weeks would pass without their conferring. James always left a batch of memos for the night editors, and many evenings I'd see one of them glance at them, then throw them in the wastebasket. However, since James passed on the publisher's instructions, as well as his own, a code had been worked out to denote Sulzberger's requests. If James said in a memo, "It is desired that . . . ," the bullpen editors understood the particular instruction came from Sulzberger, and was not to be ignored.

Sometimes I would stay in the office at night, watching the bullpen editors get out the paper. I had worked with them as a reporter, and they were always quite cordial, but it was clear they considered me a sightseer, with no authority to comment on their work. It had never been made clear whether I, as assistant managing editor, or McCaw, as night managing editor, stood higher on the office totem pole. When I once raised the point, James waved his hand and told me not to worry about it.

Sulzberger was aware of this problem, but not of the depth of it. It was not until January of 1951 that he acted to correct the situation by creating for me the new title of Executive Managing Editor, with a mandate to bridge the day-night gap. But that created some other problems.

The day-night problem was symptomatic of divisions that existed throughout the *Times* in those days. I already knew how the Washington bureau fought to preserve its autonomy from New York, and now I discovered that there were many other pockets of bureaucracy within the New York office itself. Lacking central leadership from the front office, various dukedoms had grown up, fiercely jealous of their prerogatives. The Sunday department, ruled by the brilliant and often irascible Lester Markel, was one of the most independent. To an extent, Ochs and Sulzberger had encouraged competition between the daily and Sunday staffs, but I was convinced the division had gone too far. However, so long as Markel was Sunday editor, no managing editor was able to exercise any effective influence over the Sunday department.

Another administrative problem was that the publisher's nephew Cy Sulzberger was operating as the paper's "Chief Foreign Correspondent"—in effect, as the foreign editor—from his home in Paris. Cy sought maximum autonomy for himself and "his" correspondents. He resented editing of their copy, and it was readily assumed he might take his case directly to his uncle. He seldom did, but the editors were nervous about his possible influence.

Within our office, I learned, we had both a "business editor" and a "financial editor." The two men rarely spoke, their stories often overlapped, and no one was sure exactly what was "business" and what "financial." This situation had a quite typical history. Many years earlier, Adolph Ochs had created the division to take care of another office problem. He wanted to remove a managing editor to make way for Carr Van Anda. Ochs learned that the editor was interested in business, so he made him business editor, the existence of a financial editor notwithstanding.

Once when the *Times* was host to a seminar of out-of-town editors, it happened that two of our editors—a sports copy editor and a national news editor—encountered each other at cocktails and had to be introduced. This incredible situation existed despite the fact that for years these two had worked less than one hundred feet apart. Arthur Hays Sulzberger was present and was horrified that this should happen before editors of other newspapers.

The divisions among the local, national, and foreign desks came into the open each day as their editors made their requests for space in the next day's paper. One of the first assignments Jimmy James gave me was to mediate these daily battles. Each afternoon the editors would submit slips of paper stating how much space they needed. Traditionally, each editor would claim to need about 30 percent more than he actually needed. I got revenge one day on our sports editor by giving him all the space he asked for and forcing him to admit he couldn't use it all.

When I first joined the *Times,* news coverage was handled largely along very strict jurisdictional lines—largely geographical. The city desk handled not only New York City, but all of New Jersey, southern New York, and Connecticut as far as New Haven. It didn't cover Philadelphia, but it did cover Camden, just across the river. The city desk's arbitrary—but fiercely defended—jurisdictional lines led to situations such as one I encountered in the fall of 1929. I was accompanying Ramsay MacDonald, the Prime Minister of Great Britain, on a special train from Washington to New York, but I was allowed to put into my story only what happened until the train reached Trenton. The rest of the story was handled by a city-side reporter, without reference to what I was writing.

Another difficult jurisdictional problem was between the telegraph desk and the cable desk. The telegraph editor and his desk handled all news developing in the nation outside the New York City area; it came in mostly by telegraph, about 85 percent of it from Washington. The cable desk handled foreign news, most of which came in by cable. A problem would arise, for example, when the Secretary of State made an important foreign-policy speech in Chicago. Under our strict system of news division, this would be a story for the national desk, although logic would suggest that a foreign-policy speech be handled by the specialists on the foreign desk. Another problem arose when the United Nations settled in Manhattan—should it be the property of the city desk or the foreign desk?

Later, after I started the daily news conferences, James and I were able to bend the rigid jurisdictional lines and to break through a few of them. As managing editor, I redefined the jobs of some of the desks, stressing topical rather than geographical assignments. Some editors accepted these changes only after a struggle, but most were willing to accept change when they were convinced it would produce a better newspaper.

Still another problem when I arrived in New York was that so few of the senior editors had had reporting experience. Jimmy James and I were exceptions, as Scotty Reston, Clifton Daniel, Harrison Salisbury, Frank Adams, and Abe Rosenthal would be in later years, but most of the top editors in those days were former copy editors, and too often they had scant understanding of reporters and their problems. When I was starting my career, the men on the copy desk were the aristocrats of the newsrooms. They made more money and worked more regular hours than reporters, and were more highly valued by most executives. The shift in status came with the proliferation of by-lines in the late thirties. The by-line gave the reporter increased prestige. He became a star and could command a greater salary. But, when I joined the *Times'* New York staff, the paper was still largely edited by graduates of the copy desks. Many of these men had been hired by Ochs in the First World War era and were highly resistant to any change. In their view, the *New York Times* had reached its full maturity and, if not tampered with, could be expected to remain in full flower for at least a century.

I recall an incident when I was a Washington correspondent in the late thirties. A report came over the wires that Mussolini was going to ask President Roosevelt to mediate the war in Europe. At a news conference we reporters asked Roosevelt about the report and he laughed it off as ridiculous. But a night editor insisted it was a big story and must be treated as such. I argued in vain, and finally Felix Belair and I wrote the slam-bang story he demanded, that Roosevelt had "refused" to try to mediate the war. The next day FDR quite rightly denounced the *Times* for irresponsible reporting. That is the sort of situation you encounter if your senior editors lack reporting experience and aren't willing to listen to those who have it.

No one was ever fired at the *Times*—God was our personnel director—and there was no set system of hiring beyond nepotism and patronage. I soon concluded that while nepotism was inevitable where the publisher's family was concerned, it might be less desirable elsewhere. We might lose some good men by not hiring our editors' and reporters' sons and wives, but we would spare ourselves a multitude of other difficulties.

I found that the editors of the *Times* were so busy getting out each day's paper that no one was considering the future. The paper seemed to me unnecessarily dull, and I sensed that the postwar newspaper reader might not be content to read the same *Times* he had read in the twenties and thirties.

The general rule at the *Times* in 1945 was to do things today the way we had done them yesterday and not to worry about tomorrow. There was a terrible diffusion of management. We were getting out a paper, but it was not my idea of the best way of doing it. Sulzberger had told me he had brought me to New York to inject some vigor and youth into the news staff and to tighten its organization, but he seemed at first reluctant to move aggressively, and I wondered if change would ever come. The criticisms that I and others occasionally made ran into the brick wall of James' "success" argument.

I too gloried in our success and our traditions, yet I increasingly felt the *Times* was set in its ways and smug. If the *Times* did not criticize itself, others did. I often talked with writers and editors from other papers in New York who frequented the Artists and Writers Restaurant on Fortieth Street, next to the *Herald Tribune*. They were willing, even anxious, to point out the *Times'* various shortcomings, although most of them wanted jobs on it.

When I first went to work for the *Times*, I soon learned that people from other newspapers considered it a smug, aloof, self-satisfied outfit. I'm forced to admit they were right, although there were individual *Times*men who weren't like that at all, such as Richard Oulahan. Arthur Hays Sulzberger shared my concern about our reputation, and when I became an editor I set out to make our paper more a part of the newspaper community. When I was still assistant managing editor, I became active in the Associated Press Managing Editors Association. After I became managing editor, I joined the American Society of Newspaper Editors, and in 1960-61 served as its president. In 1946 I helped found the American Press

Institute and for many years I was on its advisory board. I accepted as many speaking invitations as I could manage from state and regional newspaper groups, and otherwise tried to be a good-will ambassador for the *Times.* I tried, however, to confine my outside activities to the newspaper field, and I tried, with limited success, to discourage members of the Sulzberger family from joining the various civic and charitable groups that sought them.

One area in which I was able to cause some early improvement was that of news development. Although I had myself been a Washington political writer, I thought that too much of our national news came out of Washington. Editors liked Washington stories, and with our large bureau there it was convenient to fill the space allocated to national news with them, but I felt that we needed much more reporting from around the nation. I knew all too well, from my own experiences, how Washington reporters tended to forget there was an America beyond the Potomac. I also thought that our "political" reporting needed new dimensions. For example, instead of simply reporting that President Truman had introduced a housing bill we should take a look at housing conditions around America and tell the story not only in terms of large statistics but in terms of people and how they lived.

My efforts toward expanded news coverage were aided by the fact that my friend Arthur Krock was head of the Washington bureau, and also because most of the New York editors respected my judgment on matters related to news. Still, there were difficulties. When the night-side editors thought the day side was getting too active in developing stories and thus creating difficulties fitting them into the paper, they'd respond by leaving them out of the paper —with the explanation that there wasn't room for "all this junk." I tried not to be discouraged by these episodes. I kept in mind the motto of the *Neshoba Democrat,* the little weekly where I started my career: "Patience, Tolerance, Triumph."

I was also interested in our foreign coverage. I recall once telling James that our coverage—or noncoverage—of Latin America was a disgrace. He said no one cared about Latin America unless there was a revolution. I argued that we had a responsibility to develop an audience, that our readers should never be surprised by anything that occurred in the world. Eventually, we did send three of our best correspondents to Latin America, and then we encountered a new problem. The correspondents were unhappy to be "out of the mainstream," by which they meant London, Paris, Rome, and perhaps Moscow. In more recent years, however, the importance of reporting from trouble spots like Latin America, Africa, and Southeast Asia has meant new opportunities for ambitious young newspapermen. More Pulitzers are won in places like Vietnam and the Congo than in London and Paris.

I concluded that many of the *Times'* problems existed because Jimmy James, for whatever reason, was not providing the leadership that I thought his job demanded. I don't enjoy being critical of James, for he was a wonderful person and a great reporter. Certainly it is true that part of the difficulty stemmed not simply from his performance, but from the uneasy relationship that existed between him and the publisher, Sulzberger.

Jimmy James was a flamboyant Virginian who had excelled in mathematics at Randolph-Macon College and afterward taught math at Baltimore City College. He took a weekend job as a copyreader for the Baltimore *Sun*, and liked it so much he quit teaching and joined the *Sun* full time. The *Sun*, however, having hired him as a moonlighter, fired him for moonlighting—for working for the United Press in New York on one of his vacations. James became a press agent for a traveling show that folded in Albany, New York, where he joined the staff of the *Knickerbocker Press*. In 1915, aged twenty-five, he joined the *Times* as a copyreader, but he switched to reporting when he saw that an energetic reporter could make more money, writing at "space rates."

One night he caught the attention of the managing editor Carr Van Anda, by solving a math problem for him. Later he persuaded Van Anda to send him to Europe as a war correspondent, and he proved to be an outstanding one, with a flair for vivid colorful writing.

James also had a flair for flamboyant clothing and for high living. His many nicknames included "Dressy James" and "Jesse James." After the war he became the *Times'* Paris-based European correspondent, and soon became intimate with the *Times'* publisher, Adolph Ochs.

Ochs was then in his sixties (he was born in 1858), and although he lived an eminently respectable life in New York he liked to take time on his frequent trips abroad for a little relaxation. Jimmy James became his favorite guide and companion on these excursions, and a great affection developed between them. In 1930, when James was about forty, Ochs brought him back to New York as an assistant managing editor, and two years later he made James his managing editor. James kept his post for twenty years, and he was immensely popular with his staff. He had a gruff manner and a growl in his voice, but in truth he was a kind and generous man, probably too kind for the job he held.

When Ochs died in 1935, and his son-in-law, Arthur Hays Sulzberger, became publisher, one of the things the new publisher inherited was an unbudgeable managing editor, Jimmy James. Sulzberger was not a newspaperman in James' terms. Sulzberger had become publisher by marrying the daughter of James' patron, who was a great newspaperman. And James by his nature liked to scoff at authority, which on the *Times* was embodied in the publisher.

James had these feelings despite the fact that Sulzberger had been working for the *Times* since 1918 and was widely admired as a capable executive and an exceptionally pleasant man. Sulzberger had come to the *Times* the year after he married Ochs' only child, Iphigene. Sulzberger sometimes joked that when he came to work at the *Times* (at Ochs' insistence, incidentally) his father-in-law gave him an office, a secretary, and nothing to do. But the situation was more than a joke. It was said that Ochs hadn't wanted Iphigene to marry Sulzberger, or anyone else; he once said she had everything she needed under his roof. Thus, he grudgingly brought his son-in-law to the *Times,* but at first he showed limited affection for him.

The situation was complicated by the presence of Ochs' favorite nephew, Julius Ochs Adler, who was about Sulzberger's age. Adler had distinguished himself as a combat officer during the First World War, and after the war came to the *Times* as a business executive. The two young executives became close friends, yet there was inevitably a feeling of rivalry between them, particularly since there was some uncertainty whether Ochs would choose his son-in-law or his nephew to succeed him as publisher. (This issue was settled when Ochs, in his will, named Sulzberger, Iphigene Sulzberger, and Adler as the three trustees of his estate and, therefore, custodians of the ownership of the *Times;* so long as Iphigene Sulzberger supported her husband, he was assured of the publisher's job by a two-to-one margin.)

Sulzberger and Adler were very different sorts of men. Adler was blunt and outspoken; Sulzberger reserved and suave. Adler kept up his reserve commission after the war, and in time rose to the rank of major general, and he always referred to himself by his military rank. I felt that Sulzberger was always quite conscious of General Adler's well-known war heroism and that it affected Sulzberger's own behavior. Sulzberger's wartime tour of the Pacific theater—the one I went on—was an example. Sulzberger was determined (despite sizable obstacles created by the government) to get to the war zone. He seemed to feel guilty that he was living a good life in New York while his correspondents were risking their lives, and he often told me that if his reporters ran risks he should too. I suspect he was delighted when that sniper took a potshot at us on Peleliu. Another time, when we were aboard an overweight C-54, flying to Hollandia, a worried pilot informed us that he wouldn't be surprised if we crashed at any moment. Sulzberger's only reaction was to pick up the detective story he'd been reading and say, "Well, in that case, I'd better hurry up with this book and find out whodunit." At the time, I thought Sulzberger was simply a very cool customer, but I later believed that his coolness under fire and his determination to seek out danger were a deliberate response to General Adler's war record. When General MacArthur spoke to us fondly of "Julie" (General Adler) and his hopes of assigning "Julie" to head a combat division, I could see the impact on Sulzberger.

Jimmy James refused to be impressed by Sulzberger. General Adler was more James' sort of man, and it was no secret to me (or, I think, to Sulzberger) that James would have been happier with General Adler as publisher.

One practical result of James' attitude was that he often let the publisher make mistakes that he could have warned him about. Sometimes I'd see these coming and suggest we intervene, but James would growl, "Nah, let him go."

Sulzberger was an extremely sensitive man, particularly about his prerogatives as publisher, and I am sure James' attitude pained him a great deal, but he did not see any immediate solution to the problem. On any other paper the solution would have been easy— the publisher would have fired the troublesome editor and hired one he could work with. But that would not do for the *Times*. It was unthinkable that Sulzberger would fire Ochs' hand-picked, much-beloved editor. Sulzberger was stuck with James and he would have to make the best of it. In fact, he did, and came to have a good measure of affection for James, although the affection fluctuated with the managing editor's behavior.

I think Sulzberger must often have regarded his position as publisher of the *Times* as a mixed blessing. He was from an old and distinguished New York family, headed for a profitable career in his family's textile-import business when he married Iphigene Ochs and thus, like it or not, became the next publisher of the *Times*. He jumped to the top of America's greatest newspaper, well aware that hundreds of critical, often resentful eyes were on his every move.

He was determined to prove that he could be a worthy successor to Ochs, and in fact could leave the *Times* stronger than he found it. He made an important step in that direction early in the Second World War. Because of the paper shortage, we had to put out a smaller newspaper, and Sulzberger, like other publishers, had to make a basic decision; he could cut back on news coverage and circulation, go all-out for advertising, and thereby make a financial killing; or he could stress news coverage. Sulzberger unhesitatingly chose to stress news coverage, to the extent of rationing advertising space to our prime customers. At the same time, our main competitor, the *Herald Tribune,* chose to go for increased advertising, and in time pulled close to the *Times* in total advertising linage. Sulzberger's decision put the *Times* in a profit squeeze during the war years, but its wisdom was seen after the war. We had won new readers with our war coverage and both our advertising and circulation far outstripped those of the *Herald Tribune.*

Sulzberger's decision was very much in keeping with *Times* tradition. His father-in-law, Adolph Ochs, in 1896 when thirty-eight years old and the publisher of the Chattanooga *Times,* had bought control of the *New York Times* for $75,000. It had a circulation of 9,000 and was losing $1,000 a day. It was an era of yellow journalism in New York, a time when most papers were intensely political and the reader rarely knew what he could believe, and Ochs saw the need for a paper that would "give the news impartially, without fear or favor, regardless of any party, sect, or interest involved." Or, as he sometimes put it, "a paper that would not soil the breakfast linen."

Ochs' policy paid off brilliantly. When he started, his circulation was 9,000 at three cents a paper. His two biggest competitors were Pulitzer's *World,* with morning and evening editions totaling 600,000, and Hearst's *Journal,* with two editions selling 430,000 copies. As soon as possible, Ochs cut his price to a penny, and by 1900 his circulation was 76,260 and by 1915 it was above 300,000. Ochs believed he had achieved this success by stressing news, not political views. In his motto, "All the News That's Fit to Print," the key word was "news." In 1942, when his son-in-law was forced to choose between news and advertising, and chose news, he was simply following Ochs' policy. Sulzberger didn't like losing money, and he may not have known his policy would pay off in the long run, but he felt a binding obligation to do as Ochs would have done—to report the news. It fitted his own nature.

He felt he needed to honor the paper's traditions (he often said to me, "If I was driving a Cadillac up a steep hill, and it was running perfectly, wouldn't I be a fool to stop and check the spark plugs?"), yet he realized that the paper had to change and improve. He made it clear to me as early as our Pacific trip that he'd enlisted me to help him in that effort. Given my and Sulzberger's rapport, personally and philosophically, and given the problems between him and James, one of my biggest problems as assistant managing editor was to keep Sulzberger within channels. Time after time he would come to me with some idea he wanted carried out, and I would protest, "Mr. Sulzberger, Mr. James is my boss. Don't put me in this position." Sulzberger would reply, "Of course. You're absolutely right." And soon it would happen all over again.

One of the first things I did after arriving in New York was to spend several afternoons on a guided tour of the *Times* building. I went from the fourth sub-basement to the fifteenth floor, went in every door and shook every hand I could. I was particularly glad to get to know the printers and others in the composing room. Thanks to my early experience on the weeklies in Mississippi, I could speak their language. My tour was a thorough one; I think it is fair to say that when I was finished I knew more about the total *Times* operation than any of my fellow editors on the third floor. (Perhaps my most startling discovery was that someone had given the city police permission to use a room in our fourth sub-basement as a shooting gallery, which they were doing, quite unknown to the paper's owners.

My guide on that tour was a remarkable young man named Nat Goldstein, who soon became my friend and still is today. Nat started with the *Times* as a fourteen-year-old office boy, and by the time I met him he had become production manager, a position in which he was responsible for bringing all elements of the paper together for final publication. He had come to know more about producing the *New York Times* and more people associated in the enterprise, including advertisers and subcontractors, than any other individual. Whatever you wanted Nat could get; whatever your problem, Nat could solve it. He later rose to be circulation director.

Nat, an energetic, bright-eyed, rather high-strung young man, was kept hopping by General Adler, who dearly loved him and counted on him to solve all problems. Once General Adler, who lived on Park Avenue at Sixty-seventh Street, was bothered by the trash collectors banging cans under his window very early on several mornings. After this had gone on for several mornings at the expense of his sleep, General Adler one day jumped out of bed, put on a formal evening coat over his pajamas, and a homburg on his head, and charged downstairs to tell the trash collectors to be more quiet. He was greeted with laughter and several rude remarks. Later that morning General Adler arrived at the *Times* terribly distraught. He was not accustomed to backtalk. Finally he shouted to his secretary, "Get me Goldstein." Nat dashed in; Adler explained his problem. Nat broke in before General Adler had finished his complaint, "I'll take care of it, General," and dashed out. Just what he did remains a mystery, but no more trash cans banged beneath the General's window.

One of Mrs. Arthur Hays Sulzberger's favorite stories was of her returning from a trip to Europe and Nat's arranging for some New York policemen to come aboard her ship, get her quickly through customs and into her car.

"I can't thank you enough for what you've done for me," Mrs. Sulzberger, in her sweet way, told the officer in charge, who was an Irishman named Mooney.

"I ain't doing it for you, lady," Mooney replied. "I don't even know who you are. I'm doing it for Nat Goldstein."

Mrs. Sulzberger, somewhat flustered, said, "Oh, do you know Nat?"

"Do I know Nat? Do I know Nat?" the officer asked. "Just look what he brought me from the Pope," and exhibited a religious token which Nat had given him.

Nat was fascinated by church ritual and clergymen, many of whom were his close friends. He once raised funds for the restoration of a small chapel in a remote section of Ireland. A few months before the shipboard incident Nat had indeed had an audience with Pius XII. On his way to the Vatican Nat loaded himself down with medals, rosaries, and sundry holy objects in the hope the Pope would bless them. Sure enough, the Pope asked at the end of their interview whether he had anything he wanted blessed. So Nat, pointing to his bulging pockets, said "Yes." Nat's opening remark to the Pontiff was a question as to whether he was getting his *New York Times* on schedule. The Pope assured him he was. Nat's sacred medals stood him in great stead with the New York Catholic police. After he returned home, Nat wrote the Pope a personal letter thanking him for his courtesies. In a very short time he received a reply from Monsignor Montini, who had been his guide and sponsor during the audience. When it became known later that Montini was a likely choice to succeed John XXIII, he was hailed at Sardi's bar as Nat's candidate. And it came to pass that Montini, Nat's man, became Pope Paul VI.

One of Nat's most challenging assignments came when General

Adler ordered him to find a live tiger. General Adler was passionately devoted to his alma mater, Princeton, and he was to be the grand marshal of his class in the homecoming parade when the class celebrated its fortieth anniversary. (There were those who said that the general's love of Princeton influenced our sports coverage, and that if Yale's football team beat Princeton, Princeton still won in our sports page.) Nothing would do but that the general march in the parade with a live tiger, the Princeton symbol, at his side, and he told Nat to find him one. Even Nat was somewhat stunned by this order, and he came to me for advice. I suggested that we get in touch with Beverly Kelly, the press agent for the Ringling Brothers circus, whom we readily located in a night-spot bar in Ohio. Kelly gave us the not-very-helpful suggestion that we paint a large dog to look like a tiger. Kelly told us that the circus had found out a boxer could be made a very convincing tiger. General Adler vetoed this idea. Kelly then suggested that the tiger be carried in the back of a jeep, but Adler said no, he must lead the tiger down the streets of Old Nassau. Finally Kelly found a man in Philadelphia who had a supposedly tame, or overaged, tiger, but said that he, the owner, would have to accompany him in the parade. Adler said no again; he must lead the tiger personally. Then the man said Adler might take his chances, but the rent on his tiger was $600 a day. At that, General Adler decided he would do without the tiger.

Soon after I arrived in New York, James told me that William L. Laurence, the paper's science writer, was on loan to the Army for a secret project. James knew few of the details. He explained to me that, to maximize secrecy, Laurence's various contacts with our office had been divided among several editors, and he wanted me to handle our dealings with the Army over the reporter's financial matters. I didn't think much about this arrangement, as I was told the details had been settled. Neither James nor I knew that Laurence's mission dealt with the development of the atomic bomb. Sulzberger knew more but said nothing. Then one day in August of 1945 a man I knew from Washington, a Mississippian who was an Army captain but worked in civilian clothes, cames to see me in New York. He sat down beside by desk and asked if I knew what Bill Laurence had been doing. I said I did not, and he replied that I would soon find out. He instructed, or rather ordered, me to report to a certain building in Washington the next day. He said I should tell Sulzberger I was going to Washington on "the Laurence matter" but should say nothing to anyone else.

I left by train that evening and reported at the appointed place the next day. I was ushered into a large conference room where six or eight men, some in uniform and some not, were sitting at a long table. The man at the head of the table was introduced to me as General Leslie Groves. He was a large, cordial man with a mustache, who, I presently discovered, was head of the whole atomic-bomb program, or Manhattan Project, as it was titled. These officers asked me a few questions, evidently to establish that I was virginal so far as knowledge of the Manhattan Project was concerned. Then the officers, guided by General Groves, told me the whole story. They told me of the test in New Mexico, and the destructive force they had revealed. I found it a frightening story. They told me next that a decision had been made to drop one or more of these bombs on Japan and that bomber crews to do so were already poised for takeoff.

They were taking the *Times* into their confidence to ensure that we would print a full and accurate account of the bomb's use and development when the time came. They also felt obligated, General Groves said, because they had taken away Laurence. They showed me the documents which had been prepared for release to the press when the bomb was dropped. I assumed that Bill Laurence had helped write these documents. They said the announcement of the bombing, when it occurred, would be made by President Truman, who was then returning by ship from the Potsdam Conference. They showed me a draft of the announcement he was to make. I was told almost everything except when and where the first bomb would be dropped.

General Groves asked me to designate someone in our Washington bureau with whom they could deal when the moment came. He said they would be pleased to deal with Sidney Shallet, one of our reporters whom he knew, and I readily agreed to this. Upon leaving General Groves and his staff, I went directly to our Washington bureau and told Shallet to be ready for a major story, although I could not tell him what it was. Our bureau manager agreed to have Shallet on tap twenty-four hours a day until the event, whatever it was, occurred.

I did not get the same quick cooperation when I got back to New York. I told the night editors that a big story was coming and would be announced by President Truman. I told them I could give them no more details, but they were to call me personally any time Truman's name came into the news. One of the night editors became annoyed and said he couldn't accept any such obligation from the day side without more information. I decided we'd better have a showdown, and I told the recalcitrant editor that I was invoking full authority of the managing editor's office to tell him that he'd better do as I said. Fortunately, he agreed without further debate. I had, of course, picked a perfect issue on which to challenge the autonomy of the night side, since there was no doubt that Sulzberger would back me on the issue of secrecy for the atomic bomb.

I returned from Washington on Thursday evening, and Friday I went to Sulzberger's country home in Westchester County to report to him. Mrs. Sulzberger was giving a luncheon for several women and the publisher was out on the lawn with them. I called him aside and we walked down by the swimming pool, where I told him the story. He was visibly shaken, and I found he knew quite a bit about the bomb. When we rejoined the women they could see the concern in his face and they quietly dispersed. As it turned out, the announcement of the bombing of Hiroshima came at 11 A.M. the next Monday, August 6.

XVI

Executive Managing Editor

ONE of the first things Jimmy James said to me when I reported to work for him in 1945 was, "Turner, from now on you make no mistakes." When I asked what he meant, he told me he was giving me the same assurance Ochs had given him when he became managing editor. "With me you'll always be right whether you are or not," James said. "In this office, I may think you're crazy as hell, but when you're out in that newsroom you'll always be right."

His support, and the support and encouragement I had from Sulzberger, were a great reassurance to me. Yet I very rarely called upon either of them to back me up in disagreements that arose. I preferred to get my way by persuasion rather than by pulling rank. James, very early in his career as managing editor, had once threatened to go to Ochs to settle a dispute he was having with the bullpen. The bullpen editors gave in, but thereafter they resented and resisted James, and many of his difficulties in later years stemmed from that incident. I hoped to avoid a similar mistake.

In 1946, hoping to lessen our administrative anarchy, and to provide some central leadership, I proposed to James that we begin a daily news conference, so that the various editors might learn what the others were doing, and we might have a "cross-pollination" of ideas. James was not enthusiastic, but he agreed to the idea, provided I would carry it out as my own operation. I had expected it would turn out that way.

The format of the news conference was a daily report given about 4:30 each afternoon by the subeditors and desk heads to the managing editor (or, in those first years, to the assistant managing editor). Those attending would include the national and foreign editors, the city and sports editors, the financial editor, and the night editors—the bullpen editors, who would implement many of the decisions reached at the meeting. Other men with an interest in the next day's paper, such as the circulation or promotion managers, might also sit in.

However, they did not "sit in" at first, because we had no table or chairs. In those days, the *Times* newsroom had no conference table (a problem that was overcorrected in later years, when we had too many). At first we met, standing up, at the back of the newsroom. From time to time, James would come to the door of his office and growl something about "Catledge's Sunday-school class," but he came to have great respect for the conference, and when I was away he would conduct it. I would always report to James after the conferences, both orally and in memoranda, giving him plans for the next day's paper and also my impression of people and my forecast of coming events. When I had been away, he would report to me, and we would discuss the performances of various writers and editors, and ideas for news development.

At the daily conferences, each editor would report to me on the news he had for the next day, and soon the editors would be discussing and criticizing their own stories and those of the other departments. I think some of the editors felt that these daily meetings were a threat to their long-standing autonomy (I certainly regarded them as such), yet to a greater degree I think the meetings were appreciated for giving the paper a central focus that had not existed for a long time. I did my best to foster a feeling that group decisions were being made, in which each editor played a part. "When you go out that door," I would say, "everyone is part of our decisions." It was not always that simple, but the meetings did pull our staff together, and over the years the daily news conference has continued to provide central direction to the *Times*.

As I gained more responsibility at the *Times*, the frustrations of my job lessened, although I was never entirely happy in this period. I missed Washington terribly. It was my spiritual home. My family and I missed the more comfortable life in our large house on Wyoming Avenue. We were now cramped in a small hotel apartment with two adults, two children, a dog, and a maid.

Professionally, I missed my friends in politics, missed reporting, and couldn't believe I was finished with it forever. I had spent more than a decade becoming one of the capital's leading political reporters, and now I could see my sources and my insider's status slipping away. Trying to keep in touch, I went down to Washington every chance I had, and spent many weekends there. I continued to be active in the Gridiron Club, and in fact I was in Washington rehearsing for a Gridiron Dinner when the news came of Roosevelt's death. As the new administration took shape, with new men coming into office, I felt more and more a stranger in Washington.

One of my rudest jolts came when I attended the Democratic convention in Atlantic City in 1948. I had written the *Times*' lead news stories for the Democratic conventions of 1936, 1940, and 1944, but now another man had that assignment and I was simply a prestigious bystander. I found that status so uncomfortable that I left the convention before it was over.

I often wondered if I had made the right move in coming to New York. Or, I should say, whether the right move had been made for me, since it was at the instigation of James and Sulzberger that I came. I had decided early in my career to do what my superiors asked me to do. I felt that if I disagreed with them strongly over an assignment I should simply quit. I don't recall ever refusing an assignment in my professional life. In recent years, as an editor, I've observed that many young reporters don't feel that way. Sometimes you practically have to beg them to take an assignment that doesn't suit their immediate convenience. I'll grant that the assignments I was offered were generally desirable ones, but I do think that in an organization as freely and cooperatively administered as the *New York Times* it is important for reporters to submit willingly, if not eagerly, to leadership. As for myself, I had decided that our management probably knew better how my talents could be used than I did. The first responsibility was theirs. I loved reporting and left to my own devices I might never have left it. But, as I once put it, given a free grab I might have taken the wrong job.

My thoughts of returning to Washington ended late in 1945, when Arthur Krock made a proposal to that effect. He offered to step aside as bureau chief and devote himself exclusively to his columns, so I might become bureau chief and head of the news staff. He urged me to accept, as he was sure I'd be happier in Washington. At Krock's request, I put this plan to Sulzberger, who put his foot down on the project.

It was also during my early years as assistant managing editor that my marriage, after many years of stress, began to come apart, culminating in a legal separation in 1949 and a divorce nine years later. Throughout these years, given my personal difficulties and my professional frustrations, I kept asking myself, "Where in hell does all this lead?" It seemed to me that to be the managing editor of the *New York Times* was extremely desirable, but to be assistant managing editor was equally undesirable. My job was rather like that of the Vice President of the United States—after a while, whether you intend it or not, you spend a lot of time wondering about your boss's health.

Despite my frustrations, I declined several job offers in the late 1940s. One of them was from the administrators of the Marshall Plan, who wanted me to go to Paris as Averell Harriman's public-relations adviser. This offer came to me from Paul Hoffman by way of Arthur Hays Sulzberger, who, incidentally, suggested that I accept it for a year or so. He felt that a year in Paris would give me some of the international experience that I often complained I'd never gotten on the *Times*. He offered to make up the difference between my *Times* salary and my government salary, and promised to keep intact my standing and prospects on the *Times*. Both Hoffman and Harriman added their considerable persuasive talents, but in the end they couldn't overcome my aversion to government or political service. Also, I was bothered by my inability to speak French or any other foreign language.

Another job offer came from my old Washington contact Jesse Jones. One morning in October of 1948 he called and asked me to join him for breakfast at his apartment at the Mayfair House on Park Avenue. I walked over and had hardly seated myself when he made a startling remark: "Turner, I'm getting ready to die."

My face must have fallen, for he chuckled and went on with his story. He told me something I already knew—that he was a very rich man—and explained that he was in his seventies and was settling his affairs so there'd be no complications after his death. He said he'd have no trouble arranging for his business interests, but he was bothered about the future of his newspaper, the Houston *Chronicle*.

"I can dispose of my banks, my hotels, and my lumber yards," he told me, "but I want to leave the *Chronicle* as my monument. And that's what I want to talk to you about."

He said he had a nephew who would eventually be the paper's publisher, but in the meantime he wanted someone he could depend on to set the paper "on the course of statesmanship." He said I was his first choice to be the *Chronicle*'s new publisher, and that, financially, I could write my own ticket.

Perhaps I was tempted, I can't really recall, but at just that moment his phone rang. It was Jones' editor at the *Chronicle,* returning his calls, and as I listened Jones instructed him to have the paper come out for Thomas E. Dewey in the Presidential campaign.

When Jones finished talking to his editor, he returned to his efforts to hire me, and after stalling a few minutes I decided to be perfectly frank with him. "Uncle Jesse, it wouldn't work out," I told him. "We've been good friends with each of us sitting on his side of the desk. With that desk between us, we're about even. But, if I come around to your side, you become the boss."

"But a good boss," he said.

"Yes and no," I told him. "Frankly, you just let me hear something that made up my mind for me. If I'd been your editor, and you told me to come out for Tom Dewey, I wouldn't have been your editor ten minutes later."

He stared at me for a minute, then laughed and declared: "That's real newspaper statesmanship." (He liked the word "statesmanship.") "Well, Arthur Krock was right again," he continued. "He told me you'd turn me down. He said I could make you rich but I couldn't make you happy. But, Turner, you've got to give me a nickel for trying."

Another job offer came from the Cleveland *Plain Dealer,* which proposed to triple my *Times* salary if I would become its editor, but I was not tempted.

Whatever my frustrations, I knew the *Times* was the place for me. The memory of my unhappy experience in Chicago was always fresh, and although I was impatient at the *Times,* my future there seemed secure.

One man to whom I often told my troubles in those days, and to whose in return I listened, was Sulzberger's son-in-law Orvil Dryfoos. He had married Marian Sulzberger in 1941 and given up his seat on the Stock Exchange to come to work as an assistant to Sulzberger. Dryfoos had made this move with some reluctance, but his position was greatly helped by the considerate treatment he received from Sulzberger, who remembered well the slights he'd suffered from his father-in-law.

Dryfoos and I assumed, without ever saying it, that he would someday be publisher of the *Times* and I would someday be managing editor. However, in the late forties, with our bosses active and in good health, our advancement seemed a long way off, and both of us often felt frustrated. We felt that our careers were linked, and we became good friends, although I never felt the same personal intimacy with Dryfoos that I did with Sulzberger. Often, in those years, Dryfoos and I would take sandwiches to Central Park and spend our lunch hour sitting on a bench talking endlessly about the changes we hoped to make at the *Times*—someday.

Other young men were moving up in the *Times* organization in those days. *Time* magazine of January 15, 1945, began a story: "Two of the *New York Times'* favorite sons last week took a step up the ivy-muffled *Times* ladder." I was one of the two; the other was Scotty Reston, who had taken over my job in Washington as national correspondent.

Scotty had joined our London bureau early in the war years and quickly distinguished himself as a reporter. He later was transferred to the Washington bureau, and in 1943 Sulzberger brought him to New York to be an assistant to the publisher, with the primary responsibility of helping Orvil Dryfoos learn about the newspaper business. While in New York, Reston made a trip with Sulzberger to the European war zones, similar to my trip with AHS the next year. Scotty was restless in New York, however, and soon secured a transfer back to London, and later returned to Washington. It was clear that he was, as *Time* described him, "fast-rising." Sulzberger had in mind that he would someday take over as editor of the editorial page, but it turned out that Scotty preferred to stay in Washington.

Another rising star on the *Times* in those days was Amory Bradford, a tall, self-assured young lawyer who was hired in 1947 as an assistant to Sulzberger. Bradford was exceedingly intelligent and capable. Not long after he arrived he was assigned to work with me on a project for continued publication of the paper in case of a labor strike which was then threatened. I was highly impressed by his talents and his judgment. There was, however, a certain rigidity in his manner that foreshadowed his difficulties, years later, in the labor negotiations of 1963. That rigidity was suggested by an incident not long after he joined the *Times*. Sulzberger, as part of an economy drive, had ordered that no one be hired without specific approval from himself or General Adler. Bradford thought this was silly, and told the publisher so when a conflict arose over the hiring of a secretary in the Sunday department. A dispute arose and Bradford resigned. Dryfoos told me the publisher was "astounded" at Bradford's unyielding manner—he had, in effect, refused to carry out an order of the publisher. Sulzberger, hoping to ease the situation, arranged for Bradford to take a leave of absence, rather than to resign, and Bradford spent a year or so in London on a diplomatic mission. "He'll never come back in the same capacity," Dryfoos said, which I took to mean that the publisher was still angry about Bradford's behavior. But Dryfoos was wrong, for Bradford came back in a better job than the one he'd left, and in time he rose to be the paper's vice president and general manager. Throughout the fifties, he was one of the men relied upon most heavily both by Sulzberger and by Dryfoos.

Jimmy James was increasingly seeking my advice on matters of personnel. He always consulted me about salaries. James didn't like to disagree with anyone, so his inclination was to give a raise to anyone who asked for one. He'd say that a man was the best judge of his own needs. I felt that need should be wholly subordinated to performance when considering merit increases, and by that criterion I knew that persons who didn't deserve raises were getting them, not for stories in the paper but for hard-luck stories told to Mr. James, while people more deserving professionally were being ignored. I thought the senior editors could best decide what men deserved what salaries. I never in my career asked for a raise—my superiors always gave them to me without my asking—and I thought that was how the *Times* should operate. After I became managing editor, with full control over salaries, I rarely gave a raise to a man who asked for one. If a man deserved more money, I tried to anticipate the request and give the raise on my own initiative. As a rule, if a man asked me for a raise, I didn't think he deserved one.

By 1948 I was convinced that one of the paper's key personnel problems was its city editor, David Joseph. Joseph had been hired by Ochs in 1908 and had become city editor in 1927. He was a fine person, but he was one of those editors most resistant to change on the *Times*, and he seemed to me to have passed the age when he could provide the aggressive leadership needed in a city editor. Joseph came in each morning at ten, gave assignments to the local reporters, left about 6 P.M. and never saw their copy until it appeared in the paper the next day.

Joseph played an important part in building the *Times'* policy of always hiring three men to do what one man could do. He was always fearful that a big story would break when he had no reporters on hand to cover it. To avert this, he would send only his younger reporters out on routine assignments, and would keep a large pool of first-class reporters sitting in the office, doing nothing except waiting for the next emergency. When, every few months, a great fire or homicide would occur, we would have excellent coverage, but the months in between were frustrating for the reporters and costly for the publisher.

I discussed the situation with James and he agreed that we needed a new city editor. He asked me what satisfactory arrangement could be made about Dave Joseph and I suggested that he be made an assistant managing editor, co-equal with me. James agreed and called Joseph in to break the news to him. Joseph became furious and from my desk outside James' office I could hear him giving James a terrible time But after he calmed down he accepted the new arrangement.

I persuaded James to replace Joseph as city editor with Robert E. Garst, a copy editor of about my age, whose abilities I had come to value highly. Both Garst and Theodore M. Bernstein had come to the *Times* as copyreaders in 1925, soon after they graduated from the Columbia School of Journalism. I had found that both men shared my views about the need for change and improvement on the *Times*. I later had a hand in Bernstein's becoming head of the bullpen editors, and when I became managing editor I promoted both Garst and Bernstein to be assistant managing editors. In these two cases, and others, I was able to start assembling a staff of people who were personally beholden to me and who, I hoped, would be loyal to me when I became managing editor.

By the start of the 1950s, Sulzberger and James were clearly grooming me as James' eventual successor. James consulted me on all major decisions and counted on me to run things during his frequent absences. And in January of 1951, Sulzberger, wanting to give me increased authority to deal with some of the paper's problems, created for me the new title of Executive Managing Editor. His primary motive was to give me a mandate to bridge the gap that still existed between the day and the night staffs. As executive managing editor, I would come in around noon each day and stay until ten or so. Thus I, not the night editors, would be authorized to make final decisions when the paper was being put together each evening.

Sulzberger called me to his office one day and showed me a copy of a letter he had just sent to James, creating the new position and appointing me to fill it. His letter stressed that I was still subordinate to the managing editor, yet James might, had he chosen, have taken offense at my promotion. He did not. I went immediately to James' office, and his comment was "It's a pretty good idea, but there'll be hell to pay with the bullpen."

I think James' main reaction was to hope the change could be put into effect with a minimum of unpleasantness. He called to his office the one man most adversely affected by the new move, Neil MacNeil, the assistant night managing editor. MacNeil was a burly, soft-spoken Nova Scotian, an exceedingly pleasant man who was also one of the most independent of the bullpen editors. His superior, Raymond McCaw, had for some time been in poor health and MacNeil was in line to succeed him. In fact, when James called him in that day in January of 1951, MacNeil may well have thought he was to get the news of his promotion. Instead, he was hit with the news that I was, in effect, coming in as his boss. MacNeil was understandably shaken. He went silently back to his desk and wrote out a request for retirement.

A little later, MacNeil asked to withdraw his request, but Sulzberger thought it better to let it stand. An arrangement was reached whereby MacNeil would stay on five months, until May, before retiring. If the job of night managing editor became vacant in this period (that is, if McCaw died or retired) MacNeil was to have the title until his retirement became effective. However, it developed that the ailing McCaw had no intention of giving up his title. On the evening when Mr. and Mrs. Sulzberger went by his apartment to tell him of the arrangement with MacNeil, McCaw declared that he'd stay in his job if they had to drive him to the *Times* each day in an ambulance.

I think it was unfortunate that Sulzberger had to make me executive managing editor, but nonetheless the move was necessary. It was unfortunate because it reflected on the performances of both James and the night editors. Yet the day-night problem did exist, and my new job proved to be an effective means of lessening it.

I was helped by a turnover in personnel. McCaw's health prevented him from returning to work, MacNeil retired in May, and I was able to install Bernstein and some other men of my choice in the night editors' jobs. I was separated from my wife and able to work the long hours necessary to make the new assignment successful, and I think that throughout 1951 we were able to solve many of the day-night problems that had troubled me since 1945.

As it turned out, I was executive managing editor less than a year. James died on the night of December 3 at Roosevelt Hospital, after more than a third of a century of loyal, invaluable service to the *Times*. I have criticized James as an administrator, but I have only the highest words for him as a reporter and a friend. In an era of fabulous, flamboyant newspapermen, he ranked with the greatest.

He had been desperately ill for several weeks but was thought to be improving when suddenly his great heart stopped. I was living alone at that time, and when the city desk called and gave me the news, I went to pieces. It was as if something had snapped inside my nervous system. I was heartbroken to have lost my friend, and I was fearful that I might prove incapable of filling his shoes.

Sulzberger called me in the next day and said, "Of course I want you to take the big job, but I'm not going to make a move until a decent interval has passed."

I stayed at the same desk, performing the same duties, for two weeks. My main emotion in that period was loneliness. I missed James terribly. For seven years, we'd had a drink and a talk at the close of almost every work day, and I'd sought his advice just as he'd sought mine. Now, as I contemplated filling his job, I saw what a lonely job it was. It was good that I had the trust of Sulzberger and of Dryfoos, but I would deal with them only on the big problems. The day-to-day responsibility of running the news operation of the most important newspaper in America was about to become mine, and for the first time I fully realized what an awesome responsibility it was. I had wanted this job for at least seven years, and now that I had it I was not a little frightened by it.

Exactly two weeks after James' death, Sulzberger told me he was ready to announce his plans. That afternoon, a notice went up on the bulletin board that began:

> To the Staff:
> When death takes a valued member of an organization, it is always a sad occasion. Such it was with the passing of Mr. Edwin James. But the institution must go on, and I have today appointed Turner Catledge to the post of Managing Editor of the Times. . . .

XVII

Managing Editor

I ONCE received a letter from a man in the Midwest who said he
read the entire Sunday *New York Times,* every word of it, every
week. He was quite specific. He told me what hour the *Times* arrived
on Tuesday, and at what time on Friday, by diligently applying
himself to the task, he could finish reading it. The reason for his
letter, he said, was to ask if there couldn't be a second Sunday
Times, to occupy him from Friday until Tuesday.

The letter was quite literate and I was so intrigued that I wrote
the man asking for more details. A few days later I got another letter,
this one from a doctor, who explained that my correspondent was a
mental patient under his care, and that he'd assigned the reading
of the Sunday *Times* to him as a form of therapy.

That man aside, I do not know of anyone who reads the entire
Sunday *Times,* or the entire daily *Times* either. Nor do I know of any
one newspaper editor with the breadth of intellect to be an expert
on all the subjects—politics (local, national, international), science,
sports, society, religion, drama, crime—that must be covered in the
Times. Certainly I claim no such universality of intellect.

Yet it was necessary for the *Times* to cover all those subjects
and more, and I believed it was necessary for one editor to see that
they were covered in more depth and more detail than ever before.

As I entered my new job, I knew the *Times* was too big to be bossed by the traditional shirt-sleeved managing editor. Our news staff numbered some eight hundred reporters and editors, in New York and elsewhere, and I could deal with them only through a chain of command. I believed the *Times* urgently needed strong leadership. Only that sort of leadership, I believed, could bring such a large, tradition-minded newspaper to make the changes that were needed for its continued prosperity and growth. I wanted talent and I wanted loyalty—not to myself, but to the office I held and to the *Times*. Fortunately, over the years, I was able to find, bring forward, and utilize such able and dedicated men as Ted Bernstein, E. C. Daniel, Harrison Salisbury, and, some years later, Abe Rosenthal.

The kind of men I wanted in top positions at the *Times* were independent, creative men, thoroughbreds, and they were not the sort who could be bossed or browbeaten. I had to make them do what I wanted done, often by making them think it was what they wanted done.

Harry Truman once said he spent most of his time persuading people to do things they ought to do without persuasion, and, on a smaller scale, my job as managing editor of the *Times* was somewhat similar. I had to make an assortment of proud, ambitious, independent men work together as a team. Inevitably there were disagreements among them—I never minded, I even needed, a measure of healthy ferment—and it was my job to handle them, to mediate between them to make the most of their talents.

I wanted men with ideas, men who could do as much for me as I could for them—or more. I considered myself an expert in one subject, national politics, and in other areas I expected initiative and imagination from the responsible editors. Once I was having a difficult talk with a sports editor whose work I found unsatisfactory.

"Tell me what you want," the editor said.

"No," I replied. "That's what I want you to tell me, what I want."

Part of an editor's job is to be a problem solver, and it was my belief, no doubt influenced by my years observing the Congress, that problems aren't always best solved by plunging directly into them. Sometimes if you let a problem simmer for a while, it will solve itself. The trick is to determine how long to keep hands off. I'm sure that my cautious style sometimes annoyed E. C. Daniel, who was more inclined to direct confrontations when a problem arose, but that was how I chose to operate.

I was greatly aided in my new job by the knowledge that I had Sulzberger's full support. He was my boss, my drinking companion, and my close friend. He had groomed me for this job, he had faith in my abilities, and now he was prepared to stand behind me. Sometimes other editors would want to appeal my decisions to Sulzberger, or to Dryfoos. "Go ahead," I'd tell them, "but you'll lose." And they always did.

Both Sulzberger and Dryfoos felt as I did that it was necessary to strengthen the prestige of the managing editor's office, and we did so in a number of ways. He agreed that all raises in the news department would be made in my name. I eliminated the distinction that James had recognized between the publisher's orders and the managing editor's orders. One day, not long after I took command, I made a suggestion to Ted Bernstein which he ignored. The next day I told him I was sorry he hadn't followed my instructions, because it was something the publisher had wanted done. "Why didn't you tell me that?" Ted asked. I replied that he had best assume that anything I wanted the publisher also wanted.

Sulzberger did not want to be an aggressive, dominating publisher, hurling thunderbolts at an awed staff. His style was more reserved, more subtle, and I think more effective. He sought executives who shared his general outlook, and he tried, by word and deed, to set a tone for the paper.

On a day-to-day basis, Sulzberger made his likes and dislikes known via memoranda which we called the "blue notes" because they were written on blue paper. Hundreds of these blue notes rained down on me over the years, on great matters and small. Sometimes they were helpful, sometimes annoying, sometimes both. Sulzberger was by nature irritable about small mistakes—a shortcoming I understood because I shared it. As he read through each day's *Times,* he might see a half-dozen items that displeased him—a fact not clarified, an imprecise headline, and so on. Firing off an irate blue note to me was a form of therapy for him.

Sometimes, if he was particularly angry, he might demand to know what editor or reporter was responsible for an error. His instinct was to call the reporter or send him a note. I'd either refuse to tell him or would stall. I knew that his anger would pass soon, and that if he sent an angry note to a reporter he'd regret it within an hour. Once when he was demanding to know who'd made a mistake, I asked, "If I told you, what would you do about it?" He just laughed and said he didn't know.

Sulzberger was irritable on small issues, but the other side of the story is that he had unerring good judgment on the big issues. In that, he reminded me of Harry Truman. One of my mottos in dealing with Sulzberger was "Make no small plans," for he liked to think in big terms, and when big problems arose I never doubted his support or his good sense.

If one of Sulzberger's blue notes contained praise for a reporter's work, I sent it on to the reporter. If it was critical, and I thought the criticism valid, I would pass it on to the reporter as my own comment, for insofar as possible I wanted our reporters and editors to do their work without feeling that the publisher was constantly looking over their shoulders. In truth, however, he was. He read the paper closely and he had a very personal feeling about what he saw there—if the *Times* looked silly, he felt that he looked silly. Here, for example, is a note Sulzberger (who was then quite ill) sent me the morning after the Presidential Inauguration of January, 1965:

> Turner: This morning my nurse, who was feeling ill last night and turned in early, wanted to see pictures of Lady Bird at the Inaugural Ball. She was unable to find anything in my apartment copy of the Times. However, she found what she was looking for, hairdo and all, in the Herald Tribune and the Daily News. I was embarrassed.

Sulzberger was an ever-flowing source of story ideas, some of them good, some not. His suggestions often reflected his intense interest in our city. As he drove about, he was forever noticing new construction projects, or traffic problems, or something of the sort, that he would mention to me. For example, here are two typical blue notes from the 1950s:

> On the way to the barber shop this morning, I noticed that there are new lights at 50th Street and Lexington Avenue. Have we had a story about them?

> I am told that a lot of plants have been stolen from the planting on Park Avenue. Will you have it checked?

Sulzberger was attracted by the philosophizing of cab drivers, and their theories would often make their way to my desk. For example:

> I had a philosophic discussion with a taxi driver the other day. He claimed it was impossible to touch the hearts of New Yorkers. I claimed it could be done, but very frankly, I don't know how. It's an interesting thought. What's your reaction?

My reaction was mainly confusion, as I indicated in my reply:

I am at a loss to know exactly how to reply to your note of June 30 regarding the taxicab driver's complaint about the impossibility of touching the hearts of New Yorkers. I don't think New Yorkers are different from any other people. They may have pressures that people in other parts of the country don't have, and they may have defenses against some of those pressures.

I'd have to have more information about his major premise before being able to suggest any cure for the ills of which he complains.

Very often, Sulzberger caught mistakes that had slipped past our editors, and all I could do was promise to try harder in the future. But there were many other times when I thought his criticisms were not justified, and it would be my duty to tell him so. At such times, I would remind him that my obligation was not only to him but to hundreds of employees who were trying to put out a paper they could be proud of. He was an easy man to deal with in that regard. He understood that I could often save him from mistakes, or make him look good; I developed a technique for dealing with him when I had something unpleasant to tell him. I would begin by saying, "Mr. Sulzberger, I have something I feel it my duty to tell you. You may not want to hear it. Shall I proceed?" Naturally, when I put it that way, he had no alternative but to assure me he wanted to hear the worst.

One of the sensitive issues that arose between Sulzberger and me in my first years as managing editor concerned his nephew Cy Sulzberger, then the *Times'* chief foreign correspondent. On the very day that Sulzberger told me I was to be managing editor, I had asked him if there would be any limits to my authority over the news department. If so, I said, he should tell me before I accepted the job. Sulzberger only laughed in his disarming way. "I know what you mean," he said. "You want to know where you stand with Cy. Well, I assure you there are no strings to your job except those between you and me. You can handle Cy in your own way."

It was good to have that assurance, but handling Cy was not as easy as his uncle suggested. Inevitable administrative problems arose from Cy's dual status as our chief foreign correspondent and as the publisher's nephew. Cy had been an outstanding war correspondent, and after the war Sulzberger and James re-established for him the post of chief foreign correspondent—the same job Adolph Ochs had created for James after World War I. The job was ill defined, and given Cy's special status, he was soon functioning as the *Times'* foreign news editor, but one with a Paris address rather than a New York address. I thought this a poor way to operate. My view had nothing to do with my personal feelings for Cy, for I had known and liked him since we met in Washington in the thirties, but his free-wheeling style ran counter to my belief in a centralized news operation.

When I was still assistant managing editor, Cy's status caused one of the few instances when Sulzberger overruled me on a news decision. Cy had interviewed General MacArthur and written a six-part series on their talks. Other editors and I thought Cy's series awfully thin, and suggested that it be boiled down to one article. Cy was furious, and when his uncle heard of the dispute, he backed his nephew all the way. Sulzberger decreed not only that all six articles should run, but that the first was to be carried on the front page. Jimmy James was vastly amused by all this; he'd predicted that I'd get my fingers burned if I bucked Cy.

I thought Sulzberger had made a serious mistake. The series wasn't that important, one way or another, but the fact that he'd overruled his editors was. A few days later I told Sulzberger I had an unpleasant matter to bring up and asked if he wanted to hear it. He said he did. I said that if he continued to overrule his editors he would have a serious morale problem. I stressed that he was in a difficult position where Cy was concerned and urged him to abide by his editors' judgment.

"Those editors represent you," I told him. "They *are* you. They're not usurping power. But if Cy can walk over them, it'll leave scars that won't heal."

"Why doesn't somebody tell me these things?" he complained.

"I just did," I said.

Still, the problem continued. Cy resented any suggestions that he took advantage of his status as the publisher's nephew, but, even if he did not, he remained an aggressive, independent correspondent, and it was hard for our editors to ignore his special status with the publisher's family. The family ties were there, and, despite my admonitions, most editors treated Cy with kid gloves.

Sulzberger twice sent me to Europe to "straighten Cy out." We had some fine times together, including one delightful visit to Luxembourg when Pearl Mesta was U.S. Ambassador there, but Cy's idea of being straightened out was for me to agree with him to be his spokesman in New York; I never pushed him too hard, for I knew that Sulzberger didn't really want a fight with Cy.

My disagreements with Cy came to a head in the fall of 1953 and were reflected in a series of letters that passed between us. A number of issues had arisen, but the primary one was the degree of autonomy he and the other correspondents would have in relation to the New York office. I had asked that New York be given as much advance notice as possible if a correspondent was traveling from one country to another, or even taking a long trip within one country. Cy interpreted this as an effort by New York to exercise unnecessary and burdensome control over the correspondents. He felt that he and the correspondents were being made to "ask permission" to take trips. This was not my intent, as I tried to explain in my first letter to him:

> To my mind it is highly desirable, from the standpoint of both yourself and The Times, for the New York office to know your plans of travel as far in advance as possible. We might have some administrative or news matter I would want you to take up with a correspondent. We might have other plans for you or concerning the story you were about to cover. It is not a matter of "permission"—it is a matter of knowledge at the nerve center in New York of what the staff is doing. . . .
>
> The whole problem comes down to this, Cy: We have the task of producing, bringing in, and presenting an enormous news report. The superintendency of that task must be lodged somewhere, and the logical spot is the New York office. I am sure no one in the New York office wants to be in the position of heckling or attempting to exercise authority over minor details. But the movement of staff members from place to place, the assignment of stories and things of that kind are by no means minor.

I returned to this theme in a second letter to Cy a few days later:

> I ask you to keep always uppermost in mind that we are trying to operate a total staff; we can no longer, if we ever did, think of The Times as having a foreign service, a domestic service, and a local staff. We are all one paper, concentrating on getting out the best possible product at 229 West 43rd Street, New York City, and it is from that base the operation must be managed.

That is as good a statement as any of my belief in a unified, centrally-directed New York Times, and it is for that reason I repeat it now. The battle for central control was an endless one. It had to be fought with Cy and other correspondents, with Lester Markel's semi-autonomous Sunday department, and eventually with the Washington bureau. Some battles were won and some were not. Those that were won did not always stay won. But they were always worth fighting.

In Cy's case, the publisher moved slowly, because he did not want a showdown in which, in effect, he'd be forced to choose between Cy and me. His patience paid off, for in the fall of 1954 an opportunity arose to settle the problem peaceably. Our foreign-affairs columnist, Anne O'Hare McCormick, died, and Sulzberger named Cy to replace her. Given this opportunity to utilize his talents, Cy no longer had the time or the desire to continue his administrative role, and those duties returned where they had always belonged, to the desk of the foreign news editor in New York.

One of my first concerns as managing editor was the lamentable way the paper was written. We were famous, or notorious, for our long sentences with countless dangling phrases. I've already mentioned that when managing editor I wanted to undo that tradition. In this effort, I was immeasurably helped by the talents of my assistant managing editor.

Ted Bernstein is a small, slender, bright-eyed man who loves the *New York Times* not merely as an institution but as an edition-by-edition, page-by-page, line-by-line creation. He helped bring a new element of daring to the editing of the paper. He set new standards in the use of language. He was an ever-flowing source of ideas, and I gladly made use of hundreds of them. I have often thought that Bernstein, with his deep roots in Manhattan and his cosmopolitan interests, came closer than anyone else on our staff to embodying the educated, liberal core of *Times* readers. He could edit so well for *Times* readers because he was so truly one of them.

It was with constant assistance and advice from Ted Bernstein that I set out to attain better writing and editing. I knew that there were several reasons for our ponderous style. It had been fixed in an earlier, more leisurely era, when all forms of writing were more ornate.

The tradition had been reinforced by the fact that, as late as the 1920s, reporters were still paid on "space rates," that is, by how many words they got into the paper This did not encourage tight writing. Finally, our style was a by-product of one of our virtues — the tradition, begun by Adolph Ochs, of printing "all the news." Reporters often felt that, to be safe, they should include every possible detail in a story. Laziness could be justified as thoroughness; the reporter was spared the job of intelligent selectivity. But as the years passed there was far more news to report, and less space to report it in, so tighter writing became imperative.

A major obstacle to better writing was the resistance of many of the older reporters and editors. Some simply couldn't or wouldn't change their accustomed way of writing and editing. Others feared, quite sincerely, that shorter stories would lead to skimpy news coverage and that "bright" writing had no place in a serious newspaper. They thought change implied criticism of the work they had done in the past.

I believed the *Times* should have a dual appeal. First, it should be necessary to people who wanted to be well informed. It already was that. Second, it should be a paper people wanted to read, for pleasure as well as out of necessity. It was not that. I recall a comment about the *Times* made by an out-of-town editor at an American Press Institute seminar: "Some days I pick it up and I say, 'I'm going to read you, you son of a bitch, if it kills me!' "

I confess that I sometimes picked up the *Times* with that same apprehension. One morning I came across a story on our business page that I simply couldn't understand. I took it to the business editor, who finally had to admit he didn't understand it either. About that time, the reporter who had written the story walked by. I asked him to explain the story to me. He stammered about for a moment, then finally confessed that he'd simply turned in some corporation's handout and he didn't understand it either. That was an extreme example, but it was the sort of thing I hoped to eliminate.

As early as 1950, Sulzberger agreed to let me give out $1,000 a month in the Publisher's Writing Awards. Awards of up to $100 were given each month for outstanding writing by reporters in the various news departments. Even this incentive plan proved difficult to administer because some editors, notably the city editor and the sports editor, wanted to be good fellows and see that the money was passed around equally to all their writers. They wanted to be benign bosses, not judges. Thus I had to double-check their recommendations to make sure the money was going for good writing and not for good will.

In 1953, Ted Bernstein started a little publication called "Winners & Sinners," a mimeographed sheet distributed every three weeks, calling attention primarily to good and bad language usage in the paper. In each issue, examples of notably good and notably bad writing were reprinted. (The writer's name was attached to the good writing, but not to the bad.) "Winners & Sinners" was another useful tool in our campaign for better writing, although it too caused problems. Writers who won praise from Bernstein, but not cash from the Publisher's Awards, were quick to register complaints. Also copy editors complained that all the glory was going to reporters. To improve this situation, the Publisher's Awards were later broadened to include prizes for outstanding editing.

I did all I could to persuade our reporters that we really wanted better, brighter, tighter writing, and that we'd back them up if disputes arose with tradition-minded editors. I often told reporters that I'd bought a carload of periods and I wanted the staff to help me use them. I asked reporters to think of a story as a letter to a friend—or, as I once suggested, as a letter to a curious but somewhat dumb younger brother.

On October 26, 1953, I issued a letter to the staff that said in part:

> Brevity, simplicity and clarity are basically what we are striving for. We feel that the main news point of any story can be told in simple, short statements. We feel that it is no longer necessary and maybe never was, to wrap up in one sentence or paragraph all the traditional W's—who, what, when, where and why.
>
> I do not wish to lay down any rules. I certainly do not intend to try to fix the length of sentences, since the need varies with each story. What I wish to do most of all is to enlist your sympathetic interest and help in our general purpose. I should hope that, in striving for the particular goals of brevity, simplicity and clarity, our writers will develop individual styles, which will make their stories more readable and, hence, more attractive to our readers. Above all, it should never be forgotten that thorough reporting and sound thinking are pre-requisite to good writing.

Attached to this letter were ten "before and after" examples of leads as they had been written and actually published in other days, and how they could be improved in hindsight. I won't reproduce these examples here, but most showed how long, cumbersome leads could be fixed by breaking up the sentences and by not attempting to tell every fact in the first paragraph. Lest anyone accuse me of holding myself up as a paragon of good style, I let it leak out that several of the bad examples had been taken from stories I had written in years past.

This letter was well received, and on the following February 26 I followed it up with another, which said:

> This is more on the subject of our efforts to make The Times more readable. Since I addressed you last fall, results have been most gratifying. . . . One area in which I think we can make further improvement at once, however, is in the body of the story. I urge you to follow the purpose of simplicity and brevity throughout the entire piece. . . .

May I make this final suggestion: Try to back away from your story and ask yourself, "What does this story really mean? Just what am I trying to say?" Then say it simply.

In addition to poor writing, there was a general stuffiness about the paper. "Let's get a smile on the front page," I told our editors.

I was delighted in 1962 when *The New Yorker* carried a cartoon that showed two commuters reading their morning papers, one reading the *Times*, the other the *Herald Tribune*. The man reading the *Times* burst out laughing, and the man reading the *Herald Tribune* was staring at him with a look of amazement.

Soon after I became managing editor, the Kuklapolitan Players—Kukla, Fran, and Ollie—performed at Town Hall. One of our reporters wrote a deadpan "review" of the show which we printed under the headline:

OLIVER J. DRAGON
BOWS AS BARITONE
Member of Kuklapolitan School
Is Formidably Assisted by
Oooglepuss at Recital

With the story was a one-column picture of Oliver J. Dragon, baritone. This was the sort of humorous feature that made our traditionalists tear their hair, but I thought it was delightful, and I was pleased when Sulzberger sent me a copy of the story with "Bravo!" written across it.

Another time, in 1959, a reporter cleverly personalized the story of a runaway locomotive ("The big locomotive saw his chance. Quietly, so nobody would notice, he ran his engine a little faster. . . ."). Someone drew several cartoons which showed the locomotive with a frown on his "face" as he sat in the train yard, then grinning as he raced down the tracks. I found the drawings amusing and authorized their use. They appeared on our front page the next morning, and during the day one of our most tradition-minded editors rushed up to me in such a fury that I feared he might strike me. "Those drawings are un-*Times*like," he declared. I had to agree, although I thought being un-*Times*like now and then might be good for the *Times*.

Sulzberger had mixed feelings about my efforts to brighten the *Times*. He was himself a man with a delightful sense of humor, totally incapable of pomposity. For example, at the reception for his oldest daughter's wedding he walked around with a sign on his back that said: "If you liked the setting and the ceremony, remember I have two more." He also had a weakness for puns—a weakness I didn't share, for I loathe puns. Once I discovered a picture caption in the *Times* with a pun in every line. I rushed to the editor responsible and was giving him hell when he pulled out a blue note from the publisher congratulating him on his wit.

Still, Sulzberger was cautious where humor in the *Times* was concerned. He knew how tricky humor is, and how very subjective. He enjoyed the "review" of Kukla, Fran and Ollie, but I'm not sure he'd have approved if it had been shown to him prior to publication.

In the early fifties, I was concerned that Meyer Berger, one of our finest writers, was not being used to the utmost of his talents. Berger had written some beautiful "mood pieces" about New York City for *The New Yorker*, and I wanted him to write a regular column about the city. Sulzberger was dubious. He feared the column would be too "light," too un-*Times*like. He said he could see no reason for a column about New York; I argued that if we had a Washington column, why not a New York column? After all, we were a New York newspaper. Finally he agreed, and Mike Berger's "About New York" became immensely popular, but Sulzberger was never entirely satisfied with it. He seemed to think it should be topical and less concerned with the mood of the city. Part of the problem was that the subjects that fascinated Berger—the working people, the ethnic subcultures, the neighborhood bars and customs—were virtually unknown to Sulzberger. The *Times* had never written about that level of New York, and he wasn't sure it should.

After Berger's death early in 1959, I tried to persuade Sulzberger to name another writer to continue the "About New York" column. On February 6 I sent him a memo which said:

> I have your note about dropping the Berger column rather than have someone else do it temporarily.
> Of course, I would cheerfully do anything you want. But I make a plea that you consider it, at least for several days.
> I know how you feel personally about the column, but I think it is a very good feature, and we have many reasons to believe it is very acceptable to our readers. The one criticism I dislike most about The Times comes from people who still claim it is stodgy and lacking in human interest. This column, to my mind, is quite a brightener, and quite dignified at that.

I renewed my plea on March 23:

> I would like to have a talk with you at your convenience concerning the "About New York" column which we have let lapse since the

death of Mike Berger. I am strongly in favor of a column of this
nature, as I wrote you before, and I would like a chance to present
my arguments personally.

Sulzberger was cool to my proposal but, undaunted, I wrote him
again on May 18:

> I would like to see you at your earliest convenience to try to sell
> you some items. Not insurance. Not oil stocks. Not even Florida real
> estate.
> What I have in mind is a new "About New York" column and also
> a daily bridge column, both of which I think we could anchor on the
> page opposite the TV page with considerable appeal to readers and
> advertisers, mostly the former from whom we feel pressure for both
> of these items.

Finally, I went ahead and assigned a talented young reporter to
prepare some "dry runs" of a new "About New York" column, hoping
I might sell Sulzberger that way. On July 22 I sent him this note:

> We have been having dry-runs in preparation for a revival of an
> "About New York" column, as a substitute for the one Mike Berger
> used to do. I believe we have come upon a real "find" for this column.
> He is Gay Talese, who has proved himself not only in the dry-runs
> but also in the ordinary work as one of the finest. He is a young man
> who developed in the Sports department and has been doing some
> excellent stuff on the general staff. I refer you particularly to a story
> he had in the Sunday Magazine on the Via Veneto in Rome. We have
> four of his dry-runs in hand, which I will be very happy to show you.
> I think you will find them tremendously interesting and well done.
> I am convinced he can sustain them.

This elicited a one-sentence response from the publisher—"I'd
be glad to see some of Talese's work—that is aside from the Via
Veneto piece of which I have a copy at hand"—but he never agreed
to resume the "About New York" column. Later, however, in 1962,
when we seemed about to lose one of our most talented Washington writers, Russell Baker, Sulzberger did reluctantly agree to
let Baker begin his "Observer" column, which became highly
successful.

The bridge column, which I'd urged on Sulzberger in my memo
about Talese, was already being carried in the Sunday paper, but
Sulzberger resisted putting it into the daily despite demands from
readers. I argued that logically, morally, or whatever, if it was all
right for Sunday it was all right for weekdays. I told him I was

under pressure from the home front, since my wife, Abby, is an expert bridge player. He finally agreed to the bridge column.

Sulzberger understood home-front pressures. I never knew how many of his blue-note complaints to me represented his wife's criticisms, but I thought the percentage was high. He had once alluded to this in a joking manner. He asked me if we'd ever considered a woman for education editor. I said we had no prejudice against women, but we'd have to keep in mind that she'd direct the work of men. He scribbled in reply: "That happens in my house too."

XVIII

Changing *The Times*

ONE of my responsibilities as managing editor was to find and groom my own successor. This was important to Sulzberger, with his concern about continuity in the paper; he himself was then grooming his son-in-law, Orvil Dryfoos, to be his successor as publisher. Also, I had the fine example of the training Jimmy James had given me.

When I became managing editor, my assistant managing editor was David Joseph, whose promotion from city editor I'd arranged a few years earlier. Joseph was then in his sixties, so there was no question of his succeeding me. I tried to work with him, but I found him unwilling to assume responsibility. When I was away, work would pile up, and Sulzberger's blue notes would go unanswered. Finally I called him in and told him we'd have to make a change.

"Do you know what I'd do if I were in your place?" Joseph asked me. I stared at the kindly old man in amazement, until he repeated his question.

"No," I said finally. "What would you do if you were in my place?"

"I'll tell you," he said. "But first let me be in your place."

I stood up and let him sit down at my desk.

"Now, if I were you," he said, "I'd ask for my resignation or retirement."

I did as he suggested. I had already spoken to Sulzberger, who was prepared to make Joseph's retirement financially comfortable. I sent Joseph up to see Sulzberger, and his forty-four years on the *Times* came to an end.

I then promoted Ted Bernstein and Bob Garst to be assisant managing editors. I told Garst at the outset that although he had several months' seniority over Bernstein (and seniority meant a great deal in those days) I wanted Bernstein to be the senior of the two. I had in mind a clear division of responsibility between them. Garst would handle administrative and personnel matters, and Bernstein would be my principal assistant, with major responsibility in fundamental news development, as well as with his first love, copy editing.

Neither man performed entirely as I had intended. Garst was a capable technician but proved to have a rigid way of dealing with people, one that caused a good many problems. Bernstein, I found, didn't want as broad an assignment as I'd envisioned. He was, and is, a brilliant copy editor and a brilliant student of the language. He was also an ever-flowing font of ideas. Within his chosen area, the editing and presentation of the news, he was unexcelled But he didn't want to drop his pad and pencil to take on broader problems in news development and the operations of the paper. He had no taste for the difficult personnel problems that arose.

When I first made Garst and Bernstein assistant managing editors, I told them that it was not in the cards that either of them would succeed me, and that one of their duties would be to help me groom a younger man. They readily pledged their cooperation, although when the time actually came to catapult a younger man in over them, they exhibited some understandable reluctance.

By 1954, it was clear to me that, of all the talented young men on our staff, one stood out as I searched for a successor. He was Clifton Daniel, who had been serving as a *Times* correspondent in London and in Germany.

Daniel, who was then about forty, was a handsome and courtly man whose roots, like my own, were in a small town in the South. A dozen years or so after I was working in my uncles' hardware and grocery stores in Philadelphia, Mississippi, E. C. Daniel, Jr., was tending the soda fountain of his father's drugstore in Zebulon, North Carolina. He studied journalism at the University of North Carolina, worked for the Raleigh paper and for the A.P., and joined our staff in London in 1944. He performed ably there, and later in Bonn, and he struck me and others in New York as clearly having executive potential. He was a fine reporter, with experience in Washington, New York, and Europe, and he had shown administrative ability. He was a man of considerable charm and polish. A bachelor, he had moved easily in London's finest circles, and earned quite a reputation as a ladies' man. His combination of journalistic ability and social grace attracted the attention of Sulzberger, who liked his executives to be, like himself, worldly men.

There was no doubt in anyone's mind that, if I was to pick a successor a decade or so younger than myself, Daniel was the man. One day, after I had discussed him several times with Dryfoos, Sulzberger called me into his office and suggested—as if it were an original idea—that I consider Daniel. I said that was a fine idea. Bernstein and Garst also were enthusiastic about Daniel, and we discussed how to move him along. Our plan was to keep Daniel abroad for two more years, then bring him home for some reporting in the United States and executive training in New York. Dryfoos was very much for this plan, because when I was away he did not feel at ease in dealing with Bernstein, and Daniel seemed more his sort of man.

Early in 1954, Daniel was home on leave from his station in Bonn and I told him of my plans. He was highly pleased, although he thought his prospective advancement was rather slow paced. However, when I told him we were looking for a new correspondent in Moscow, he jumped at the chance. After a training period at Columbia University, he arrived in Moscow in the late summer of 1954, filled with enthusiasm. But he found the assignment a most difficult one. The weather was bad, the living conditions were bad, and the government's treatment of foreigners was bad. He soon developed ulcers and lost twenty or thirty pounds, and when he went to Geneva after a year to cover a Big Four conference, three of our men wrote me to report how thin and weary he looked. On AHS's urging, I ordered him to return to the United States, and his entry into an executive job thus came ahead of schedule. Daniel became an assistant to the foreign news editor and, a little later, an assistant managing editor.

An important factor in my selection of Daniel was his proven ability as a reporter. One of the *Times'* biggest problems in those days was that almost all of its editors came up from the copy desks and had little or no reporting experience. I was an exception, as Jimmy James had been, but at the next level almost all the editors were deskmen. I think one of my most important contributions was advancing talented reporters like Daniel, Harrison Salisbury, James

Roach, Tom Mullaney, and Abe Rosenthal to top editorial jobs. I sometimes told these reporters-turned-editors that I was bringing them in to stud—using them for breeding purposes.

Soon after Daniel came to work in New York, in the fall of 1955, he met his future wife, Margaret Truman. I happened to witness their first meeting, which took place at the Manhattan home of George and Evie Backer. The playwright Robert Sherwood had just died and his widow, Madeline, was staying with the Backers. She was in such low spirits that Evie Backer suggested they have a few friends in to lift the gloom. Madeline said she'd like to see Turner Catledge and hear some of his stories about the South. Evie called and asked me to dinner, and since her husband was out of town, she suggested I bring "Danny," as she called Daniel, whom she'd known in London. I did, and as we four were having our after-dinner coffee, in walked Miss Truman, accompanied by Alan Campbell, Dorothy Parker's former husband. Daniel and Miss Truman soon fell into conversation. I recall him sitting at the end of the sofa twirling a charm on his watch chain. After an hour or so Campbell and Margaret left and Evie, who was quite a matchmaker, started in on Daniel about seeing more of her. "Now there's a girl for you, Danny," she said several times. Finally, as we were leaving, Daniel laughed and said, "Relax, Evie, I'm having lunch with her the day after tomorrow."

Daniel and Margaret had much in common, and the outcome of their whirlwind romance never surprised me. For one thing, both were prominent: she a President's daughter, he a well-known journalist and man-about-town in New York and London. But, beneath the glitter, there were other attractions. Both were from small towns and each was the only child of adoring parents. Both came from a Protestant background, and neither would have married anyone who was not wholly acceptable to his parents.

I was an usher at their wedding in Independence, Missouri, in the spring of 1956, and later a godfather to their first child, Clifton Truman Daniel. One of my fringe benefits was getting to know Margaret's father better. I recall one Christmas when my wife Abby and I invited the Daniels over for cocktails. It developed that Harry and Bess Truman were spending the holidays with them, and we urged them to bring the Trumans. (From that night forward the Catledges rated high with the porters, doormen, and elevator operators in our building.) When Harry Truman walked in, Abby asked him what he'd like to drink.

"Bourbon, bourbon," he said.

"A little bourbon?" she asked.

"Who the hell said 'little'?" he snapped.

Daniel and I were to be closely associated for more than a decade; while I was managing editor, he was my first assistant; later, when I became executive editor, he succeeded me as managing editor. It was, as far as I was concerned, an excellent relationship. He and I have different styles in directing subordinates, but we think alike as far as newspapers are concerned, and I have the highest regard for him both personally and professionally.

Daniel's weaknesses included a streak of impatience in his dealings with subordinates. He was respected but not always liked. He was a perfectionist and something of a pedagogue. His daily news conferences, when he inherited them from me, were referred to by one of our high executives as Daniel's course in "Journalism One." He is a man with sharp edges, sometimes abrupt and short-tempered, and these qualities would eventually keep him from succeeding me as executive editor.

For more than a decade, Daniel was my principal assistant. During that period the *Times* passed through a period of self-renewal, making, in my opinion, crucial steps into the modern era of journalism. As I describe some of the changes we made, I must stress my indebtedness to men like Daniel, Bernstein, and Harrison Salisbury, a brilliant reporter whom I advanced to assistant managing editor in the early sixties.

One problem in the early fifties was our local coverage. Prestige on the *Times* had traditionally gone to the foreign correspondents and to the Washington bureau. We took our local staff for granted, and as a result its morale was low, its performance uninspired. When James was managing editor, he tried never to assign returning foreign correspondents to our local staff, which he considered too great a comedown. Often he would send them to Washington, if he could not offer another prestige foreign assignment. His attitude was shared by other top executives, and in time the local staff came to have a low opinion even of itself. Ambitious young reporters joined the *Times,* as I had, with the hope of getting assignments in Washington or abroad. We were a cosmopolitan newspaper, not a metropolitan one.

I understood this point of view, but I wanted to change it. I believed the New York office *is* the newspaper, and it should have first-rate coverage and first-rate status within our organization.

Part of the difficulty was that our "local" coverage was so vast. Our city editor directed not only the usual coverage of fires, crime, and local politics, but also the cultural, social, financial, and political news of one of the world's great cities. It was almost impossible to find a city editor who could satisfactorily direct the coverage of all the aspects of our amazing city.

I made some progress in the late forties when I arranged the replacement of Dave Joseph as city editor by Bob Garst. Garst had chosen an outstanding reporter, Frank Adams, as his assistant city editor. When I promoted Garst to assistant managing editor, he urged that Adams succeed him as city editor. I agreed to this, but Adams, for all his knowledge of local political affairs, did not handle the coverage of cultural affairs as well as I had hoped. I tried breaking cultural coverage away from the city desk, but that wasn't successful. The problem was not really solved until I brought Abe Rosenthal in as metropolitan editor in 1963. At that time, Frank Adams became our chief editorial writer on local affairs, and has done an excellent job. And even Abe's appointment proved only a temporary solution, since his talents soon won him promotion to assistant managing editor and then managing editor.

As this chronology might suggest, I had no master plan, no magic formula for solving the paper's problems. I was dealing with people, talented, sensitive, sometimes stubborn people, and they were constantly surprising me, one way or the other. I proceeded by trial and error, always pragmatic, trying to learn from experience. I had no rigid rules, for the people and problems I dealt with were always changing. We were working in an era of change, and in that state of flux rigid rules were not much help.

If I may digress, I would like to tell about the way the *Times* covered a certain event that occurred during these days of change, one of the biggest, and most tragic, stories our local staff ever covered. It began in the first minutes of Thursday, July 26, 1956. The second edition had closed and the city room was quiet as, in the wireless room, operator Bernard Murphy idly turned in on 500 kc., the short-wave ship distress frequency. Murphy and other radio operators often twirled those dials, but rarely heard anything of interest. This night was different.

At 12:03 A.M. Murphy jumped to a typewriter and tapped out a fragment of Morse Code he'd overheard: "Position 40.32 N, 69.45 W . . . inspecting our damage." Then he rushed out and told Tom Mullaney, who was acting as late man in the newsroom bullpen, of the apparent distress call. Minutes later, as a rewrite man was checking the message's latitude and longitude on charts in the shipping news office, Murphy overheard another message:

"12:21 A.M.—S.S. *Stockholm* says: Badly damaged. Whole bow crushed, No. 1 hold filled with water. Have to stay in our position. If you can lower your lifeboats we can pick them up."

Thus did the first news arrive of the collision between the Italian Line steamship *Andrea Doria* and the Swedish Line's *Stockholm* off Nantucket.

Mullaney moved fast. He told the man on the picture desk to get out photos of the two ships, and he ordered the art department's late man to prepare a two-column map showing the point of collision. Next he called news editor Ernest von Hartz, Orvil Dryfoos (then an assistant to the publisher), and me, and the three of us hurried from our homes to the office.

A 12:35 message made clear that a disaster might develop: "From *Andrea Doria*—we are too bending [listing]. Impossible to put boats over the side. Please send lifeboats immediately." Mullaney stopped the presses, and decided to try for a new edition at 2 A.M.

Don Janson, late man on the city desk, pulled a rewrite staff together. Max Frankel was assigned the lead story, and the outstanding job he did on it did much to further his career. Victor Lawn of the rewrite desk wrote a history of the two ships, and Phil Benjamin wrote a story on notables among the ships' passengers. A half-dozen copy editors checked the stories and wrote headlines for them.

Soon after I arrived at the office, I ordered a plane chartered to take several reporters to Boston, where it seemed that the survivors of the collision would likely be taken. The chartered plane left La Guardia Airport at 3:45 A.M. and arrived in Boston forty-five minutes later, but our reporters then learned that all rescue ships were bound for New York, not Boston.

At 2:34 the presses began moving again, with a banner head over Frankel's one-and-a-half-column story. I called Ted Bernstein and the city editor, Frank Adams, and they reached the office about 4 A.M. Fresh material was added to the story at 3:59 and 6:23, and a cleanup edition went on the presses at 7:33 A.M. It was 8:29 when they finally stopped. A total of 740,000 papers had been printed, 540,000 with the *Doria-Stockholm* story. At that point, we had reports of injuries among the passengers of the two ships but no reports of fatalities.

Throughout the night, we at the *Times* felt a special excitement because we knew that one of our best men, Camille Cianfarra, then our Madrid correspondent, was aboard the *Andred Doria,* returning to the United States on home leave. We looked forward to his dramatic, eye-witness account of the collision. Frank Adams put in a ship-to-shore telephone call to him at 5 A.M., certain he was among the survivors, but Cian, as we called him, could not be found. Our excitement turned to concern, then to grief as in late afternoon we learned that Cian, his daughter, and his stepdaughter were among the missing, and that his wife, Jane Cianfarra, although a survivor, was injured.

Cian was an immensely popular member of our staff. He was a high-spirited individual, who loved laughter and a good time, and he was also a brilliant reporter. During his years in our Rome bureau, he developed unsurpassed contacts in the Vatican, often getting the *Times* exclusive stories, and he wrote two books, *The Vatican and the War* and *The Vatican and the Kremlin*.

Thus, grief overhung my news conference Thursday afternoon as we made plans for our second day's coverage of the disaster. The assignment sheet for that day included the names of twenty-seven of our staff members. Cian's assignment, for an eye-witness account, was later crossed out.

The next morning, Jane Cianfarra asked me to come to her room in St. Clare's Hospital. She was still not sure whether to believe the reports that her husband and two daughters were dead. I had to confirm that this was apparently true.

The two missing girls were Joan Cianfarra, who was eight, and Linda Morgan, fourteen, Jane's child by a previous marriage to Edward P. Morgan, the news commentator. That afternoon, Friday afternoon, we at the *Times* received a report that Linda had been found alive, saved by something close to a miracle. She and the others in her family had been sleeping in their staterooms, virtually at the point where the *Stockholm* struck the *Andrea Doria*. Linda was somehow scooped up into the twisted bow of the Swedish ship, and later found trapped there. She too was brought back to a New York hospital. When we received word of this, we sent a reporter to the hospital to confirm the child's identity. When it was certain, I rushed back to St. Clare's Hospital to tell the child's mother, but found that Ed Morgan had arrived minutes earlier with the wonderful news. It was the only bright spot in a terrible disaster.

Hiring and firing, at all levels, was my constant concern. I have a feeling that the time to fire a man is when you hire him. I instituted a consensus approach to staff recruitment, whereby no man was hired unless he had passed the muster of the top six or eight editors. I hoped this would break down cliques within our staff and make all our editors feel responsible for the new man's success. I also began a practice whereby men hired to be correspondents in

Washington or abroad would begin by working a few months in New York. I hoped this would instill in them a loyalty to the home office and an awareness of its needs and purposes.

When I became managing editor, I knew we had a good deal of deadwood on our staff. I had no wish to fire anyone, but I wanted the *Times* to have the finest newspaper coverage in America, and I did not think that goal was compatible with our past personnel practices. Nor did I think it any favor to keep a man in the job if he was not performing satisfactorily. Another important factor in my thinking was a "freeze" Dryfoos put on the staff's total number.

There were many reasons for the problems. Sometimes a foreign correspondent had been unable to adjust to life back in the United States. Often, as a reporter grew older, he lost the energy or the imagination that he'd once possessed. This can be a painful process, for reporting is primarily a young man's game, and yet there are not enough editorial or executive jobs for all those who want them as they grow older. Also, our standards were rising, and sometimes men were performing as well as they ever had, but weren't up to our new requirements.

I made a list of men I didn't think were performing adequately, and over the months I called them in for confidential talks. I told them I had no intention of firing anyone, but that they had no hope of advancement on the *Times*, so perhaps they would wish to seek other opportunities. I believe that without exception these men got good jobs elsewhere—for men with experience on the *Times* were in demand. And I think that by dealing candidly with these men I served their long-range interests, as well as those of the *Times*.

The other side of the story is that we were building a younger, better-paid, more capable staff. With Dryfoos' help, I began a system of merit raises, whereby editors down the line could recommend men for special attention. This policy had the desired result. When I became managing editor, we were losing too many capable people to the news magazines, radio and television, or public-relations jobs. By paying better salaries, and making it possible for talented young men to advance faster, we reversed that trend. I maintained that an editorial expenditure was not an expense, it was an investment— an investment in personal talent.

We tried, throughout the fifties and early sixties, to improve all elements of our news coverage. I was impressed by the way the news magazines had broken their coverage into departments and were providing detailed, expert analysis in each area. I thought we should do more of that, and increasingly we did. In Washington, we assigned the talented Anthony Lewis to cover law and the Supreme Court. I hired my fellow Mississippian, Craig Claiborne, as our food editor, and he was a success in that job and as a guide to New York restaurants.

We had for years treated obituaries as important news. A man's death was often an opportunity to look at his life as a whole, both the good and bad sides of the record. But we thought our obits could be even better—I sometimes said I wanted to "liven up the obits"—and we chose one of our copy editors, Alden Whitman, to do that job. Whitman was given status, a raise, and the authority to travel over the world gathering material for obituaries. The excellent job he has done is well known, and I think has improved standards of obituary writing in all newspapers.

During the fifties and sixties, we opened new bureaus, or expanded existing ones, in San Francisco, Detroit, Boston, Hollywood, Los Angeles, Chicago, Des Moines, Houston, and Atlanta and New Orleans. This expansion cost money but Sulzberger and I thought the "investment" would pay off.

One of my ideas was that as fresh figures appeared in the news we should carry sketches of them. As it was, we could cover such people in a few lines in a news story, or, at the other pole, in a full-length profile in the Sunday *Magazine*, but there was no way to cover them at length in between. I urged Lester Markel to run some profiles, but he chose to stay with the full-length treatment. Thus, with Ted Bernstein's initiative, we began the daily "Man in the News" columns. This format was not without its drawbacks. Some days, there would be no candidate of much interest in the news. Still, I think the feature added a desirable element of human interest to our coverage.

It was during my editorship that the *Times* began to carry news-analysis articles in the daily paper. To do so was a break with tradition and, as such, was not accomplished easily. The *Times* had always recognized a clear line between news and opinion, with the latter limited to the editorial page and the Sunday paper's *Magazine* and *Week in Review*. News analysis is, of course, neither pure news nor pure opinion but something in between, an attempt to explain and interpret the news. The danger is that the writer will go beyond analysis into editorializing.

Some members of our editorial-page staff, particularly John Oakes, opposed news analysis in the news columns. Oakes, who is Mrs. Sulzberger's cousin and a man deeply concerned with preserving tradition on the *Times*, believed that the news columns should be limited to "hard news," that is, they should give the "who, what, where, when," but not the "why" of the news. The editorial-page staff may also have felt that for the news department to begin news analysis was an invasion of their domain. Lester Markel, the Sunday editor, also at first resisted, primarily, I think, for jurisdictional reasons. But in time he agreed that changing times had made changes necessary in our presentation of the news and he wound up applauding our efforts at analysis and interpretation in the daily paper.

My own views had also changed. My background was that of a "hard news" man. I had not been an advocate of news analysis. Yet as political issues grew more complex and more personal to readers, and as politicians became more adept at distorting them, I increasingly saw the need for analysis of the news. Television was another important factor, for it increasingly gave people their hard news, while adding to their need for explanations.

Our first news analyses were written by two of our most qualified men, Scotty Reston and Russell Porter. Reston wrote on politics and Porter on economics. In order that their analysis pieces would be recognized as such, we used a new headline type with them, which we called the S-P head—for Scotty and Porter. This was later replaced by what we called a Q head. Sulzberger was not sure that even this head was warning enough for the reader, so we began the half-column insert saying "News Analysis," which left the reader no doubt as to what he was reading.

Once Reston and Porter began to write news analysis, it was only a matter of time until pressure from other talented reporters would force us to let them write it too. I did insist for some years that there be only one news-analysis piece per day. In recent years this rule has been relaxed, as perhaps it should have been.

My background as a political reporter made me particularly interested in improving the quality of our political coverage. I thought that, like our sports and financial writing, it tended to be too much for insiders. Our political writers tended to plunge too deeply into factional infighting, and our Capitol Hill reporters too often got hopelessly entangled in parliamentary maneuvers. I knew, for in my day I'd been among the worst offenders.

I wanted political stories written for the consumer—the reader, the taxpayer—not for the politicians. If a story told of a billion-dollar tax bill passing Congress, I wanted it explained up high that this meant five dollars or ten dollars or whatever for each taxpayer. I would ask: "What does this do to me?" Ten dollars out of his own pocket meant more to the reader than a billion out of the national budget. Too often Washington reporters insisted on describing every legislative action as a "victory for the President" or "a defeat for the President." I wanted to know if it was a victory or a defeat for our readers.

I tried to question all the assumptions of our political coverage. Were the traditional "scouting trips" before elections—those trips I'd so enjoyed—really the way to find out what the reader wanted to know? We tried sending teams of reporters. We began using computers on election night—thus attempting to satisfy the American lust for predictions.

One of the most nerve-racking nights of my life came on the night of the 1960 Presidential election, when I let the *Times* print a story virtually predicting Kennedy's election. The early returns showed Kennedy far ahead of Nixon, and our initial story, perhaps reflecting our own prediction as well as the returns, said Kennedy had won. The story was written by Scotty Reston, with several of us looking over his shoulder. Our eight-column headline said, KENNEDY ELECTED PRESIDENT. Had Nixon won, it would have ranked with the Chicago *Tribune*'s 1948 DEWEY WINS fiasco.

Around midnight, with the first edition on the street, the returns began to change, and it appeared that a Nixon victory was possible. By that time I was in a terrible condition—I found myself hoping that a certain Midwestern mayor would steal enough votes to pull Kennedy through. I could have had our lead rewritten, and softened, to reflect the new uncertainty. Instead, I made another decision of questionable wisdom. I stopped the presses. Other editors and I were convinced that final word of Kennedy's victory would come any minute. The minutes dragged on for two hours, with the newsdealers screaming for their papers. Finally, after two hours, we crawled back off the limb a bit, softened our prediction, and got some papers out. Our competitor, the *Herald Tribune*, had avoided the guessing games that night, and sold some additional papers as a result.

Our first two editions that evening made no predictions. Our third edition declared that Kennedy had "piled up such a spectacular lead in the states east of the Mississippi River" that "he seemed almost certain to be elected the thirty-fifth President of the United States."

Our fourth-edition story began with the declaration that Kennedy "was elected yesterday the thirty-fifth President of the United States." We held with that in our fifth edition. Then came the late returns, our uncertainty, and finally, in our "7 A.M. Extra" edition, a more cautious lead that said Kennedy "appeared to have won the election" as President.

The publisher then, Orvil Dryfoos, backed my decision, although he was pacing the newsroom floor as he awaited the returns. Bob Garst, then an assistant managing editor, gave the best advice that night. "Don't get ahead of the news," he warned, but we ignored his good advice. I heard that Arthur Hays Sulzberger was upset by what had happened, but his only comment to me, said very softly at lunch the next day, was "I think we should have gotten out some papers."

In my final years as editor, in the late 1960s, we began to have a new sort of problem in our political coverage. The war in Vietnam, growing racial tensions, and other factors had radicalized many talented young journalists. Some didn't want to work for the *Times*, with its demands of objective reporting, and some who did come to work for us often chafed at our requirements. They wanted a journalism of commitment, and resented those of us who seemed to hold them back. They were a new generation, and we editors could no longer take it for granted that they were devoted to the ideal of objectivity and impartiality.

We are all caught up in a time of political passion. Our newspapers have contributed to this intensity. We have reported in detail America's social explosions—the riots, the shoot-outs, the demonstrations but have we been so alert and so bold and so thorough in reporting the conditions that led to them?

A riot does not begin with an inflammatory speech by an "outside agitator." It begins years before in the decay of neighborhoods, in the deterioration of schooling and housing and medical services, in the inability of my generation to understand the yearnings and frustrations of the young. Among the rarely-reported causes of the social explosions we report is the indifference and shortsightedness of the middle-aged. To the extent that social conflicts arise because people are uninformed, responsibility lies uncomfortably close to our newsrooms.

I think our papers must continue to strive for objectivity and impartiality. But we must seek more than objectivity. We must have a new dimension to our journalism. We must give society a deeper, truer picture of itself. As an editor, I hoped we could harness the enthusiasm and commitment of our young reporters within the format of our newspaper. We cannot print news stories that hail the Black Panthers as heroes, but we can have stories that describe what they actually do, or that describe the social conditions that create black revolutionaries. I think that in the long run that sort of reporting will give newspaper readers a truer insight into the radical's cause.

Religion was another major area in which I hoped to improve our coverage. It seemed to me to be a growing force in American life in the postwar years. You saw this, at one level, in the success of evangelists like Billy Graham, and at another in the new social involvement and intellectual ferment among young clergymen. Yet, when I turned to our religious-news coverage to see these forces reflected, I was disappointed. I had hired our religious-news writer, a clergyman's son, when I was assistant managing editor, but he had fallen into the rut of covering institutional religion—sermons and conventions. We editors, of course, were partly to blame for his falling into the rut.

Our coverage was quite haphazard. We used to pay young reporters $5 to write a brief notice on a sermon. They went about this assignment with all due cynicism, usually sending for an advance copy of the sermon and never seeing the inside of a church or synagogue. Eventually, I ordered that we stop reporting routine sermons. There was a tremendous outcry from the clergy, but no corresponding outcry from our readers.

I wanted a more sophisticated coverage of religion as a social and intellectual force, but finding the right man to provide this was not easy. E. C. Daniel, Salisbury, and I talked to several leading theologians and one of them recommended John Cogley. Cogley was then fifty years of age, a scholar, a liberal Catholic who had written for *Commonweal* and was on the staff of the Center for the Study of Democratic Institutions. Part of our urgency in finding a new man was that the Vatican Council was forthcoming and we wanted first-rate coverage of it. We hired Cogley, at a high salary, and he did an excellent job. It happened that, because of a heart attack, he did not stay with us long, but in that time I believe he raised the standards of religious news writing on newspapers all over America.

Perhaps I should say a word about Sulzberger's attitude toward religion. Sulzberger was not a religious man. He was, however, Jewish by birth and that fact caused two problems. First, some of his fellow Jews thought they had a special "in" at the *Times*; second, Sulzberger was sometimes concerned that people would think the *Times* was a "Jewish newspaper."

I never realized until I became an editor of the *Times* how many factions there are among Jews. Sulzberger was caught in an endless crossfire between the Zionists and the anti-Zionists, the Orthodox and the Reformed, and various other factions. His main interest was to stay out of these religious wars, as we called them. Sulzberger himself was originally non-Zionist and would never go to Israel. I remember Ben-Gurion once saying to me, "I'll get Sulzberger yet."

One issue that did concern Sulzberger, and that kept recurring, was whether as a matter of style we should refer to "Jesus" or to "Christ." The point is that while everyone agrees there was a man named Jesus, not everyone agrees that he was "the Christ." Thus, it was our style to refer, whenever possible, to Jesus, and to speak of Christ only in direct quotes or in the clear context of the Christian religion. That was our style, but "Christs" often slipped through, and I would usually hear about them in a blue note from Sulzberger, who knew he would soon be hearing from the Jewish community about them.

As far as our staff was concerned, we tried to keep religion from being any consideration, but it inevitably was in people's minds. When I first joined the *Times*, it was widely believed that Ochs would never have a Jew as managing editor or editor of the editorial page. When I became assistant managing editor, our bullpen was largely Catholic, and there had been criticism that our news coverage had been affected by that fact. When I began to put new men in the bullpen, it happened that my first appointees were Jewish. "Let's don't go from a Catholic bullpen to a Jewish bullpen," Sulzberger told me. Another time he commented on the high proportion of Jewish by-lines, but for the most part we gave no thought to the matter.

I tried never to let religion be a factor in my personnel decisions. I sometimes thought that some of our Jewish editors preferred to work with other Jews. I suppose that some of our Southern editors preferred to work with other Southerners. That is only human, but I think most of us judged a man by his professional ability and not by his religion or lack of it. In following that principle, it was inevitable that we'd hire a considerable number of Jews in our community of New York.

I do recall one instance when the religious issue arose. Arthur Krock sent a man he knew to see Fred Meinholtz, the head of our communications department, about a job. Fred, a big, gruff-spoken German, asked the man if he was a Jew. The man said he was. "Then I can't hire you," Fred declared.

The man reported this back to Krock, who called me in justifiable outrage. I called Fred in and asked him what he'd told the man.

"I told him I couldn't hire him because he was a Jew," Fred said candidly.

"Good God, Fred," I said, "that's contrary to our policy and it's also against the law. You may wind up in jail."

"Well, what am I supposed to do?" Fred moaned. "I'm looking for a man to work the Jewish holidays."

When I became managing editor, our sports department seemed to me to be in a state of stagnation, to epitomize the worst of the "do-it-today-like-you-did-it-yesterday" attitude at the *Times*. With a few notable exceptions, the writing was sloppy and ingrown, chock-full of clichés and belabored literary allusions. This was at a time when television was interesting millions of Americans in sports for the first time, including many women, but our sportswriters always assumed that the readers knew their special slang and their references to sports heroes of the past. Much of the appeal of sports is the appeal of the nostalgic past, and our sports department was awash with sentimentality.

I recall that one day I was watching a baseball game on television and was intrigued to see one of the New York batboys leap into the arms of a Detroit player after the visitor hit a home run. At our news conference, later that afternoon, I asked our sports editor what happened. He didn't know and, until I pressed him, wasn't much interested in finding out. But eventually we learned the story. Normally, the home team supplies the batboys, but this day not all the New York batboys had shown up. It happened that the Detroit catcher's son was traveling with the team, so he had been suited out in a New York batboy's uniform, and when his father hit the home run, it was quite natural for him to leap joyously into his arms.

It was a nice little story, but one we'd have missed if our sports department had had its way.

I wanted crisper, more imaginative, more informative sports writing, and I decided I would have to have a new sports editor to attain it. I wanted to promote someone from within the department, and in time I decided that James Roach, who was then covering racing for us, was the man for the job. Jim was a good reporter and a fine writer. I made him assistant sports editor and, after a year, editor, the former sports editor having agreed to retire. I was able to make this shift, and several others, because Sulzberger and Dryfoos were willing to make retirement quite attractive financially to certain editors I thought were blocking progress and should be replaced. That is, they were willing to pay men higher-than-ordinary retirement benefits, or in some cases to allow men to retire before they reached the official age for retirement.

Under Roach, our sports pages soon began to have new ideas, better writing, and broader coverage. Some of our best writers started out in the sports department. The changes were not easy, and some of the old-timers in the department doubtless resented them, but the result was to turn one of our weakest departments into one of our strongest.

Jim Roach was only one of several dozen talented men I discovered within the organization and tried to make full use of. Tom Mullaney of our financial and business news department was another. Tom had studied financial affairs in college with the intent of becoming a journalist who specialized in that field. I found him to be one of those dependable, well-informed men who always have answers for any question you put to them. In the summer of 1962, when we were about to begin our West Coast edition, I told Dryfoos I thought Mullaney was the man to be its editor. I had two reasons for wanting the appointment. First, I knew Tom would do a fine job. Second, the training would prepare him for bigger assignments in the future.

Tom was then serving as assistant financial and business news editor, and I knew he aspired to the editor's post when it became vacant, and thus might be fearful of going to California. So I took Tom to breakfast one morning and made him my offer: if he would agree to be editor of the West Coast edition, and the job of financial-business editor became available, I would give him his choice of staying on the West Coast or returning for the editor's job. He readily agreed to do this. When the financial-business editor's job did open up, Tom chose to return and take it.

Both Tom and his predecessor, Jack Forrest, a witty little Scotchman, did a lot to improve the writing on our financial pages. When I came to New York, our financial writing was such gobbledegook that I didn't think even Wall Streeters could understand it. Once in the forties I attended an American Press Institute seminar at which someone criticized our financial writing, and I was astounded and embarrassed to hear one of our senior editors reply that our financial page wasn't written for the average reader. I didn't say anything then, but I made up my mind that I'd try to change that policy, if indeed it was a policy. After all, most people who invest in the stock market are average people, including a lot of women. In the early fifties, when I began my effort to improve the writing on the *Times*,

I stressed the financial-business section, on the theory that if we could make their stories understandable, we could make anything understandable.

There were many others I came to rely upon. Lewis Jordan, our news editor, was a man almost obsessed with the quality of our paper—it had to be the best, and his efforts helped make it so. In the bullpen, which had been such a source of difficulty when I first came to New York, I had as assistant news editors men like Larry Hauck, Robert Crandall, and Tom Daffron—and I could sleep well at night confident that if troubles arose they would handle them capably or would call me if necessary. Richard Burritt, who had the title of assistant to the managing editor, had the thankless job of dealing with the Guild on a day-to-day basis and handling personnel matters for me. Emanuel Freedman, our foreign news editor, had the difficult task of dealing with our most touchy, most independent-minded writers.

Men like these are the heart of a newspaper. The public may not hear much about them, but no paper could exist without them. I did all I could to seek them out and to see that they were well treated and content. I sometimes compare them to the linemen of a football team—they don't run with the ball but they open up holes in the opposing line so the backs can get through, and most important of all, they cover the fumbles. If you took them out, the whole team would collapse.

Once the Supreme Court issued its 1954 school-desegregation decision, it was clear that race relations would be one of the great continuing stories during my years as editor. I once told Sulzberger that the unfolding race-relations drama was the biggest sociological story in American history, and I wanted to see it reported as such. Even before the Supreme Court decision, I wanted to see us write more about race relations, and also to employ Negro reporters. While I was still assistant managing editor, in the late forties, I persuaded Jimmy James to hire our first Negro reporter. However, the man we hired, who had been working for a labor newspaper, found it almost impossible to be objective when covering stories involving race. Once he admitted to me he'd invented some quotes for A. Philip Randolph, because he was sure he knew what Randolph meant to say, whether or not he said it. After several incidents, we had to let him go. Finding qualified Negro reporters in those days was almost impossible. When a young Negro named Lahymond Robinson showed promise, we arranged for him to work part time while he finished college, then join our staff. By the middle and late sixties we were able to hire a number of talented young black reporters, although keeping them was always hard, because the demand for them had become great.

Sulzberger was sensitive to this issue and urged me to find qualified Negro reporters. After we'd hired them, there was the question of whether they'd be assigned mainly to race-related stories. We tried to avoid that. One morning Sulzberger sent me a blue note saying he'd seen Lahymond Robinson's by-line on a race-related story and asking why this had been done. We tried to keep in mind the pressures our Negro reporters worked under. Often they had trouble getting hotel accommodations, or service in restaurants, or being seated at public dinners, both in the North and South. Once I offered one of our most talented Negro reporters the job of chief of our Albany bureau. He told me candidly that he and his family were settled in a mostly-white suburb of New York, they and their children were accepted there, and they just couldn't bring themselves to pick up and start over again in another city.

In the early fifties, before the Supreme Court's school decision, I persuaded James to name our first full-time correspondent in the South. The man we sent was Virginia-born John Popham. He made Chattanooga the base for his far-flung travels, and he was later hired by the Chattanooga *Times*, and became its managing editor. Later, a series of fine reporters covered the South for us, and special correspondents were sent South to help on big stories. During the riots at the University of Alabama in the fall of 1956, I wanted to send a reporter who knew the college and town but would remain objective; my choice was a young reporter who was from New Jersey but had attended the University of Alabama, Gay Talese.

Being a Southerner, loving the South, and knowing all too well its sins against the Negroes, I think I had a special feeling for, and concern about, the unfolding racial drama. Yet I tried to keep my own emotions out of our coverage and out of my own performance as editor. The editorial page expressed the *Times'* views about race relations; my job was to see that we had the best possible coverage of the race story in the South, and later in the North.

I admit I was overly optimistic in the first weeks after the Supreme Court decision. All was quiet for a while, and I thought the South might accept the desegregation of schools and public facilities peaceably. With Orvil Dryfoos' approval I sent a team of reporters to investigate the Southern mood. Their findings were also optimistic, and we printed a story reflecting that optimistic view.

We had underestimated the resistance of the average Southerner to integration, and the capacity of Southern politicians to stir those deeply-held prejudices and fears.

In trying to be unemotional about events in the South, the acid test came with the news in 1964 about the murder of three civil-rights workers in Neshoba County, near my home town. As that story unfolded—the three men disappeared, then their bodies were found, and later there were arrests—we sent several reporters to cover it. I would usually talk to the reporters before they left and after they returned I would want to know all I could about how my little home town was responding to this tragedy.

But our reporters told me that my friends and my relatives, although greeting them politely, would rarely discuss the murders with them. They closed ranks against outsiders. Worse, within the community few voices were raised to condemn the murders. The "good people" of the community were intimidated. They feared both physical violence and economic retaliation if they denounced the murders or the Klan, which was responsible for the murders. A friend in Philadelphia wrote me a long troubled letter several months after the murders, describing the atmosphere there. The local attitude, she said, was to cry "hoax" when the three civil-rights workers were said to be missing, and then "they asked for it," after their bodies were found. As newsmen flocked to the town, it came to see itself (not the dead men) as the "victim" of the affair, and to blame the news media for once again lying about the South. I was told that some of my old friends thought I had let the town down because of the *Times'* extensive coverage of the murders. But I felt the town had let me down. Or perhaps I had just expected too much.

Our society coverage was another of my concerns. I wanted to see it broadened, so that instead of concentrating on the doings of the rich and glamorous it was concerned with women's news in general. Women, after all, make up half our readers, and half the world, yet when I joined the *Times* they were rarely heard of on our pages, unless they were among the Four Hundred.

Even as we enlivened and expanded our "news" approach to society coverage, the fact remained that a considerable amount of our space was given over to engagement and wedding announcements. These things are a terrible nuisance to editors. There are no exact standards to judge which girl's engagement or wedding is worthy of announcement in our pages, yet decisions must be made. We print only about 15 percent of the announcements submitted, and the pressures are often fierce. Still, from a news standpoint, people want to read about engagements and weddings, especially of their friends and acquaintances, so they're here to stay. I ordered the first Negro society item into the paper, with picture, in the early 1950s.

I have learned over the years that a newspaper must be extremely careful in checking out all such announcements. Sometimes people will call in the engagement of two people who hate each other, as a practical joke. Also, young women have been known to announce their engagements prematurely, as a means of nailing reluctant suitors.

One of our first steps toward broader women's coverage came toward the close of the Second World War when Mrs. Sulzberger insisted that we begin a food column. Jimmy James told the story of how she pulled him off to one side at a party at her estate and hounded him until he agreed to a food column. Slowly, we began to expand into what we called the Four F's—Food, Fashion, Furnishing, Family. Mrs. Sulzberger was highly interested in this trend, although her interest did not always make things easy.

The main instrument of the *Times'* new look at society and women's news was to be a talented young woman named Charlotte Curtis. Charlotte sometimes said that Clifton Daniel invented her, which was largely true, but I think her career also reflected a desire that many of us came to have for a fresh look at women's news.

Charlotte had been working as a reporter in the women's news department and wasn't happy there. She wanted to switch to general assignments under the city desk, but Daniel had the excellent idea of putting her on "society" coverage. He gave her a mandate, which suited her own instincts, that society should not be covered with wide-eyed awe, but with the same objectivity and skepticism and even humor that would apply to any news story. The idea that society should be covered "straight" was a sensation and Charlotte was an overnight success. Her writing was bright and witty and, at its best, had a sociological dimension. The more intelligent society people appreciated that they were being treated intelligently, not like children who have to be flattered and protected. Charlotte became something of a celebrity herself, and went on to become our women's news editor.

Miss Curtis' talents were much admired by the Sulzberger family, although occasionally her new approaches to women's news caused problems. This happened once or twice when someone in the publisher's family felt that their friends had been written about too

lightly. And there was another sort of problem that often arose. The
Sulzbergers are, in the style of life and their tastes, conservative
people. They do not hang pictures of soup cans on their walls, or
buy plastic furniture, or wear Mod suits or extreme mini-skirts, or
enjoy books with excessive profanity or plays in which people go
naked. Thus, they were frequently displeased as, throughout the
fifties and sixties, our coverage of fashions, furnishings, and the arts
increasingly publicized styles and trends which they found distasteful.

There was one conversation I must have had with Mrs. Sulzberger a hundred times. She would refer to a picture of a drawing
room with its period furniture and lovely antiques, and she would
say, "Turner, why don't you do a story on a pretty room like this?"

"Mrs. Sulzberger," I would reply, "it's not news."

"Oh, but it is," she would insist.

I never enjoyed disagreeing with Mrs. Sulzberger, although my
job sometimes forced me to do so. She is a charming, very feminine
woman, a woman you instinctively love and want to please. She is
also a woman of substance, one with a deep concern about social
issues and the *Times* treatment of them. I can remember Arthur
Hays Sulzberger confiding to me in 1956 that he was having "a
hell of a time" with his wife, because she favored Adlai Stevenson
for the Presidency and he preferred Eisenhower. On that issue, his
wishes prevailed, but on many others her impact on the paper was
considerable.

She had a maternalistic feeling toward the *Times*, and for good
reason. Since her father bought the paper in 1896, it has had four
publishers—her father, her husband, her son-in-law, and her son.
Thus, beyond her personal charm and intelligence, she occupies a
special role as an embodiment of continuity at the *Times*.

For more than sixty years, the *Times* has been her overriding
concern. Her father taught her to keep an eye out for news stories,
and she passed on countless ideas to me and others. Sometimes that
could be a problem, for her most casual remark would be treated as
a command by some editors and reporters. I recall Jimmy James
saying to her once, "Little lady, you don't know the power of your
own words."

She had a great interest in community affairs. The city parks
were a special concern of hers, and sometimes when she would urge
more stories about parks and I would suggest that we had exhausted
the subject, she would insist, "But, Turner, parks are news!" She
was approached by a great many civic and charitable organizations,

which wanted her to serve on their boards or steering committees, and it rarely occurred to her that they were trying to use her to get publicity. But, whenever she accepted some title or chairmanship, we would soon hear from the group's publicity director. I did what I could over the years to discourage the Sulzberger family from such involvements, although the newspaper publisher has never lived who didn't have special interests and use his paper to advance them.

Her strictly traditionalist tastes inspired many exchanges between us. I never really convinced her that a Duncan Phyfe chair is not news, but one made of plastic is. I had many notes from her over the years, in which she expressed her opinions in a good-natured but candid manner. One typical note came a few years ago after we'd carried a picture spread on the somewhat bizarre decorations in the home of a Philadelphia doctor. Mrs. Sulzberger said:

> Turner:
>
> If Exhibit A—the home furnishings pages from today's *Times Magazine*—means that we had to go all the way to Philadelphia to find such a tasteless and ugly home, then it is good news.

I replied:

> Dear Mrs. Sulzberger:
>
> I have your note about our take-out on the ——'s Philadelphia town house in last Sunday's Magazine. I am very sorry you didn't like it. This is an old house which was given a new type of treatment, and I had entertained the hope that you might approve of the piece as an illustration of what some people do with buildings of this sort.
>
> Thank you, nonetheless, for your note.
>
> Affectionately,
> Turner Catledge.

Punch Sulzberger is very much his mother's son where furnishings are concerned, as this memo from him suggests:

> Turner:
>
> When you talk with Charlotte on Monday, I wish you would tell her that I have had it when it comes to this absolutely way-out crazy furniture that we have been showing in our Magazine. Frankly, if [the home-furnishings editor] has no more sense that what she has displayed in Sunday's Magazine, I would suggest that you replace her with someone who has more traditional taste. I would be happy to help with the selection.
>
> Punch.

These exchanges, like all my exchanges with the Sulzbergers, were carried out with good humor and full respect for the other's opinions. Mrs. Sulzberger found a good deal that she liked in the *Times*, as well as things she didn't like. In 1967 she sent her son a note that said:

Dear Punch:

In all the notes and letters I have been sending you I forgot to tell you that I think our daily coverage of home decorations is good. Today is an example of a particularly good article on what people buy.

I.O.S.

Punch sent this note on to me, and wrote across it: "Wonders never cease."

A more serious exchange took place in the mid-sixties when Mrs. Sulzberger sent her son Punch, then the publisher, an irate note suggesting that our women's-page writers had been taking a "What's wrong with Society?" attitude.

I was disturbed by her note. I felt that, while Mrs. Sulzberger might have had cause to be unhappy with a particular article, her note had made general comments that were unfair to the various writers and editors involved. I therefore felt a responsibility to send a memo to Punch which stated my own view on the issues that his mother had raised. It said in part:

Particularly as to the work of Charlotte Curtis: Miss Curtis doesn't, in my opinion, take a "what's wrong with society?" attitude. On the contrary, she thinks that society is interesting and influential, although she is obviously amused by its foibles, as many of her readers also seem to be. Some people probably imagine that Miss Curtis's work in the society field is offensive to the people she writes about. I think this is far from the fact. I have yet to see a letter of complaint from a single person about whom she has written in these pieces. I have had numerous telephone calls in praise of her work by people about whom she has written. She becomes lastingly friendly with many of the people she writes about. . . .

Let me point out in passing that Miss Curtis has been sought after by a number of other publications who want to exploit exactly what she was doing for the New York Times up to the time she became women's editor.

The Times offers no hospitality for stories that are snide and deliberately hold respectable people to ridicule. One may get by occasionally, but that's the penalty—or the luxury—of having a big organization of sensitive and clever people.

XIX

The Eastland Investigation

IN 1955, Sulzberger, I, and other executives of the *Times* faced one of the hardest issues ever to confront the newspaper. A Senate Internal Security Subcommittee, headed by Senator James Eastland of Mississippi, began public hearings into the alleged influence of Communists on American newspapers. The investigation centered on the *New York Times*. Of thirty-eight witnesses asked about present or past Communist affiliation, twenty-five were from the *Times*. Sixteen of these held positions in the news or editorial departments, and six of these admitted having been Communist party members at some time in the past.

The hearings patently were politically inspired. Eastland, a segregationist and a reactionary, was using his investigative power to try to smear the nation's leading liberal newspaper. But that was not the real issue to us at the *Times*. We could withstand Eastland's attacks. The harder questions related to our internal relationships on the *Times*—to the element of trust and respect that had to exist among the publisher, his editors, and the reporting staff if the paper was to function.

What was to be our policy toward employees who had once been Communists before they came to the *Times*? Toward employees who refused to discuss their politics with us? To employees who pleaded the Fifth Amendment when summoned before the Eastland subcommittee? Toward employees whose testimony caused contempt-of-Congress charges to be brought against them?

I might say that these questions caused little difficulty at most other newspapers whose reporters were shown to have had Communist ties. At other papers, almost without exception, such reporters were fired summarily. Such a policy was expedient at the time, with the passions of McCarthyism still running strong. But we at the *Times* believed we had an obligation to our employees, to our own consciences, and ultimately to the court of history, to conduct ourselves in a fairer and more rational manner.

Our policy was not reached easily. On the contrary, it was arrived at only after months of intense debate and after the most anguished deliberation by the publisher. Sulzberger was being pulled in opposite directions by two of his deepest instincts. On the one hand was his deep personal abhorrence of Communism; on the other was his protective and paternal feeling toward employees of the *Times*.

It would be impossible for me to overstate what a high standard of honesty and objectivity Sulzberger expected of his reporters. He was acutely aware of the trust that millions of people put in the *Times*, and he expected every reporter to live up to that trust, just as he himself tried determinedly to do. In 1950 Sulzberger wrote a poem for his son Punch which indicates the depth of his concern. At one point, Sulzberger declared:

> The careless doctor may poison and kill a patient.
> The careless newspaperman has the power
> To poison the minds of vast multitudes.

The poem concluded, speaking of the role of the newspaperman:

> He is one of the chosen Knights of Democracy.
> He is one of those who will gird our country
> With the knowledge that will make and keep it strong.
> No matter where the struggle may lie
> He is a combat soldier battling for the Lord.

Given these passionate beliefs, it is easy to understand that Sulzberger's first impulse was to fire newspapermen who had been Communists and who now refused to cooperate with us or with the Congressional investigators. Still, there were those of us with access to Sulzberger, including Scotty Reston, John Oakes and me, and the *Times*' lawyer, Louis Loeb, who believed that no rigid rules should apply, that each case must be judged on its own merits, and that we must be guided by understanding and compassion. There was to be a long battle between Sulzberger's anti-Communism and his basic decency and fairness.

Louis Loeb and I were Sulzberger's leading advisers on the issue. We worked on the problem day and night. I believed that a *Times* employee, like any other American citizen, should be free to exercise any constitutional right, including the Fifth Amendment protection against self-incrimination. Such action does not provide a final presumption of guilt or deserve punitive reprisals. At the same time, when our employees were named as former Communists, they had an obligation to give the *Times* management a full, candid accounting of their political histories. Only by so doing could they maintain the trust and confidence both of management and their fellow workers that were essential if our newspaper was to function effectively on the course we had set.

Sulzberger and I were not in total agreement at the outset, but eventually he accepted the position that Fifth Amendment pleaders should not be fired for exercising their constitutional rights. I think that Sulzberger's behavior in this crisis was one of his finest hours. The story of that crisis begins with a pathetic individual named Harvey Matusow, a man whose career was all too symbolic of the national sickness we call McCarthyism. Matusow was born in the Bronx in 1926 of Russian-born parents. In 1944, after graduating from high school, he entered the U.S. Army, and it was while serving in Europe in 1945-46 that he first became interested in Communism. After returning to New York late in 1946, he was active for several years in Communist party affairs. For a time he was a full-time telephone operator at the Communist party's headquarters on East Twelfth Street. In 1950, however, he fell from favor with party officials, and he offered his services to the FBI as an informer. He functioned as an FBI informer for about six months. Then, early in 1951, he was expelled from the party and also was called into active duty in the Air Force reserve.

In August of that year he was a psychiatric patient at the base hospital at the Wright-Patterson Air Force Base, Dayton, Ohio. While in the hospital, Matusow read newspaper stories about the testimony of FBI informers and perhaps began to imagine himself as a national figure, writing and lecturing as an ex-Communist. He went to the base chaplain and asked permission to deliver anti-Communist talks to youth groups. The chaplain referred him to the base public-information officer, at whose suggestion Matusow wrote a seventy-one-page account of all he knew about the Communist party.

Matusow was again a psychiatric patient in the base hospital from October 1 to 12, 1951. In November he appeared before the House Committee on Un-American Activities, and in December he was released from the Air Force and became an employee of the Ohio Un-American Activities Commission.

It was on October 8, 1952, that he made his first charges against the *New York Times.* The Senate Internal Security Subcommittee called him to Salt Lake City, where it was investigating the International Union of Mine, Mill and Smelter Workers. In response to the question, "Have you attended Communist party schools in which instruction was given with respect to infiltration of labor unions?" Matusow replied:

"For instance, the American Newspaper Guild, of which I am a member now, might be an illustration. In 1950 I attended Communist party meetings, caucuses, in the Newspaper Guild in New York. It has a large membership and is not a Communist-dominated union, but in New York City today there are approximately 500 dues-paying Communists working in the newspaper industry.

"The *New York Times* has well over one hundred dues-paying members. Time, Inc., has seventy-six Communist party members working in editorial and research. . . ."

The wire service covering this hearing ignored Matusow and his charges. Two weeks later he spoke at the high school in Great Falls, Montana, under the auspices of the local American Legion, and he was quoted in the local paper as having said: "The Sunday section of the *New York Times* alone has 126 dues-paying Communists. On the editorial and research staffs of *Time* and *Life* are seventy-six hard-core Reds. The New York bureau of the Associated Press has twenty-five."

His charges circulated in the anti-Communist underground. Eventually they reached Sulzberger, who was sufficiently concerned to get in touch with an official of the U.S. Department of Justice, who assured him he had no information whatever indicating Communist influence on the *Times.* The charges did not die, however. On January 14, 1953, they made their way into Walter Winchell's column. This led Sulzberger to send General Adler to see J. Edgar Hoover, director of the FBI, who said he had no information to support Matusow's charges, and added that Matusow was a generally unreliable character. Later, Hoover suggested that the *Times* contact Matusow directly. We attempted to do this, by letter, in May of 1953, but Matusow could not be found.

On September 15, 1953, the Matusow charges surfaced dramatically at an unexpected place—a meeting of the Sales Executives Club at the Waldorf-Astoria Hotel. Robert R. Young, then chairman of the board of the Chesapeake and Ohio Railway Company, was speaking on the subject of high taxes, and declared:

"Suppose we organized ourselves and all began to ask in our advertising, if 100 percent taxation is Communism, just what is 92 percent taxation? There are many different and effective ways to ask that question. . . . Instead we allow our advertising patronage to go by default into the hands of those who feel differently about our System than we do. . . .

"I got from Senate testimony that there are at least 500 dues-paying Communists on New York City papers. The *New York Times* has over 100 dues-paying members and *Time* magazine has seventy-six. . . ."

I wrote Young asking for the basis of his remarks. He replied:

I quoted directly from a report of the Senate Internal Security Subcommittee hearings of October 8, 1952, covering testimony taken under oath.

On further investigation I have found that the witness whose testimony I quoted in this instance may be unreliable.

Unfortunately those in a position to know such things obviously are not reliable. That, of course, was the argument the defenders of Hiss used against the testimony of Chambers.

It is disconcerting that I never saw in the Times a report or refutation of this sworn testimony.

I later met with Young at a lunch arranged by Thomas J. Deegan, Jr. He steadfastly refused to admit that he had been wrong to repeat Matusow's charges.

It happened that ten days after Young's speech we at the *Times* finally made contact with Matusow. On September 25, he called from Reno, Nevada, and demanded to talk to an executive. He spoke of being bothered by his conscience and wanting to change his story about the *Times*.

We arranged for Matusow to go to Los Angeles to be interviewed by our correspondent there, Gladwin Hill. When Hill pressed Matusow to tell him what specific Communists he knew on the *Times*, Matusow named two commercial-department employees whom he had met at Guild meetings, a news-department clerk who had been fired, not for being a Communist but for failing to perform his duties, and two writers who had never been employed by the *Times*. When Hill asked how Matusow had arrived at the figure of 126 Communists on the *Times*, the ex-Communist said this was "essentially an unverified estimate based on impressions I received" as a member of the Newspaper Guild in New York.

Matusow's admissions to Hill were incorporated in a sworn affidavit. With this in hand, Sulzberger on September 30 sent a letter to members of the Sales Executives Club which concluded:

> The statements are untrue and the witness who made this statement had repudiated it voluntarily and under oath.
>
> I write you not because of any thought that you may give credence to the charges but because of my deep concern of the fact that they were repeated by a man of Mr. Young's reputation before such an audience. Our record here at the Times is made every day and we are proud to stand on it.

With that, we thought the Matusow episode was closed. We were wrong.

Matusow was called before the Eastland subcommittee in February and March of 1955 and examined at length about the affidavit he had given us. The fact that Matusow could name only one alleged Communist in the *Times* news department, the clerk who had been fired, was awkward to the subcommittee's counsel, J. G. Sourwine, who preferred Matusow's earlier statement that there were 126 card-carrying Communists on our staff. Thus, the subcommittee's "Report on the Significance of the Matusow Case," issued April 6, 1955, ignored the informer's sworn recantation and relied on his earlier allegations. The subcommittee was not about to let the facts spoil a good witchhunt.

While the subcommittee was readying itself for its move against the *Times*, we learned that one of our Washington reporters had at one time belonged to the Communist party. (I will not use the reporter's name, or the names of the others described in this narrative. In most cases they are matters of record, but I see no reason to repeat them here.) On September 27, 1954, Walter Winchell's column stated: "A former editor of the Red *Daily Worker* in New York has named a *New York Times* reporter as a Communist—still covering Washington and Senator McCarthy."

The reporter in question went to Scotty Reston, head of our Washington bureau, and told his story. In 1937 he had been a young reporter on the *Long Island Press* at the time its staff went on strike. A dozen of his fellow reporters were Communists and they urged him to join the party. They stressed its progressive program, its opposition to Fascism and its panaceas for war and poverty. He joined but was soon disillusioned and left the party. He joined the *Times* in 1947, nine years after rejecting Communism.

If that had been all there was to the reporter's story, his would not have been a difficult case, given our high regard for him as a reporter and as a man. The complicating factor was that Winchell's charge—"still covering Washington and Senator McCarthy"—was partly true. This reporter had for some months been assigned to the "security beat." Unknowingly, we had assigned an ex-Communist to report on investigations into Communism. This put the *Times* in an awkward position.

Reston sent us a full report. He had assigned this reporter the previous November to present full, thoughtful coverage of the entire McCarthy phenomenon. Reston added, in his report: "At that time, the *Times* itself was under organized attack, and I said to him that we could not assume that McCarthy would not try to investigate the *Times,* and subpoena the man on the beat. Therefore, I urged the greatest care in preparing for the assignment, in writing his copy and keeping careful records."

After a few months on the security beat, the reporter told Reston he'd prefer another assignment. Apparently, he feared his name might come up in investigations. He should, of course, have refused the assignment in the first place, and his failure to do so disturbed Reston.

"I do not think he was fair to the paper or to me or to his other colleagues in the bureau," Reston wrote. "If I had responsibility for other sections of The Times, where no political material was handled, I would not feel that this record had destroyed his usefulness to the paper. To fire him outright would seem to me to be too utterly drastic, and an unnecessary cruelty not only to him but to his wife and three children. But I am clear that he has forfeited the confidence of this bureau and cannot continue to do the kind of work expected of him here."

Sulzberger and I agreed that the reporter should be reassigned to the New York office, to handle nonpolitical assignments under the city desk. I explained the situation to the city editor, Frank Adams, who was anxious to do whatever he could to help. I reported back to Sulzberger:

> I want to assure you we will do everything within our power to make this as smooth as possible. Unfortunately, of course, we are not dealing with an ideal, or even simple, situation; we are dealing with unpleasant alternatives.
>
> Furthermore, the subject is very sensitive and the case itself perhaps may get "hot." We must look forward to the possibility of publication of these moves, either correctly or distortedly, in gossip columns.

But I agree with you that it is something we must face and work out to the greatest good, or at least the least harm, to the man and to The New York Times.

The matter ended there. The reporter was restricted to noncontroversial assignments for a time, but eventually became one of our top political reporters. His subsequent career fully justified the faith we placed in him.

Other executives and I were highly gratified that Sulzberger had agreed to this course of action. I sent Sulzberger a note saying, "It is a rare experience in a lifetime to be associated with someone like you." Frank Adams told the publisher: "For nearly thirty years I have been proud of being a *Times* man, but never quite so much as today."

We knew the decision had not been easy for Sulzberger. One of the strongest pressures in the other direction came from General Adler, who took a hard-line view toward the former Communists, and who, from his office opposite Sulzberger's on the fourteenth floor, was not timid about expressing his view. General Adler often used military analogies, and once he told me, with reference to the ex-Communists, that if he had a fellow with him in the trenches whose Americanism was in doubt he'd know how to handle him. Another time he told me that he had no patience with anyone who didn't choose his way of life. I said, "General Adler, I would like to choose your way of life, but I can't, and most people can't." After Sulzberger made his decision on the handling of the Washington reporter, he noted General Adler's disagreement in a memo which said: "In case it proves to be the wrong course, I think it is only fair to include in the file a statement that had the other end of the fourteenth floor been the deciding vote in the matter, the decision would probably have been different."

I was pleased with the resolution of this case, but in retrospect I see what a relatively easy case it was. The reporter had been a Communist only briefly. There was no question about his objectivity as a reporter. He cooperated with us fully and was willing to cooperate with the FBI and the Eastland subcommittee, as he later did. The harder cases were still ahead of us.

On June 29, 1955, the Eastland subcommittee opened an investigation into the influence of Communism in the news media. Its star witness that day was an ex-Communist who told, among other things, about his role in a Communist cell at the Brooklyn *Eagle* in the 1930s. He named some twenty persons he said belonged to that cell; two of them were men who had later joined the news staff of the *New York Times*. His allegations, added to those of Matusow, set the stage for an all-out investigation of the *Times*.

Before and during that investigation, Louis Loeb and I interviewed all but two of the former Communists in long sessions in my office. When one would come to see me, I would ask him to encourage others to talk to me. I stressed that we intended no punitive action. On the contrary, we wanted to know the facts, so that we and the employees could prepare for the expected onslaught from the Eastland subcommittee.

I found that most of these men were willing, even anxious to talk about their pasts. They had lived with their secrets for a decade or more, and now they wanted to get them off their chests. Most were looking for support, for sympathy, for consolation, even to purge themselves of feelings of guilt. Most, too, were highly concerned about protecting the *Times*.

These interviews were often emotional, sometimes painful, yet they were not without their lighter moments. One man, declaring his political innocence, pulled out a card proving him a member of the Republican party—he was the only card-carrying Republican I ever met. Another man told me he didn't know if he'd been a Communist; he said he'd stayed drunk for a year or two and he might have joined anything.

Often the way a man conducted himself in the talks with me and Loeb determined how we dealt with him. Sulzberger, throughout 1955, was still uncertain how we should handle employees who took the Fifth Amendment, but we were all agreed that we could not retain and support employees who refused to cooperate with us. All three of the former Communists we fired during this period (two were fired outright; one resigned under pressure) were men who chose not to cooperate with us.

One of those fired was the number-two man on the financial copy desk. This man learned that his name had been mentioned in the investigation, and he came to see me. He said that during his two years with the *Times* he had not been affiliated with the Communist party. He would not comment beyond that. I told him that his attitude made it difficult for us to retain him as an employee. I said I thought we were entitled to know whether he had been a member of the Communist party, when, and why he had ceased to be. He refused to cooperate and we asked for his resignation. He did not agree to resign, and several days later, just before he was to appear before the subcommittee, under subpoena, he and his lawyer met with Loeb and me again. This time, the copy editor told us he'd been a member of the Communist party prior to 1942, but refused to discuss the matter further.

Before the subcommittee on July 13, he invoked his Fifth Amendment privilege against self-incrimination. Sulzberger sent a telegram firing the man before he had completed his day's testimony. Sulzberger stressed that the dismissal was the result of the man's entire course of conduct, not just his use of the Fifth Amendment, but obviously the latter was an important factor. I fully agreed with Sulzberger's decision. It was clear to me after talking to the man that, if he was no longer a member of the party, he was still emotionally and intellectually involved with Communism, and he had no business handling copy for our financial page. The man took his discharge to the Newspaper Guild, but the Guild eventually dropped the case.

During the hearings in January of 1956, two more of our employees invoked the Fifth Amendment, a copy editor on the foreign desk and an assistant book-review editor. Both men were uncooperative with me and Loeb, and both were fired by Sulzberger. Once the assistant book editor's Communist affiliations came to light we checked back and found that he'd let his politics influence his selections of reviewers for books on politics and economics.

These three men chose not to cooperate with us; a larger number of the former Communists did cooperate, and received our support. A young copy editor told us of his past Communist involvements but challenged the subcommittee's inquiries into his political beliefs as a violation of his rights under the First Amendment. He was cited for contempt of Congress, fought his case in the courts, and won. Throughout the litigation he remained on our staff, meanwhile becoming a well-known writer and critic of folk music.

Another copy editor chose to inform us fully about his membership in the Communist party in 1935-49. When he went before the Eastland subcommittee he answered questions about his own political involvement, but refused to name other Communists on the ground that the subcommittee's inquiry was a violation of the First Amendment. He too was cited for contempt, but his position was eventually upheld by the Supreme Court. He later switched from copy editing to reporting and remains today a valued member of our staff.

In another case, a deskman in the Sunday department told the subcommittee he had joined the Young Communist League in 1937, remaining active until 1942, but he declined on grounds of conscience to name any of his associates. He too was cited for contempt and his position upheld on appeal.

It was only after the most intense thought and debate that Sulzberger came to accept these men's right not to answer the subcommittee's questions about their past political associations. His original view was stated many times. In a letter drafted in mid-1955, to an employee who pleaded the Fifth Amendment, Sulzberger declared:

> It is my opinion that as a member of the New York Times staff, it was your duty to answer the questions put to you by the committee and that your refusal to do so has ended your usefulness as a reporter. Even though he may have the legal right to do so, a reporter who refuses to answer questions on the ground that the answers may incriminate him, immediately destroys the confidence in his objectivity that is essential for his work.

But even as the investigation continued over the fall and winter of 1955 a battle was in progress for Sulzberger's mind.

I and others felt, in the first place, that we simply couldn't fire people for taking the Fifth—either a man has certain constitutional rights or he doesn't. Sulzberger was also coming to recognize that some men, as a matter of individual conscience, felt compelled not to cooperate with the Eastland subcommittee, and he saw that, however much he might disagree with them, he had no right to impose his beliefs on them. He saw, too, that the *Times* would have to live with his decisions for many years. As John Oakes wrote to him on January 2: "I am very much concerned that anything we write in the future on basic civil liberties and Bill of Rights problems will be weighed against our own actions and statements in this critical situation."

Sulzberger's acceptance of this view was made clear on January 5, 1956, in an editorial entitled "The Voice of a Free Press." The editorial written by Charles Merz, then director of the editorial page, reviewed the facts about the investigation, stated our policy toward Communists and ex-Communists on our staff and our determination to judge each man's case on its own merits, and continued:

> We may say this, however. We do not believe in the doctrine of irredeemable sin. We think it is possible to atone through good performance for past error, and we have tried to supply the security and the favorable working conditions which should exist in a democracy and which should encourage men who were once misled to reconsider and to reshape their political thinking.
>
> We have judged these men, and we shall continue to judge them, by the quality of their work and by our confidence in their ability to perform that work satisfactorily. It is our own business to decide whom we shall employ and not employ. We do not propose to hand over that function to the Eastland subcommittee.

Nor do we propose to permit the Eastland subcommittee, or any other agency outside this office, to determine in any way the policies of this newspaper. It seems to us quite obvious that the Eastland investigation has been aimed with particular emphasis at The New York Times. This is evident from several facts: from the heavy concentration of subpoenas served on employes of this newspaper, from the nature of the examination conducted at earlier hearings by the subcommittee's counsel, Mr. Sourwine, and from that counsel's effort, at those hearings, to demonstrate some connection between a witness' one-time association with the Communist party and the character of the news published in this paper.

It seems to us to be a further obvious conclusion that The Times has been singled out for this attack precisely because of the vigor of its opposition to many of the things for which Mr. Eastland, his colleague, Mr. Jenner, and the subcommittee's counsel stand—that is, because we have condemned segregation in the Southern schools; because we have challenged the high-handed and abusive methods employed by various Congressional committees; because we have condemned McCarthyism and all its works; because we have attacked the narrow and bigoted restrictions of the McCarran Immigration Act; because we have criticized a "security system" which conceals the accuser from his victim; because we have insisted that the true spirit of American democracy demands a scrupulous respect for the rights of even the lowliest individual and a high standard of fair play.

If this is the tactic of any member of the Eastland subcommittee and if further evidence reveals that the real purpose of the present inquiry is to demonstrate that a free newspaper's policies can be swayed by Congressional pressure, then we say to Mr. Eastland and his counsel that they are wasting their time. The newspaper will continue to determine its own policies. It will continue to condemn discrimination, whether in the South or in the North. It will continue to defend civil liberties. It will continue to challenge the unbridled power of governmental authority. It will continue to enlist goodwill against prejudice and confidence against fear.

We cannot speak unequivocally for the long future. But we can have faith. And our faith is strong that long after Senator Eastland and his present subcommittee are forgotten, long after segregation has lost its final battle in the South, long after all that was known as McCarthyism is a dim, unwelcome memory, long after the last Congressional committee has learned that it cannot tamper successfully with a free press, The New York Times will be speaking for the men who make it, and only for the men who make it, and speaking, without fear or favor, the truth as it sees it.

XX

Covering Culture

CULTURE GULCH is the name an office humorist gave the part of our news room wherein labor our critics and cultural-news reporters. In my years as editor, however, Culture Gulch was no joke; perhaps no part of the *Times'* coverage caused me more concern.

Today, looking back, we see that a cultural avalanche was under way in America in the 1950s. The fact was not so clear at the time, for cultural change does not come all at once, but in bits and pieces. At the time, we could only be sure that people in New York were talking about exciting, controversial developments in music, in painting, in the theater, and these developments were not being adequately reflected in our newspaper.

Nor was the story confined to Manhattan. Postwar prosperity made possible rising interest in the arts nationally. The national level of education was rising, and television was popularizing new tastes and trends. All across the land, a new cultural era was beginning, one in which art and artists were increasingly the cutting edge for social and political change, as well as artistic change.

I saw these new stirrings, and so did Clifton Daniel, when he returned to New York in 1955. During his years in London, Daniel had been impressed with the level of criticism in English newspapers. He and I agreed that the *Times* was weak in its criticism and even weaker in news coverage of cultural affairs. We thought our readers deserved better coverage. We thought the *Times* would have to do a better job to maintain its pre-eminence. To an extent, we simply wanted to exploit a new area of news.

Cultural affairs had for years been handled casually. We chose our critics often for the wrong reasons: seniority, or because a reporter had an interest in books or music and no one else wanted the job. Sometimes this haphazard system turned up a Brooks Atkinson or an Olin Downes, but more often it did not. We found, as we tried to recruit better critics, that the best-qualified men were usually in academic life, and often took a dim view of writing for a daily newspaper. The other side of the matter was that they often lacked an ability to write in the clear, simple style and with the speed we required.

Editors often preferred to deal with some general reporter or sportswriter-turned-critic, who at least spoke the newspaper language, than with experts in the arts, who often seemed to be pretty odd ducks. I recall an exchange Jimmy James had in 1948 with our music critic, Olin Downes. Downes was a supporter of Henry Wallace for the Presidency, and had spoken at Wallace's nominating convention in Philadelphia. James was concerned to see one of our critics so actively involved in politics, and called Downes in to discuss the matter. Downes vigorously asserted his right to political activity, and finally James growled, "Okay, but just don't get so wrapped up in it that you say Henry Wallace can play the piano better than Paderewski."

As Daniel, Harrison Salisbury, and I worked to improve our cultural coverage, we were often breaking new ground. No daily newspaper in this country had tried to provide both the quality and the quantity of criticism and cultural news we wanted. The level of writing we desired was found only in a few magazines. Our job was made more difficult, and our mistakes more serious, by the fact of the immense influence of the *Times* in cultural affairs. "I've got power I don't want," Brooks Atkinson used to complain, well aware that his reviews could make or break a play. All our other reviewers don't have the same impact as our drama critic—we can close a new play, but we can't close *Aïda*—but theirs was still formidable. Since we started our Saturday art page, I've often seen people in galleries using it as their guide to what they should see and buy, and I'm sure dealers use it in establishing their prices. None of us were entirely comfortable with this make-or-break power over the arts, but I feel no need to apologize for it. If our critics are more influential than those of other newspapers and magazines, it is perhaps because they have over the years shown themselves to be reliable guides.

Yet increasingly we tried to counterbalance our critics' impact by having separate reviews in the daily and Sunday papers. The most clearcut example is in book reviews. Our daily reviews are written by a permanent staff. They must, for reasons of space, be extremely selective in what they review, and there is a certain institutional quality to their reviews—that is, they are clearly our reviewers—and, we hope, a certain consistency. The Sunday *Book Review* is a different sort of operation. It is in effect a magazine about books and the book world. The reviewers are generally not our employees, and one page might have a review by an ultra-liberal and the next page a review by an ultra-conservative. It is, thus, something of a forum.

Punch Sulzberger, with his love of neat organization, repeatedly suggested to me that we consolidate the daily and Sunday book-review staffs, which now operate on different floors of the *Times* building. His suggestion was perfectly logical but, despite my own admitted liking for centralization, I thought the dual operation better. It allows us the luxury of diversity. It permits conflicting voices to be heard in our pages. For example, when Gay Talese's book on the *Times* appeared, our staff reviewer was largely critical of it, but an outside writer, writing in the Sunday *Book Review*, praised it.

A system of checks and balances operates to a lesser degree in other areas, in that we invite outside writers to contribute to our Sunday entertainment section. Still, a balance is almost impossible. When Walter Kerr began writing Sunday theater pieces for us, we hoped they would offset the make-or-break effect of Clive Barnes' daily reviews, but we found that readers—and theater people—continued to regard the first-night reviews as the crucial ones.

I usually detected a certain ambiguity in the way theatrical people regarded our critics. Most of them were like Sam Goldwyn. If our movie critic, Bosley Crowther, had praised one of Sam's extravaganzas, he'd say, "That Bosley Crowther is a very fine man, very sensitive, very intellectual." But if Crowther had panned a Goldwyn epic, Sam would say, "That fellow Boswell Carruthers—what's his name?—what's the trouble with him, anyway?"

Still, the fact remained that we never (nor did any publication I know of) achieved perfection in our criticism. Some critics were better than others. That was one reason that the selection of a new critic was such an agonizing process for Daniel and me. We were leaving the field where we were experts and entering one in which we were well-meaning amateurs. We were dealing with people we didn't know, largely on the recommendations of others, yet the prestige of the *Times* was involved and we would feel responsible for the critic we hired.

Often we faced an initial decision either to promote a "second-string" reviewer already on the staff or to seek a prestigious outsider. We found it hard to build up our number-two reviewers. Sometimes the top critics didn't want their assistants viewed as possible successors; they took the attitude, "*Après moi, le déluge.*" It was also a fact that when you hired a critic you were buying his reputation, his standing in the intellectual community. A little-known critic, given the chance, might do better work than a famous authority, but that was a hard gamble to make. When Brooks Atkinson retired, he suggested a talented news editor, a man with extensive knowledge of the theater, be named to replace him. But we simply didn't think we could name an unknown to replace Brooks Atkinson. Without a reputation, he would have been especially vulnerable to the sniping that confronts any major critic.

To me, as editor, a good critic was worth his weight in rubies. Not a critic you always agreed with, for that is impossible, but one whose judgment you trusted. When you had such a man, you had to give him a chance to grow in the job. You had to defend him when he was under fire. Sometimes it was the weakest critics you defended most stoutly, knowing your responsibility for putting them there. Yet, if a critic clearly was not working out, you had a duty to the paper to remove him, as gently and gracefully as possible. These were the ways I thought we should handle critics; admittedly we didn't always meet these standards.

One of Daniel's and my first major decisions came in 1959 when we had an opening for an art critic. Aline Saarinen had been writing art criticism for us but she was not available full time. She urged us to consider John Canaday, who was then in charge of the division of education of the Philadelphia Art Museum. We talked to Canaday, were impressed by him, and hired him. Ho soon proved to be, despite his gentle manner, a strong-willed, often controversial critic. He is also an excellent critic, and we always considered our choice a happy one.

Canaday's first column, on September 6, 1959, declared: "We have been had. In the most wonderful and terrible time of history, the abstract expressionists have responded with the narrowest and most lopsided art on record. Never have painters found so little in so much."

This and many more criticisms of contemporary art aroused much indignation in art circles. On February 26, 1961, we printed a letter attacking Canaday's views that was signed by fifty artists, critics, collectors, and teachers. This letter inspired some six hundred more letters, about 90 percent of them supporting Canaday. I was not interested in the statistics, but I took the controversy as a good sign. At least our critic was taking a stand, and people cared what he was saying.

An incident involving Canaday, not long after he joined us, prompted a memo from me to Sulzberger in which I stated my view on the proper relationship between publisher and managing editor in dealings with the news room. The incident arose when we reproduced (or tried to reproduce) a modern painting, only to have it come out as a blur. Sulzberger sent Canaday a note which the latter interpreted as criticism. (The incident was ironic, in that Canaday's dim view of much modern art was quite similar to Sulzberger's own view.) Canaday was upset, and when I learned of the incident, I sent Sulzberger the following memo:

Mr. Sulzberger:

I think it would be much more appropriate and effective for you to direct to me the remarks you intended for Mr. Canaday about the illustrations with Miss Ashton's art column of November 3.

In the first place, there are a number of people other than Mr. Canaday who should share the blame for this snafu, and that is exactly what it was. In fact, he perhaps was the least involved. The ones most blameworthy are members of the bullpen, which is a direct adjunct of the office of the managing editor. The bullpen knows, and shares, our feeling about this business of trying to use monotone cuts in illustrating stories about painting that depend entirely or substantially on color for interest.

Secondly, even if he were more directly involved, Mr. Canaday is a new man in our office and is feeling his way around. We must expect a few errors from him. He is a fine, intelligent, sensitive man. It is true, of course, that he is theoretically responsible for what goes into the art columns, even when a story is also done by someone else —in this case by Miss Ashton. And it is also true that he is directly responsible to the managing editor, who, in turn, is responsible *for* him. Under all the circumstances I would not want him to have a note of this temper directly from the Publisher.

Thirdly, and finally, and generally speaking, I would strongly suggest that you send criticisms about the news product directly to me so that I can make the corrections at the spots where they are needed. I think the Publisher keeps himself in a much better position to deal with the staff at arm's length, especially in the matter of criticisms. The managing editor is the one who should get the blame when things don't go right. He is in a more immediate position to do something about them.

T.C.

Sulzberger replied good-naturedly the next day:

Dear Turner:

I have your note about my "art" memorandum. Okay, forget it. I sent it to Canaday because I thought he'd be personally sympathetic. It was in no sense meant to be a criticism but maybe I didn't make it clear.

If you want me to send my bleats about art to you, get ready, brother!!

A.H.S.

No job is harder to fill than that of drama critic. We need a man who is able to write intelligently about everything from Shaw to Shakespeare to *Hair* and *Hello Dolly!* He must write well. He must be tough and honest, yet respect the vast power he wields and exercise a degree of restraint and compassion.

In 1965, Daniel, Salisbury, and I were searching for such a man. When the distinguished Brooks Atkinson retired some years earlier, he was replaced by our music reporter, Howard Taubman, but this did not prove satisfactory and Taubman was named critic-at-large— a broad assignment that he made the most of. The man we all saw as Atkinson's obvious successor, the *Herald Tribune*'s Walter Kerr, was not willing to quit the *Herald Tribune,* although it was obviously in trouble. We tried without success to interest Robert Brustein of Yale. We talked to Kenneth Tynan, whose work for *The New Yorker* we'd admired, but Tynan had returned to England and wanted to stay there.

Finally, we settled on Stanley Kauffmann, then a critic for *The New Republic*. Kauffmann had had experience as an actor, director, playwright, and critic, mostly of films. His work for *The New Republic* showed a good deal of writing ability. He had extensive talks with Daniel and Salisbury, was interviewed by me and others, and on January 1, 1966, he came to work as our drama critic. It was agreed that he would stay a minimum of eighteen months, but we hoped he would stay for many years. As it turned out, he was with us only eight months.

The *Times'* drama critic is exposed to a great deal of second guessing within our own organization. The publisher and his family and the paper's top executives probably do not fancy themselves experts on opera or ballet, but we are all part of the theatrical neighborhood of Times Square, and we think we know the theater. Some of my close friends included Martin Gabel and his wife, Arlene Francis, Bob and Kay Preston, and Frederic Loewe, and I was never unaware of their views. I had a passing acquaintance with the producer David Merrick and was always amused by his waspish comments on our drama critics. I suppose the height of my theatrical involvement came when Howard Teichmann made me an offstage character in his 1958 comedy, *The Girls in 509*. The play concerns two Republican ladies, played by Imogene Coca and Peggy Wood, who secluded themselves in a hotel suite when Roosevelt beat Hoover in 1932, and are found a quarter century later by a professor of journalism who thinks I have hired him to write for the *Times*. After he discovers the two hermits, he calls me to ask what to do, and we have several excited conversations. Teichmann generously dedicated the bound volume of the play to me, saying:

To
TURNER CATLEDGE
gentleman journalist
who nightly played his role faultlessly, whose behavior before, during, and after each performance was exemplary—whose good humor
and graciousness are deeply appreciated.

If a critic has a great deal of prestige, or a great deal of agility, he can withstand the second guessing and the pressures that accompany it. Stanley Kauffmann, unfortunately, was a victim of those pressures.

We all liked Kauffmann personally and admired his intellect and his integrity. We did feel, in his first weeks, that his writing was not as clear as it should have been. We knew how well he had written in the past, and we tended to think that he had "frozen" when he started with the *Times*, a reaction we had seen before. An editor who was among Kauffmann's biggest fans told me in a memo: "You had to have a dictionary to read the first piece he wrote for The Times."

Kauffmann soon became involved in a controversy over his wish to review a preview performance rather than the actual opening-night showing. He felt that the hour or so between a play's final curtain and our deadline didn't allow time for a thoughtful review. He was quite right, and reviewing previews later became customary, but the initial controversy added to his difficulties.

An element in the reaction to Kauffmann was simply that he was a very serious critic, with high standards, and this inevitably won him the dislike of many actors, writers, directors, and producers who make their living off the commercial Broadway theater. His critics said he was a snob, he was too highbrow, that he didn't like Broadway, and in time their complaints got back to all of us at the *Times*.

The decision to replace Kauffmann as our daily reviewer was made largely by Punch Sulzberger, and I think several factors contributed to it. His mother was displeased by a piece Kauffmann had written about homosexuals in the theater. Arthur Hays Sulzberger was bothered, I think, by the amount of criticism of Kauffmann he had heard from friends and business associates. Finally, I think Punch, who had succeeded to the publishership following Dryfoos' death, was disturbed at having a controversy on his hands. He was frankly uncertain of his own judgment in the matter, and this made him uncertain of other people's judgments.

On August 8, after Punch had received some criticism of Kauffmann, and we had discussed the matter, I sent him the following memo:

Punch:

This is with reference to the criticism of Stanley Kauffmann, The Times' drama critic. The memo is occasioned by your report to me of criticism made by Joseph Verner Reed to the Chairman and Mrs. Sulzberger. Let me deal with this first.

I am sure Mr. and Mrs. Sulzberger realize that Mr. Reed is not a completely disinterested witness. He is head of the American Shakespeare Festival Theatre at Stratford, Connecticut, and Mr. Kauffmann has recently declared that the artistic fortunes of that theater have been somewhat on the wane. These views, I am sure, are sincerely held by Mr. Kauffmann and were arrived at after considerable contact and professional observation.

I hasten to add, however, that Mr. Reed is by no means the only critic of Mr. Kauffmann's work. Mr. Kauffmann is a very serious and provocative theater critic. He is not perhaps as graceful and readable as some others—certainly not as witty. He is perhaps more highbrow and intellectual than daily readers are accustomed to, but he is by no means a nobody from nowhere.

Mr. Kauffmann came to us with a very substantial reputation, particularly as a film critic. His book, "The World on Film," has recently been published by Harper and Row and has had excellent reviews. I think his reputation as a drama critic may very well grow as he gains confidence and strength and people become used to what he is driving at. He has gone through a period of intensive hazing, both on account of his opinions and his insistence on attending previews in order to have more time to judge theatrical works. He approaches the theater as an art form more decidedly, I believe, than any other critic. This runs counter to the views of some of his critics who regard the theater more as show business or a form of entertainment. They want the kind of light criticism that he does not give.

However, there are other opinions of Mr. Kauffmann's talent held by people who are just as distinguished in the theater as Mr. Reed and other of Mr. Kauffmann's critics. For example, we have received letters from Edward Albee and Richard Bissell, the playwrights; Frederick O'Neal, president of Actors' Equity Association; Eric Bentley and Howard Mumford Jones, both distinguished critics themselves; Mrs. Ben Hecht, widow of the author and playwright; Zeke Jabbour of the Ypsilanti Greek Theatre; John R. Goetz of the Minnesota Theatre Company, who runs the Guthrie Theatre in Minneapolis; Charles L. Mee, associate editor of the American Heritage Publishing Company; Alfred de Liagre, the producer; George Tabori of the Berkshire Theatre Festival and Stanley Edgar Hyman of The New Yorker and a few others, all of whom have warm words of praise for Mr. Kauffmann, some of them even ecstatic. Mr. Daniel tells me that these are by no means all the fan mail Mr. Kauffmann has had. He selected these letters because they are from persons whose standing is comparable to that of Mr. Reed.

I don't have to tell you that no drama critic keeps in favor always with all the people all the time. We have heard in recent years a great deal of praise for Brooks Atkinson and of a yearning for the good old days when he reviewed for The Times. I share that yearning, but I also have a vivid recollection of the missiles that used to be directed toward The Times when Mr. Atkinson took a play apart, as he often did. We even had producers undertake to have us agree Mr. Atkinson would not be sent to review their plays. The life of a New York drama critic is not an easy one, especially as he has so much power over the success or failure of a production.

T. C.

Then we learned that Walter Kerr was at last available. He wanted to write a Sunday column but was willing to write daily reviews for a time. We knew the theatrical world was anxious for us to take on Kerr, and of course we wanted him. To Punch, hiring Kerr seemed an ideal way out of the Kauffmann problem, yet Punch wanted very much to keep Kauffmann on the staff in some other capacity than daily critic. I agreed with this solution.

I asked Daniel to tell Kauffmann we were hiring Kerr to write daily reviews and to see if some other assignment could be found for Kauffmann, perhaps a Sunday column. Kauffmann, understandably dismayed, declined to take another assignment, and we agreed to fulfill our financial agreement even though he would cease to write for us.

Daniel, too, was upset by the affair, quite justifiably so, both by the decision and by the fact that he hadn't been consulted on it.

After Daniel finished his talk with Kauffmann, I asked the critic to come to my office. I told him the decision to replace him had been made by a consensus of our executives and that I had been part of that consensus. I made that statement, despite my earlier memo in support of him, because of my belief that if you are part of an organization you have to accept responsibility. You argue your position in private, but if the decision goes against you, you make yourself part of it. If you can't do that, you leave. I had defended Kauffmann, but I also thought he had not been a satisfactory daily reviewer, and I agreed that to replace him with Kerr would without question be for the good of the newspaper.

Kauffmann was a perfect gentleman throughout our talk. I had the feeling he felt sorry for me because I had a dirty job to do. At one point, he said quite calmly, "The *Times* has dealt with me irresponsibly." I could not disagree. I thought that we might have worked with him to enliven his style of writing. Or we could have found some arrangement whereby he would have finished out his eighteen months. I thought Punch's decision showed an unnecessary touch of nervousness. But I became part of the decision and I was glad we were able to get Kerr. Later, Kerr got the Sunday column he wanted, and our dance critic, Clive Barnes, became a successful daily theater critic.

Fiction, in the postwar era, used ever-increasing amounts of profanity and ultra-realistic descriptions of sex and violence. Court decisions ended virtually all restraints on what could be put in books. This caused some problems for newspapers and their reviewers. The Chicago *Tribune*'s editor, my friend Don Maxwell, was so offended by some "dirty" best sellers he happened to read that he ordered that the paper's "Best Sellers" list be changed to "Among the Best Sellers," so they would not be required to list "dirty" books. A somewhat related issue arose in an exchange of memos between me and Arthur Hays Sulzberger in November of 1964. He sent me the following letter:

Dear Turner:
    I want your advice in determining a matter of policy. The question is whether or not we should accept the advertising of books which are patently and flagrantly "dirty."
    It is not an easy question to resolve. Our general rule has been that we pass on the advertising submitted to us but not the content of the books. We don't want to be censors, but we do want to maintain high standards for our advertising columns.
    Recently I ordered a specific departure from our usual practice.

Someone gave me to read a copy of a novel entitled "Candy." In my opinion, the book was so filthy that I asked the advertising department not to print further advertisements for it. As you can imagine, there was a great deal of discussion of this action in the publishing world.

Now another book comes along. We are asked, "How can you reject the advertising of 'Candy' and take ads for 'Last Exit to Brooklyn'?" Well, I looked at "Last Exit to Brooklyn" and it is dirtier, although a more serious literary effort, than "Candy."

I was the one who put in the rule about censoring the advertising content only and not the book, and yet I am the one who is now suggesting that the rule be changed. However, the arguments against doing so are strong. It is said that to decline the advertising for some would be unfairly discriminatory, leaving only the alternative of reading and appraising all questionable books before they are advertised. On the other hand, we have a right to refuse access to our readers to any distasteful product. And when we know about dirty books that are, in one way or another, brought to our attention, shouldn't we refuse to take ads for them?

We have touched on this question of advertising freedom in another context in a couple of editorials, copies of which I am enclosing.

Yours,
A. H. S.

I replied:

Dear Mr. Sulzberger:

This is in reply to your communication of November 10 asking advice on our policy of accepting advertising for books which are "patently and flagrantly dirty."

Although I abhor such literature, I think our old rule of accepting this advertising on the basis of its own content and not the content of the books is the one to follow. Should a book be barred from the mail, or otherwise be banned by a local authority, then the question might be different. But, I feel The Times should bend over backward not to appear to be censors of books it advertises. Once we embark on a policy of accepting or rejecting advertising on the basis of the contents of the books, then we have taken on a responsibility for judgment that we might find rather hard to discharge. It is only when we apply such a policy that we have to compare the degree of dirt between "Candy" and "Last Exit to Brooklyn."

The exchange over *Candy* and *Last Exit to Brooklyn* recalls an earlier episode when I served on the 1963 Pulitzer Prize advisory board that refused to honor Edward Albee for *Who's Afraid of Virginia Woolf?*

Pulitzer Prizes are awarded by a three-stage process. First, there are juries of experts in the different categories (journalism, drama, poetry, et cetera) which submit recommendations to an advisory board. The advisory board, on which I served three four-year terms, consists of twelve newspapermen and the president of Columbia University. Our advisory board gives its recommendations to the trustees of Columbia, who vote the awards.

The advisory board sometimes overrules the juries of experts, and, more rarely, the trustees overrule the advisory board. In 1962 the trustees refused to give the biography prize to W. A. Swanberg for *Citizen Hearst*. They said the subject of the prize-winning biography should be someone who would inspire the young.

I was always aware of my lack of qualifications in several categories, and was therefore almost always willing to back the experts. Most of my colleagues on the advisory board felt the same way.

I recall once when one of my colleagues, the editor of a great Midwestern paper, was serving on our poetry subcommittee. He told us about some poetry that was printed in several directions across the page. He said he wasn't sure if it was great art or a joke. He went on to say that his own poetic tastes ran to the Hoosier bard James Whitcomb Riley. In fact, he recited to us from Riley's great work "The Wreck of the Monon," culminating with the unforgettable couplet:

> Some poor wretch was heard to say,
> "Cut, oh cut, my leg away!"

My colleague's recitation from "The Wreck of the Monon" became an annual highlight of our deliberations.

Our humor failed us, however, during the *Virginia Woolf* deliberations. I had seen the play on its opening night, found it exciting and interesting, and had no hesitation about voting for it. However, a majority of my colleagues on the advisory board thought the play too "dirty" to deserve the prize. One or two had reached that judgment without bothering to see the play. I thought it unfortunate that the majority acted on "moral" rather than theatrical grounds, but they prevailed and no prize for drama was given that year. A controversy ensued, including critic John Mason Brown's resigning from the nominating jury. I was embarrassed by the episode. I thought the majority had made us all look silly, nonprofessional, and rather like a bunch of mountebanks. However, that is a risk you run if you agree to serve on a committee.

XXI

A Trip to Russia

IN the late spring of 1957 I visited *Times'* bureaus in fifteen
European and Near Eastern nations. The highlight of my tour was a
twelve-day visit to Russia—my first—and the highlight of that visit
was an hour-and-fifty-minute interview with Nikita Khrushchev, who
then headed both the Soviet government and the Soviet Communist
party. I was well aware that twelve days in Russia and two hours
with Khrushchev did not make an expert on Russia or Communism,
yet the trip did open my eyes to much I had not previously understood about that great nation, and left me with a hunger to know
far more about it. I had scheduled my visit to Russia first on my tour,
in early May, partly because I wanted to be there for the annual
May Day celebrations, and partly because I wanted to get behind
me what I thought would be the least pleasant leg of my trip. In
this latter assumption, I found I had been quite wrong.

I flew from New York to Moscow, with a change of planes in
Copenhagen, and I was met at the airport by Bill Jorden, then the
Times' chief Moscow correspondent, and also by an Intourist guide
with a car and chauffeur. My guide suggested we go straight from
the airport to my hotel, the National, but Bill Jorden had another
plan. He wanted to go directly to a reception at a hotel where the
Japanese Ambassador was staging a celebration on the occasion of
the Emperor's birthday There he hoped I'd meet some Russian big-

wigs. That's what we did, with a quick stop at Jorden's apartment for me to put on a clean shirt, and thus it was after only an hour or so in Russia that I got my first look at Khrushchev.

The Russian leader was the focal point of the Japanese reception. He was standing in the center of a group of Japanese diplomats and newspapermen. Nikolai Bulganin, the titular head of the Soviet government, was also present, smiling and chatting, looking rather like a Kentucky colonel at an after-Derby party, and it was to Bulganin that I first spoke.

Before leaving New York, I had sent telegrams to Khrushchev, Bulganin, and other Russian notables, requesting interviews. I had also been advised by Daniel and Salisbury to attend all the diplomatic receptions I could and to use a "brassy" approach; that is, if I saw a bigwig, to walk right up and start asking questions. That's what I did. The worst they could do was to refuse to talk to me, and that had happened many times before in my reporting career.

Jorden introduced me to Bulganin, who shook my hand and (with Jorden acting as interpreter) asked me how long I was going to stay and where I would visit. When I told him, he gave me a "Tut, tut, you should stay longer and see more." Others began to gather around us. I asked Bulganin if he had ever visited my country. No, he said, but he'd love to. He spoke of the need for personal exchanges between high government officials. "See these people?" he said, indicating the Japanese around us. "We had misunderstandings. Now they come to see us and we talk the same language."

Bulganin proposed a toast, and we were downing some vodka to the mutual happiness of our two countries when Khrushchev joined us. He was cordial, bouncy, and red-faced. A throng of reporters and diplomats were following him. He was talking about guided missiles and the reporters thought they were hot on the trail of a story. Just then Foreign Minister Gromyko entered the conversation as an interpreter. He looked at me questioningly as if to say, "Haven't I seen you somewhere before?" I reminded him that we'd met in Secretary of State Jimmy Byrnes' suite at the Savoy Plaza in New York, about a dozen years before. Gromyko asked me to give "Jimmy" his regards the next time I saw him. Meanwhile, Khrushchev and his entourage drifted away, and I was not to continue our talk until my last day in Russia.

The next morning, I had the pleasure of meeting Alexei, who was to be my Intourist guide throughout my trip. Alexei told me he was thirty years old and had taught school in Siberia for several years before his health failed him. He had given up the teaching job, which paid him two thousand roubles (about $2,000) a year, for the guide's job, which paid only half as much. But he liked the guide's job, he said, because he met "such nice people" and also because he got to travel around Russia on an expense account.

On May Day, I witnessed the huge parade and public demonstration in Red Square, and later that day I encountered "the girls," an amazing group of eighteen American women who were touring Russia. They were women who worked in radio and television on home shows, cooking programs, and the like. They were led by Mrs. Beatrice Johnson, who ran a television home show in Kansas City, and who made a specialty of organizing touring parties like this one. I learned that they had been greeted at the airport that morning by a band and several hundred cheering Russians.

When the girls learned who I was, they told me about their plans to visit the Soviet leaders. I started to tell them to spare themselves the embarrassment (after all, I was editor of the *New York Times*, and I wasn't sure I'd get to see the Soviet leaders) but I held my tongue rather than disillusion them.

Imagine my surprise two days later when, on my return from a trip to a collective farm, I discovered the girls had seen both Bulganin and Marshal Zhukov, the third member of the Russian Big Three. We invited Mrs. Johnson to have dinner with Bill Jorden, Max Frankel, the second man in our bureau, and his wife, and me, and she told us the whole story. Yes, the girls had seen Bulganin and Zhukov "and what interesting and nice people they were." Each woman had taken a turn sitting in Bulganin's chair. They had interviewed him on what he liked to eat, what he liked in women's hats, and similar matters of feminine interest. Zhukov, "that nice general," had given each of them a medal. I asked Mrs. Johnson how she had arranged these meetings. It turned out she had done it all by telephoning Bulganin's office direct from Kansas City.

Alexei and I went on quite a round of sightseeing, I asked Max Frankel's lovely wife, Tobi (the former Tobia Brown, who had been a *Times* correspondent at Barnard College) to join us, as she'd only been in Moscow two weeks and hadn't seen many of the sights. The three of us visited, among other sights, a collective farm, the ancient monastery at Zagorsk, about sixty-five miles from Moscow, and the Lenin-Stalin tomb.

From our first meeting, Alexei had been urging me to visit Kiev and Leningrad. I guessed he had a girl in both ports. I was half right—he had a girl in the Intourist office in Leningrad. I followed his advice, however, and visited both cities.

All our time in Kiev and Leningrad I was hoping for word that I would be granted an interview with Khrushchev or one of the other Soviet leaders. The night before I had left Moscow I had attended a party given by Leonid Ilyichev, head of the press department of the Foreign Ministry, at the Moscow Press Club. I had renewed my plea for an interview and Ilyichev, who was quite drunk, assured me he was doing his best to work things out, and promised me he'd locate me in Kiev or Leningrad or anywhere else, if the interview came through. When I left the party, Ilyichev toasted me: "Here's best to the *New York Times*; of course, what I think is best for the *New York Times* and what you think best for the *New York Times* are greatly different. But here's to the difference."

I was in Leningrad, two days before I was to leave Russia, when word came that Khrushchev would see me the next day. I flew to Moscow and got a good night's rest. My appointment was set for 2:30 P.M. and at 2:10 a car picked me up at my hotel. Jorden and I were whisked over to the Communist party headquarters, three blocks north of the Kremlin, arriving at 2:20. We were immediately ushered in to see Khrushchev, accompanied by Ilyichev. We were with him until 4:10.

Khrushchev bounced out from behind his desk and extended his hand to greet me. He was cordial, good-humored, and entirely self-assured. He invited me to sit near the head of a long wooden table, half-covered with a runner of green cloth. He took a seat opposite me. An interpreter sat at the head of the table, between us; Ilyichev sat beside his boss; and Jorden sat beside me. Behind Khrushchev on a wall was a portrait of Marx and on the opposite wall was one of Lenin. The office was neatly appointed but not lavish, and I found it difficult to realize that this was the headquarters for the Communist world.

I began by briefly describing my visit to the USSR. I thanked him for receiving me and asked if I might ask a few questions.

"Please do," he said.

I told him that my questions were not intended to be argumentative but solely to get a clearer idea of his views, which I would pass along to the readers of the *New York Times*. I explained that I was in charge of the "factual" part of the *Times*, and that I had little or nothing to do with forming the editorial policy of the paper. To illustrate, I said that, whereas the *Times* editorially had supported Eisenhower for President, I had twice voted for Stevenson, a fact well known to my superiors. He didn't seem to understand, or perhaps he simply didn't believe me.

I began asking my questions from the list that I had prepared with the help of Harrison Salisbury, Clifton Daniel, and Jorden. At no point did Khrushchev balk or bridle at a question; on the contrary he seemed to enjoy the talk and he warmed up as we went along.

It would serve no purpose to detail the interview here. His remarks to me rated a long lead story in the next day's *Times,* but there was no earth-shaking news in what he said—it was simply that he'd said it, in considerable detail. His main points included the following:

—That the surest if not the only way to avoid war was for the U.S. and the U.S.S.R. to find a joint way to ease tensions.

—That any big-four conference should be carefully prepared in advance.

—That the question of Europe was a "knot" that created disputes.

—That any settlement in Europe might entail setting up a continuing body dominated by the United States and the Soviet Union, and that such a body would mean the dissolution of NATO.

—That the problem of Germany should be left to East and West Germany.

—That selfish people in the United States are "carrying on a policy of balancing on the brink of war," and that the people of the United States were "cleverly tricked in the election campaign" to follow warmongers. He had particular scorn for Secretary of State Dulles and his talk of "liberation" of Eastern Europe. He commented: "You consider our system is a slave system. We consider your system. Marx wrote about it more than one hundred years ago. It would be better not to talk about it."

If Khrushchev's message was the familiar dogma of his government, his words were nonetheless often colorful. For example, he declared, "The case of international tension is like a cabbage. If you tear off the leaves one by one you come to the heart. And the heart of this matter is relations between the Soviet Union and the United States." At that point, he slapped the green top of the table to emphasize his point.

During the periods while he was speaking in Russian, prior to the translation, I several times lapsed into reflections. I tried to feel the importance of this occasion, tried to impress upon myself that I was sitting at the very heart of the "international Communist conspiracy," in the presence of the chief engineer of the apparatus, before one of the most important men in the world, as far as the chances of war and peace were concerned. I could accept all this intellectually, but I couldn't feel it emotionally. I felt instead a sense of disgust that this man, with his toughness and crudeness bulging through any show of good manners, should be in such a position, that my generation had allowed the world to get into such a state as to be troubled in any way by this table-thumping braggart. I resented the fact that I was obliged to regard him as important material for an interview.

At the end of the interview, Khrushchev came around to shake hands and wish me well. He brought up again a little side exchange we'd had about his coming to the United States. He said with a chuckle that he couldn't come as a tourist without being fingerprinted and he didn't like that. I pulled out my Defense Department accreditation card with my fingerprints on the back of it. I told him that in America no one took offense at being fingerprinted for such documents.

"Then you must be a criminal," he said with a laugh.

A moment earlier, as he cut off the interview, he had said he'd like to continue but—he said with a laugh—he had to go out "and meet the Mongolian delegation." After we withdrew to the main corridor, he passed us, tipped his little hat, and said in perfect English, "Off to see the Mongolians."

After leaving Khrushchev's office, we went directly to the *Times* office (which doubled as Bill Jorden's apartment) and reconstructed our notes. Then I wrote my story. Jorden said that, as I was a tourist, I might be able to telephone my story to London without going through the official censors. I chose to go through the censors, however; I wanted to see what, if anything, would be cut. We sent a copy of my story to the telegraph offce and in an exceptionally short time we received word that it had been approved in its entirety and sent on to New York.

After my account of the interview appeared in the *Times, Pravda,* the Communist party newspaper, reprinted it, using nearly nine columns, including five on the front page. *Pravda*'s version of the interview differed from mine on only one point. Khrushchev told me that he had spoken of Stalin's shortcomings in the past and would continue to speak to them in the future. In *Pravda*'s version, the promise of future criticisms was omitted.

Later, Tass, the Soviet news agency, accused the *Times* of distorting the major points of the interview. Apparently, this referred to an editorial we carried on the interview, which said, "In a startling, but not exactly new maneuver, Mr. Khrushchev has in effect proposed a deal between Soviet Russia and the United States for the

division of the world." That was, of course, the opinion of the editorial writer, but I'm sure that Khrushchev would never believe that
I was entirely uninvolved in that editorial commentary.

I left for Stockholm soon after filing my story. I took Bill Jorden
with me, as I thought he deserved a holiday after playing host to me
for several days. Jorden's office-apartment was plush by Russian
but certainly not by American standards. Even more disturbing were
the Frankels' living quarters. Max and Tobi were living in one room
at the Metropole Hotel. Tobi was cooking on an electric hotplate in
the one room, which served as bedroom, sitting room, library, solar-
ium, and pantry. Their canned goods were stored in a clothes closet,
and dishes were washed in the bathroom. I felt rather guilty, therefore, when I checked into the wonderful Grand Hotel in Stockholm.
I appeased my guilt a little by giving Jorden a holiday and by autho-
rizing him, while in Stockholm, to buy the Frankels an electric re-
frigerator. On our way to Stockholm, we had time to stop off for a
few hours in Helsinki. Jorden spent the stopover drinking one glass
of Finnish milk after another, the milk laced with aquavit.

I realized, after leaving Russia, that I had gone there with many
preconceptions, and that for the most part I had undersold Russia,
or viewed it too harshly. Obviously, my visit was limited and I was
far better treated than most visitors. But I did not see the universal
drabness I had expected; rather, I saw women with colored dresses,
silk stockings, ample makeup, and well-made clothing. And the
attitude of the people was not what I expected. I had anticipated a
courteous but cold and suspicious reception. I rather thought the
people I dealt with would be inefficient and not concerned with the
comfort of a Westerner. Instead, I was treated cordially everywhere.
I found only affection toward the American people, despite the belief
of many Russians that the United States government wanted to
make war on Russia. In essence, they respected us in the way we
respect them, as distinct from the iniquities of our government.

It struck me that if I, the editor of a great newspaper, had such
misconceptions about Russia, then we in newspapers, magazines,
radio, and television needed to do a far better job in informing our
fellow Americans about the great nation that so occupied our political
thoughts. I left Russia with a view that has since become much
more evangelically anti-Communist. That view is that we in the
United States can only profit by knowing more about the Russians
as people, that we are foolish if we think we can separate them from
their government, and that the world will be better off if we take
the Russians as they are and do all we can to learn more about them

and abandon any idea of dragging them along our sawdust trail.

My trip to Russia had one further, quite unexpected dividend. A few weeks after I returned to the United States, I delivered a speech on my trip to a meeting of the American Society of Newspaper Editors in San Francisco. Among those in the audience were my old friend George Healy, editor of the New Orleans *Times-Picayune*, his wife, and their guest, Mrs. Abby Ray Izard, a widow who lived in New Orleans. Mrs. Izard fell under the spell of my oratory, which I repeated, in various settings and forms, during the next seven months until she became Mrs. Turner Catledge.

XXII

Two Controversies

PERHAPS no man in the world has stirred more intense emotions among Americans in the past decade than Fidel Castro. His revolution was greeted with curiosity and enthusiasm in the early months of 1959, but these responses gave way to anger and disillusion in 1960 as he veered toward Communism. People who were unperturbed by Communist regimes in Russia and China were outraged to find one ninety miles from Miami. Our national outrage led John Kennedy to approve the ill-conceived, ill-fated Bay of Pigs invasion in April of 1961. It led, too, to Kennedy's taking us to the brink of nuclear war in October, 1962, when he learned the Russians were installing offensive missiles in Cuba. Even today, when we seem to have learned to endure Castro, our fear of "another Cuba" colors and often corrupts our policies toward all of Latin America.

Given the depth of national feeling about Castro's revolution, it is not surprising that twice in my years as managing editor matters relating to Cuba caused intense concern and debate among the publisher, myself, and other of our senior executives. I am referring to our attitude toward Herbert Matthews' controversial writings about Castro and to our coverage of the buildup for the Bay of Pigs invasion.

I was in sympathy with Castro's revolution, as I am in sympathy with most revolutions. Along with many people in the United States,

I applauded his overthrow of the dictator Batista. I met Castro early in 1959 and didn't think he was then a Communist. He was certainly a megalomaniac, but I don't think he knew what he was politically. My impression was that if our government had moved quickly and skillfully we might have made him our ally, as unquestionably he wanted to be, and Cuba might have become a model for revolutionary, yet non-Communist change in this hemisphere. That, of course, did not happen. The Eisenhower administration chose, instead, to treat Castro with suspicion and rudeness, and to no one's surprise we drove him into the arms of the Russians.

It is not widely known, but Castro's first trip to the United States after he took power in Cuba came about because a group of newspaper editors got high at the New York restaurant "21" one winter afternoon and came up with a wild idea.

George Healy was president of the American Society of Newspaper Editors that year, and he needed a speaker for the society's April meeting. George happened to be in New York early in January of 1959 only a few days after Castro took power, and he invited the three members of his program committee to lunch with him at "21." The three were Don Maxwell, my old friend from the Chicago *Tribune*; Alicia Patterson of *Newsday*; and me. Unfortunately, I had a touch of the gout and couldn't join them. George, Don, and Alicia made themselves comfortable in the upper room of "21," put away a few martinis, and began tossing out names of possible speakers.

They'd reached Harold Macmillan when George Healy and Don Maxwell asked almost in chorus, "What about Castro?"

Don Maxwell, who was trained under Colonel McCormick at the *Tribune* and therefore believes anything is possible, immediately put in a call to his correspondent in Cuba, Jules Dubois, who said he'd see what he could do. The party then made its way to my apartment on Eighty-first Street, minus Alicia, whose husband, Harry Guggenheim, a former Ambassador to Cuba, had been anti-Castro, and who had already begun to have some wifely reservations about the whole business. George and Don arrived at my place about three or so, and I'd no sooner poured them a drink than Dubois called from Cuba to say Castro was in the bag.

A few Congressmen and State Department functionaries grumbled that the ASNE had sidestepped protocol in its invitation to Castro, but he nonetheless arrived on April 15 for an "unofficial" eleven-day visit. "Unofficial" meant that when Castro came to Washington Eisenhower went to Georgia to play golf. But almost everyone else was fascinated by the bearded thirty-two-year-old revolutionary, and he drew large, enthusiastic crowds wherever he went. He threw the whole city into a monumental traffic jam. Even our gathering of editors, who gave him only a skeptical smattering of applause at the start of his speech, cheered him loudly at the end.

Castro came by for a drink with the ASNE officers before his speech. He was accompanied by his bodyguards, six or eight boys about twenty years old who were wearing dirty fatigues and carrying empty rifles. A bar had been set up, and the bodyguards soon discovered that if they asked for drinks they'd get them free. They sampled manhattans, martinis, and Lord knows what else, and soon most of the bodyguards were passed out on sofas. Castro however, was safe enough. Someone asked him a question and he spent the next two hours answering it. Castro, it occurred to me, made Hubert Humphrey look like Silent Cal Coolidge.

It was exactly two years after that visit that the U.S.-sponsored Bay of Pigs invasion was carried out.

There has been a good deal said and written about the *Times* coverage of that invasion and, most importantly, of the period just before the invasion, when rumors and reports of it were spreading through the hemisphere. Most of the attention centered, correctly, on an article by Tad Szulc that appeared on our front page on April 7, ten days before the invasion. Arthur Schlesinger, Jr., the historian, later said, quite incorrectly, that the *Times* had "suppressed" Szulc's story of the coming invasion. Schlesinger was correct in that we had not printed all we knew or thought we knew. Clifton Daniel, in a speech he delivered in 1966, did much to clarify this episode, but I made the decision on how to handle Szulc's story and I think I should give my own account.

To my knowledge, the first suggestion that the United States was training Cuban exiles for an invasion of Cuba appeared in *The Nation* of November 19, 1960. Its article quoted an American educator, recently back from Guatemala, as saying that the CIA had established a base there and was training Cuban counter-revolutionaries for an invasion of Cuba. *The Nation* said it had no first-hand knowledge of the situation, but suggested that it should be investigated by U.S. news media with correspondents in Latin America.

We at the *Times* agreed, and we sent Paul Kennedy, our Central American correspondent, based in Mexico City, to get the facts. Kennedy's story, beginning on page one with a three-column headline and a map, was published on January 10, 1961. The article began:

RETALHELEU, Guatemala, Jan. 9—This area is the focal point of Guatemala's military preparations for what Guatemalans consider will be an almost inevitable clash with Cuba.

There is intensive daily air training here from a partly hidden airfield. In the Cordillers foothills a few miles back from the Pacific, commando-like forces are being drilled in guerrilla warfare tactics by foreign personnel, mostly from the United States.

The United States is assisting this effort not only in personnel but in material and the construction of ground and air facilities.

The story went on to quote the Guatemalan President as saying the military preparations were purely defensive, and at its end we carried a story quoting charges by Foreign Minister Raúl Roa of Cuba that the United States was training mercenaries in Guatemala and Florida for aggression against Cuba. I don't think that anyone who read the story would have doubted that something was in the wind, that the United States was deeply involved, or that the *New York Times* was onto the story.

In early April, rumors of an impending invasion were spreading. According to Arthur Schlesinger, the editor of *The New Republic* sent him the galleys of "a careful, accurate and devastating account of CIA activities among the refugees" and asked if there was any reason why it shouldn't be published. President Kennedy asked that the editor not print the story, and he agreed.

It was about that time that Tad Szulc discovered the impending invasion. Tad Szulc is one of those wonderful reporters who is news prone. Wherever he goes, things happen. I remember, when we sent him to Spain, I thought, "Look out, Franco." (Actually, Franco survived Szulc, but the U.S. Air Force mislaid one of its A-bombs off the Spanish coast shortly after Tad arrived.) Szulc stumbled onto the invasion story when, on his way from Rio de Janeiro to Washington, he stopped in Miami to visit friends. He soon sniffed out the invasion plans and, thinking this too important to discuss by phone, flew to New York to tell us what was happening. I called Dryfoos down to my office and Szulc told us the story—that an American-backed invasion force was massing in Florida and elsewhere for an attack on Cuba. I directed Szulc to return to Miami and sent several other reporters to help him dig out the full story. On the way down, Szulc stopped in Washington and spoke to Scotty Reston about the matter. Scotty talked to CIA Director Allen Dulles, who pooh-poohed the notion that his agency was involved in an invasion of Cuba.

Szulc's story soon arrived, a full and dramatic account of the invasion plans. However, two points about the story bothered me. First, Szulc declared the invasion was "imminent." This bothered me because it was a prediction. If we made the prediction, we ran the risk of being wrong, or at least of enabling the government to make us wrong by changing its plans. I felt we would be safer—we would stay within the facts—if we said the Cuban exiles were massed, they had been trained for an invasion, and they were anxious to launch the invasion—but not say the invasion was "imminent." The tendency to predict is one of the strongest and most dangerous urges of newspaper reporters. (Actually, Szulc himself had reservations about predicting the specific time of the invasion. He was reasonably sure it was scheduled for April 18, because he had learned that the government had ordered complete radio silence that date. Szulc was hesitant to put that specific date in his story, however, so he simply wrote that the invasion was imminent. He was one day off—the invasion was at dawn on the 17th.)

My second concern was his specific reference to CIA sponsorship. I didn't doubt that our cloak-and-dagger men were deeply involved, but the government has quite a few intelligence agencies, more than most people realize, and I was hesitant to specify the CIA when we might not be able to document the charge. I thought it best to use more general terms, like "U.S. officials" and "U.S. experts" in the story.

My concern was to supply the same standards of news and accuracy to this story that I would to any story. I was not worried so much about protecting the government as about protecting the *Times* When people talk about newspapers serving the public interest, I am sometimes forced to admit that I'm never sure what the public interest is, beyond its needs for accurate information. Orvil Dryfoos, however, was deeply concerned by the question of the national interest. If we revealed the invasion plans, would we be tampering with national policy? And would we be responsible if hundreds, even thousands, of Cuban exiles died on the beaches of their homeland? (I suspected that Castro already knew about the pending invasion, and the real question was not whether we would be responsible for deaths during the invasion, but whether, however unfairly, we might be blamed for them.)

On Thursday, April 6, the day before we carried Szulc's story, Dryfoos called Scotty Reston in Washington to get his opinion. Scotty's comments reinforced Dryfoos' own concern and hesitation. Reston warned against printing anything that would suggest an invasion was in the works or might otherwise upset the government's plans. He also pointed out that an invasion ten or twelve days off is not "imminent."

The difference between Reston and me was one of degree. I was willing to say that an invasion was planned but not that it was imminent; Reston would have preferred no reference to an invasion at that point.

Scotty is famous for his political scoops; he has spent much of his career in hot water for printing stories the government didn't want printed. At the same time, in some instances, including this one, Scotty is impressed by pleas that printing certain stories might go against the national interest. I think this sensitivity, this sometimes statesmanlike approach, grows out of Scotty's great and deep love for this country. He came to this country from Scotland when very young, and perhaps his affection for it is even greater than if he had been native born. I remember well his fascination with America and American folklore when we made a political scouting trip across the country in 1944.

In the case of the Bay of Pigs story, I think Scotty allowed his news judgment to be influenced by his patriotism. My own interest was less elevated—I wanted to print the story, as fully as possible.

I thus found myself in the middle of the debate. Some editors wanted to run the "imminent" story, and to run it as it was originally dummied into the paper, as the day's lead story, with a four-column head.

Yet Dryfoos, supported by Reston's concern, had serious questions whether any story might not go against the national interest. (I should make it clear that Reston never tried to push his view; as always he gave his opinion when it was sought, but recognized that the decision had to be made by the responsible editors in New York.)

I told Dryfoos that we had to have a story, and a major one, since something was clearly brewing in Florida. I told him that, by removing the prediction of an imminent invasion, and the reference to CIA sponsorship, he would be on solid news ground. He agreed, and the story was edited and published in accordance with my views.

A second controversy arose that Thursday afternoon over the size of the headline for the story. After the changes were made in its text, I ordered the headline changed from four columns to one. The original story, predicting an "imminent" invasion, would have deserved the four-column head, but the edited version didn't in my opinion. Ted Bernstein, the assistant managing editor, and Lew Jordan, the news editor, came to my office to appeal for a reconsideration. They believed their own news judgment, on the size of the head, was being overruled for political reasons. They also had the impression that the invasion was coming the next day. They insisted on a personal explanation from Dryfoos. I was angered by this questioning of my own responsibility, but I called Dryfoos, who explained his belief that the story must be played down for reasons of national security.

Their concern, incidentally, was not over the wording of the story, simply over the size of the headline. I thought this was putting the cart before the horse, to say the least.

But the fact remains that after all the changes were made we ran a thousand-word story, starting on page one, that made it perfectly clear to any intelligent reader that the U.S. government was training an army of Cuban exiles who intended to invade Cuba. Let me quote the opening paragraphs of Szulc's story, which appeared under the headline

ANTI-CASTRO UNITS
TRAINED TO FIGHT
AT FLORIDA BASES

Force There and in Central
America Is Reported to
Total 5,000 to 6,000

MIAMI, Fla.—April 6. For nearly nine months Cuban exile military forces dedicated to the overthrow of Premier Fidel Castro have been training in the United States as well as in Central America.

An army of 5,000 to 6,000 men constitutes the external fighting arm of the anti-Castro Revolutionary Council, which was formed in the United States last month. . . .

Cuban leaders here expect that it will be possible to coordinate the activities of the external forces—those trained outside Cuba—and the internal forces when the time comes for a major move against the Castro fortress in Cuba.

The recruiting of Cubans—which has been proceeding since last summer, is being discontinued as the anti-Castro leaders believe that their external forces have reached the stage of adequate preparation.

The external forces, many of them highly trained in landing, infiltration and sabotage operations, are now concentrated at two major camps in Guatemala

and at a base in Louisiana, not far from New
Orleans. . . .

Most of the instruction given to the anti-Castro
forces was reported to have been centered in the
Guatemalan camps where infantry and artillery
units are being trained by United States experts.

But special instruction has been available in
small camps in Florida. Reports said that some of
the air and paratroop units are in the Louisiana
camps.

The story went on at some length, but the point is that it limited
itself to what we knew to be true—that anti-Castro forces were in
training, aided by American officials and with the intent of invading
Cuba—but not that the invasion was coming at any specific time or
that those Americans were specifically CIA men.

The Bay of Pigs invasion, as everyone knows, followed ten days
later and was an unrelieved calamity.

President Kennedy, to his credit, took full responsibility for the
disaster. However, that did not prevent him, in a speech a week
later, from suggesting to members of the newspaper profession that
they "re-examine their own responsibilities." He suggested that newspapermen, with respect to every story, ask, "Is it in the interest of
national security?"

Two weeks later a group of newspaper editors, including myself,
met with Kennedy at the White House to discuss the issue at greater
length. We asked him for examples of newspapers' prematurely
disclosing security information. One example he cited was Paul
Kennedy's story in January about the training of anti-Castro forces
in Guatemala.

I noted that the information had previously appeared in *The
Nation*.

"But it wasn't news until it appeared in the *Times*," Kennedy
replied.

Later Kennedy said to me in an aside, "Maybe if you had printed
more about the operation you would have saved us from a colossal
mistake." He told the same thing to Dryfoos. But his logic seemed to
me faulty. On the one hand, he condemned us for printing too much
and in the next breath he condemned us for printing too little. He
wanted it both ways, and he did not change my view that the newspapers, not the government, must decide what news is fit to print.

The controversy about our handling of the invasion plans continued for some time. Clifton Daniel said in his 1966 speech: "My

own view is that the Bay of Pigs operation might well have been canceled and the country would have been spared enormous embarrassment if the *New York Times* and other newspapers had been more diligent in the performance of their duty." Scotty Reston, however, has said, "It is ridiculous to think that publishing the fact that the invasion was imminent would have avoided this disaster. I am quite sure the operation would have gone forward."

With the benefit of hindsight I think that we might have printed more and, if we had, we might have caused the cancellation of the invasion. But that judgment is based on knowledge I did not have at the time—that the invasion was in fact imminent and, most important, that it was destined to utter failure. What if Castro's Cuba had indeed been ripe for "liberation" by the CIA and the Cuban exiles? Should we then have upset the invasion plans? That, I say again, is the sort of speculation and would-be statesmanship I think a newspaper editor should avoid. Our job is to print the facts, insofar as we can ascertain them. That is what we did, and I think we have nothing to regret.

The case of Herbert Matthews is, to my mind, a more difficult one. Herbert was a brilliant foreign correspondent, one of the most brilliant in *Times* history, yet in the 1960s he became emotionally involved with Fidel Castro to such a point that I and other editors questioned his ability to write objectively about him. Matthews' case says something about the need of a newspaper to protect its credibility, even if the individuals may sometimes suffer in the process.

Matthews was born on January 10, 1900, and joined the *Times* as an office boy when a young man. At one point, he was Arthur Hays Sulzberger's office boy, and Matthews' wife later was Mrs. Sulzberger's secretary. Sulzberger was godfather to Matthews' only son, and Matthews was one of the few members of our staff who called the publisher Arthur. The personal intimacy and affection between Sulzberger and Matthews intensified the publisher's distress when he became convinced, in the 1960s, that Matthews had erred as a reporter and thus embarrassed the *Times*.

Matthews' brilliant career as a foreign correspondent carried him to Peking in 1929 to report Chiang Kai-shek's triumph; to Addis Ababa with the Italian army in 1936; to Spain in 1939; to Italy, India, and North Africa during the Second World War; and to be our bureau chief in London after the war. By 1949, as Matthews himself was nearing age fifty, he was ready to give up his life as an expatriate. We offered him a position on our editorial-page staff and he accepted it. He would have fewer by-lines there, for we tried to minimize news writing by editorial writers, but his vast knowledge of world affairs could be put to good use. In the early fifties, when we were passing out some new titles, I tried to persuade Sulzberger to name Matthews an associate editor, but the publisher would not agree.

Matthews was an extremely sensitive man. I never saw him laugh; I did see him smile, faintly, on occasion. He was a fearless man, ready to run any risk in pursuit of a story. He was also politically committed and concerned, given to deep emotional involvement in the stories he wrote.

The climax of Herbert Matthews' career came at dawn on February 17, 1957, when, after an all-night drive from Havana to the eastern end of Cuba, after penetrating army lines at the foot of the Sierra Maestra Mountains, after a long slippery climb in the dark, he met Fidel Castro, the revolutionary leader whom the world then believed to be dead. The government of General Fulgencio Batista had declared that Castro was dead, Batista himself apparently believed it, and so did most people in America. But Matthews found Castro, interviewed him, photographed him, and wrote three long articles that appeared on February 24, 25, and 26, and established that Castro was very much alive, and stood a good chance of overturning the Batista dictatorship.

When Castro marched triumphantly in Havana on January 1, 1959, Matthews hurried to Cuba and wrote the first of his reports on Castro's Cuba. His stories reflected the excitement and enthusiasm with which many Americans, and a vast majority of Cubans, greeted Castro's victory. They also reflected Matthews' own admiration for Castro, whom he viewed as a man of destiny. "The hunted young man who for three hours whispered his passionate hopes and ideals into my ear in the gloomy jungle depths on February 17, 1957, is now the chief power in Cuba," began one of Matthews' stories in January of 1959. "In the eyes of nearly all his compatriots, Dr. Fidel Castro is the greatest hero that their history has known." Famous for having found Castro in 1957 and clearly the American journalist who was closest to Castro, Matthews not illogically became identified with Castro in the public mind.

The great question about Castro in that period was whether his revolution was, or would become, Communist. Matthews addressed himself to that question in an article we printed on July 15, 1959, after Castro had been in power more than six months. His conclusions were:

> This is not a Communist revolution in any sense
> of the word and there are no Communists in posi-
> tions of control. . . . Castro is not only not Commu-
> nist but decidedly anti-Communist. . . . Premier
> Castro and his followers have made it clear that, as
> Cuban patriots working for Cuba and the Cuban
> people, they are against Communism, since the Reds
> have entirely different aims and loyalties.

It was the next year, in 1960, that Castro turned to Communism,
or some form of it, prompting the anger and disillusion in the
United States that culminated in the Bay of Pigs invasion. Right
wingers who had always suspected Castro of Communism were glad
to point the finger at the *Times* and at Matthews for having been
naïve, or even for having aided the creation of a Communist state
in Cuba. They carried pictures of Castro with the inscription: "I
got my job through the *New York Times*." As Matthews himself
wrote, in 1967: "When Cuba's *Jefe Maximo* and his government
turned Communist and later almost brought on a nuclear war, somebody had to be blamed. I was."

The criticisms troubled Sulzberger and they troubled me. We did
not mind being attacked by the right wing; that had happened before
and it would happen again. We were troubled, rather, by a belief
that the critics were in part correct, that Matthews had used poor
judgment and had lost his cool in his coverage of Castro, and that
his articles had to some degree misled our readers. We discussed the
matter at length, and we agreed that Matthews had diminished his
standing as an objective reporter on Cuban affairs, and that some
limitations should be placed on his work on that subject.

Matthews continued to write editorials for us, and he often
contributed signed pieces to our editorial page. Some of these were
on Cuba—a piece on January 2, 1966, for example, which began:
"The Cuban revolution begins its ninth year today as a strong, completely Communistic, personalized and struggling state." Matthews'
critics chose not to notice his changes in judgment about Castro.

On at least two occasions we declined to publish articles by
Matthews on Cuba. In 1963 and again in 1966, as a member of the
editorial page, he visited Cuba and upon his return offered to write
long articles for the news department. In both cases, we declined the
offer. To put it simply, I felt that Matthews, despite certain obvious
changes in judgment, had lost his credibility as a reporter on Castro,
and that to print his articles would do the *Times* more harm than
good.

I reached the decision with reluctance, but I thought it was necessary to protect the *Times* credibility. If the *Times* has been a force for good in this country's national and international affairs, and I believe it has, it is because the newspaper has earned a high reputation for responsible reporting and reasoned editorializing. Yet a great newspaper is to some extent a political institution; to maintain its power it must sometimes use its power sparingly. It must set priorities and decide on which issues it will push ahead and on which it will bide its time. And, like Caesar's wife, it must keep its reputation above reproach.

This does not mean a newspaper should run from criticism. I think the *Times* demonstrated, in the Eastland episode and many others, its willingness to stand by its people if it believed they were right. But in Matthews' case we were concerned that he, and we, had not been entirely right, and we thought it best not to stir up the issues a second time. It was not an easy decision, or one I was fully satisfied with; in retrospect I have the haunting thought that Matthews was more sinned against than sinning.

XXIII

Strike

LABOR relations were among my continuing interests as a *Times* executive. We were struck about ten times during my quarter century as an executive and other strikes were narrowly avoided. At the beginning of that period, strikes were something new to the New York newspaper business. In earlier years, both labor and management had taken the attitude "the show must go on." Arthur Hays Sulzberger once told me that he would never allow a strike to occur over an economic issue—he'd fight on a matter of principle, but he'd rather grant higher wages than see the *Times* closed down. In the years after the Second World War, however, as unions became more demanding, he had to adopt a tougher attitude, so strikes were inevitable. He was under pressure from other publishers, too, who knew that they would have to pay whatever wages the *Times* agreed to pay. Yet the other New York papers were in stronger financial positions than we were. All the others were either part of a newspaper chain or were backed by a sizable family fortune. The *Times* had to stand on its own.

Given my instincts toward conciliation, I was pained whenever negotiations broke down, leaving labor and management locked in bitter strike. Yet I never feared or resented the Guild the way Sulzberger did. He shared Adolph Ochs' paternalistic attitude toward *Times* editorial employees and he viewed the Guild as a personal affront. It was an intruder that came between him and his employees. In time, he accepted the Guild intellectually, but he never really accepted it emotionally.

My own feelings were mixed. I was never a Guild member, but only for lack of opportunity. When I was with the *Times* in Washington, the Washington bureau was not included in the jurisdiction of our Guild contract. When I went to New York, I became part of management. I sympathized with the Guild's purposes, yet at first I shared Sulzberger's fear that the Guild would create divided loyalties among our staff. I wanted one hundred percent loyalty to the *Times*, and I saw the *Times* not as a company or an institution but as a collection of creative people, working together freely. But my fears faded as the years passed. I don't recall an instance where Guild membership influenced the way any reporter handled a political or labor-related story. On the contrary, Guild members always stressed total objectivity in writing about strikes, negotiations, and the like, even in the cases where they were personally involved.

The Guild's desire for a union or closed shop was repugnant to Sulzberger, and while he lived he was able to preserve the right of our editorial employees *not* to belong to the Guild if that was their wish, although they would share in Guild-negotiated benefits. Sulzberger didn't want any *Times* employee to be forced to belong to an organization that took political stands, as the Guild did because of its membership in the CIO. His aversion to the Guild was intensified by the fact that in the thirties our Guild unit was dominated by Communists. They even published their own paper, called *Good Times,* and sometimes confidential memos from the publishers' files would turn up in its columns. Eventually, after a knockdown battle, non-Communist elements took over our Guild unit.

As assistant managing editor I worked with the Guild in the process of "slotting," or defining, all our editorial jobs so wage standards and working requirements would be more precisely set. I found the process useful, for it gave me a better grasp of our far-flung editorial operation. In general, I thought the Guild, if properly handled, could be quite useful to us in the management ranks. In any event, the Guild was obviously there to stay.

When I became managing editor, I ceased to be directly involved in negotiations with the Guild. I felt that the chief executor of the Guild contracts shouldn't be involved in negotiating those contracts. For one thing, angry words sometimes fly across the bargaining table that can come back to haunt the negotiator. I continued to be indirectly involved in our labor relations, however, both in my role as an advisor to the publisher and in my personal dealings with the paper's employees. It was a practice of mine to stand at the front door of the *Times* whenever a strike ended and greet our employees as they returned to work. Some of my fellow executives objected to this, but I had to work with these people, and I felt that a bit of personal warmth might help ease the strains caused by the strike.

Sulzberger's attitude was one not of diehard resistance toward unions, so much as of sadness. He regretted that the growth of unionism lessened his ability to guide the paper in the fatherly manner he preferred. On December 7, 1953, the day Sulzberger marked his thirty-fifth anniversary with the *Times*, the paper was not publishing because of a strike by the photoengravers. This unhappy state of affairs inspired Sulzberger to write a poem, after the style of Gilbert and Sullivan, which concluded:

> He worked very hard and he never watched the clock
> And he polished up the handle on the big front door.
> By dint of hard labor he rose to the top
> And in thirty-five years the Times was no more.

As it happened, that strike ended the next day.

In 1958, during a drivers' strike, all the New York newspapers shut down. Our Guild members were willing to come to work, although we would have been justified in not allowing them to do so as long as the strike continued. A good deal of money was involved, in wages and benefits and Sulzberger's business advisors urged him to include the Guild in the lockout. But Sulzberger commented that Christmas was coming on, and the *Times* had a cash surplus, and he could imagine no better way to spend it than on his editorial staff. So they came to work and were paid their full salaries. Later, as a way of saying thank you, the Guild presented Sulzberger with a scroll that made him an honorary member. He was tremendously touched— that gesture epitomized the sort of warm, personal relationship he wanted with his employees.

Thus, his disillusion was all the more when the Guild joined in the great strike of 1962-63. That nearly broke his heart.

The strike began on December 8 as a strike by the typographers against the *Times*, *News*, *Journal-American*, and *World-Telegram & Sun*. The other papers in the Publishers Association suspended operations, but the New York *Post* resumed publication on February 28.

Orvil Dryfoos was the *Times* publisher who had to contend with the situation. He had become publisher in 1961 after nearly twenty years spent preparing for the job. Sulzberger had retired, wanting to set an example of *Times* executives stepping down at a reasonable age; Sulzberger, however, took the title of Chairman of the Board, and continued a lively interest in the paper's operations. He and his wife still had final say in any major decisions.

Dryfoos and his father-in-law had much in common, in that both were intelligent, modest, cautious men. There was one significant difference between their styles of operation as publisher, however. Sulzberger injected himself into editorial matters often, while Dryfoos almost never did. Sulzberger never wanted it forgotten that he was the publisher, while Dryfoos was more apt to tell me: "That's an editorial matter—you decide it." One reason for this was that Dryfoos was new in the publisher's post (and had the former publisher looking over his shoulder), whereas Sulzberger, by the time I got to know him, had had years of experience and far more confidence. In any event, Dryfoos' determination to stay out of editorial decisions was important after the strike in an episode involving his close associate Amory Bradford.

Bradford was vice president and general manager of the *Times*, and Dryfoos relied on him heavily in business affairs. As Bradford's power had increased, so had the aloofness and impatience I had first noticed back in the late forties. He often had a "don't bother me" attitude toward subordinates, or those he took to be subordinates, and this manner would become a factor in the strike.

The Publishers Association chose Bradford as its chief negotiator in the dispute. His opposite number was Bertram A. Powers, president of the International Typographical Union's New York local. Powers was then forty-one years old, a tough and ambitious man, and a relentless negotiator. Powers had quit high school at seventeen to become a printer, and a sharp personal antipathy soon arose between him and the aristocratic, Yale-educated Amory Bradford. Many of those involved in the negotiations believe that the personality clash between Bradford and Powers needlessly prolonged the strike. I was not present at negotiations sessions, but I know that Abe Raskin, our labor expert, when he conducted extensive interviews for his history of the negotiations, began by doubting that two men's personalities could affect such a great economic conflict, but soon changed his mind.

As the strike dragged on, week after week, tempers sometimes grew short. Often, several of us, including Punch Sulzberger, Harding Bancroft (then in effect Bradford's assistant), and I would sit with Dryfoos in the publisher's office awaiting news about the negotiating sessions. When Bradford would appear, he sometimes made it clear he was annoyed at our presence and wished to report only to Dryfoos, out of our hearing. He was, of course, under a tremendous strain himself, but I think that as the strike continued Dryfoos came to have second thoughts about Bradford's talents as a negotiator.

I had one clash with Bradford during the strike that was perhaps typical of the temper of that time. I called Dryfoos' office to pass on some information about the strike. Bradford answered the phone, and when I told him what I'd heard, he snapped: "I already know that. Don't waste my time with junk like that." I was outraged. A minute later Dryfoos, who'd overheard the conversation, came to my office. "Let's keep calm," he said. "Everyone is wrought up." I told him I would keep calm, but that I didn't intend to accept that kind of treatment from Bradford or anyone else.

As it turned out, Bradford continued to be a center of controversy even after the strike ended. As the end seemed to be nearing, we made plans to inform our readers of the news they'd missed.

One of the biggest stories during the strike was the strike itself, and we asked our labor specialist, Abe Raskin, if he would undertake a detailed analysis of it. Abe immediately pointed out that, from what he knew then, an honest account of the negotiations might not make some people on the publishers' side of the table, notably Bradford, look like paragons. We told Abe to write it the way it happened, and he did so, brilliantly.

Raskin's story was long—it filled two pages of the *Times* of April 1, 1963—and marvelously detailed. It devoted only a few paragraphs to Bradford's role in the negotiations, but those paragraphs contained comments that Bradford could not be expected to enjoy. Raskin first described Bradford as "handsome, articulate and aloof," and continued:

"One top-level mediator said Mr. Bradford brought an attitude of such icy disdain into the conference rooms that the mediator often felt he ought to ask the hotel to send up more heat. Another mediator, who called Mr. Bradford the possessor of the keenest mind on the management side, said he operates on a 'short fuse.'" Raskin went on to say that the other publishers admired Bradford's "independence and assurance although they are occasionally galled by his imperiousness."

That was all. As criticism goes, it was moderate; men in public life are more harshly written about every day. But Bradford was not in public life, strictly speaking, and he did not expect to be criticized in the newspaper he served as vice president and general manager. Soon after Raskin turned in his story, a copy reached

Bradford. I may have shown it to him myself, or Dryfoos may have. In any event, he protested to Dryfoos. He argued that the strike was old news, which needn't be written about, and also that the story contained inaccuracies.

To Dryfoos' great credit, he refused to intervene in any way. He took the position that the decision on whether or not to publish the story was an editorial matter and thus was for me to make. At one point, I was in Dryfoos' office when Bradford called to complain about the story. "Talk to Turner," Dryfoos told him, but Bradford insisted that he wouldn't talk to me. Eventually he did come to me. He made it clear he did not want the story published, or at least those portions about him. He insisted there were inaccuracies in the story, but he refused to tell me what they were.

Dryfoos at first declined to read the article, but I insisted that he do so, since he was himself a figure in it. He walked up to Central Park to read the story, and when he returned he dropped it on my desk and said, "It's absolutely amazing. The decision is yours, but if you run it I have one comment." He then told me one detail that had been lacking in Raskin's original draft, involving Dryfoos' intervening with Bradford and outside mediator Theodore W. Kheel when both men had threatened to leave the negotiations. Aside from this factual matter, Dryfoos had no more to say about Raskin's article.

I've since considered that hands-off attitude a great tribute to Dryfoos' integrity. I'm not entirely sure that Arthur Hays Sulzberger would have similarly abstained. More likely he would have wanted to discuss specific points or phrases in the story. Sulzberger would probably have asked if we had ever published anything like Raskin's story before. His instinct would have been to seek a precedent as a rationale for printing the article, or not printing it.

Dryfoos did suggest that I ask Bradford's friend and assistant, Harding Bancroft, to read the article for possible inaccuracies. This was during the final weekend of the strike, March 30, 31. Bancroft was at his country home, but he came to my apartment about midnight Saturday. After he read the piece, Bancroft laughed and said, "Jesus, what a piece of reporting!" I asked if he saw any inaccuracies. "Not a single thing that I know about has the slightest error," he said. "You've got to print it."

Print it we did, on April 1, when we put out our first paper in 114 days. The story caused a sensation in the newspaper business. Many editors frankly told me that they wouldn't have printed such candid remarks about one of their own executives. Bradford, to his credit, took the story in his stride, and made no further comment about it.

Raskin's story was only one episode in that long, agonizing strike. It was a painful time for all of us who thought that New York wasn't quite the same without the *Times*. It was terribly frustrating to see news breaking and to be unable to get it into the paper and to our readers. Some weeks after the strike ended, my wife, Abby, delivered a speech at the annual convention of the American Society of Newspaper Editors in Washington, in which she described, in a light-hearted manner, what it was like living with a managing editor who was unable either to manage or edit. She said in part:

"Having no newspaper to manage, he became over-interested in the management of the house. He started out in the kitchen. He rearranged the icebox. For days we couldn't find anything we wanted. He cut off the dishwasher. Said his mother never had one. Then he turned to cooking. He told me his mother used to make the best fried corn in the world. Said he'd show us how to do it. Well, he did. But we've had to have the kitchen repainted.

"On April Fool's day, my editor stormed out of the house as if it were on fire. No, the house wasn't on fire but he was. His paper was back in business. Oh, how relieved I felt for the moment. I was glad to have him run back to his old, gray mistress, the *New York Times* —at least she used to be old and gray, but now under his loving care she's getting fatter and sexier every day."

The strike ended on the morning of Sunday, March 31. John Bambridge of *The New Yorker* was present and wrote a long "Talk of the Town" piece on our reactions to the strike's end. There is space here to quote only a few highlights from Bambridge's piece:

> It was now eleven-twenty. No word of importance had been received from the meeting. When something did happen, the newsroom was expected to be the first to know, and, as a result, a number of people from other departments had taken up temporary residence there. Three of these visitors—Ivan Veit, business manager for promotion and circulation; Nat Goldstein circulation director; and Irvin Taubkin, promotion director— were sitting around a desk near Catledge's office. . . .
>
> At eleven-twenty-five Catledge, who was as restless that day as Frank Adams or any of the rest of the staff, came out of his office and glanced out the window. Three men were standing across the street. Robert Garst, an assistant managing editor, said that

two of them were from the composing room and the
third was from the pressroom. Turning away from
the window, Catledge said he was about to watch
the television program "The New York Times of the
Air," and invited anybody who would like to see it to
join him. We accepted the invitation, as did Goldstein and Salisbury, and followed him into a small
lounge adjoining his office. The program was
watched intently and with very little comment,
though when Marjorie Hunter, of the Washington
Bureau, came on, Catledge said, "That's the best
hairdo she's had." Presently, the program was inter-
rupted for a switch to Gabe Pressman, the N.B.C.
newsman, who was covering the photoengravers'
meeting. When he appeared on the screen, standing
just outside the meeting-room doors, he explained
that reporters were not allowed inside, but that, in
the best tradition of keyhole journalism, he was following developments by keeping his ear pressed to
the crack of the door. Catledge smiled. Pressman
then held a microphone to the door, and a voice he
identified as that of the Union's president could be
heard telling his audience that he hoped nobody,
upon leaving the meeting, would "say anything that
would be detrimental to the union."

"That could be a good sign," Catledge remarked.

Pressman gave some background information,
said that the vote would be taken soon, and promised
to return whenever there were more developments.

Frank Adams appeared in the doorway. "The
vote is underway," he said, and left.

Goldstein rubbed his hands. "They're wet," he
said, looking surprised. "I'm in a cold sweat."

As the program continued, Catledge got up,
walked into his office, came back, stood in the doorway, and then sat down on the arm of a sofa.

At this moment, Irvin Taubkin darted his head
around the door of the lounge and said, "It's been
approved!"

Catledge stood up. . . . Walking out of the newsroom, Catledge said, "It's passed. The strike seems
to be over. There will be a meeting right away in my
office." He motioned to ten or twelve of his staff, who
followed him into his office and sat down at an oval
table.

"Gentlemen, I hardly know how to express it,"
he began. He hesitated for a second. "We'll just go

to work. We're going to put out a paper tomorrow.
We want to get out an abnormally good paper. Let's
be very alert in handling continuing stories. For
example, our people know scarcely anything about
the football scandal that's been going on down
South. We will have to fill them in. It doesn't have
to be long—a paragraph or so—but on these continuing stories go back and loop in what's happened.
We hope to have an eighty-page paper tomorrow. It
will be in four sections—twenty-eight and twelve,
twenty-eight and twelve. Eighty pages is an ideal
paper. We're going to try to cut off copy at seven, so
we can get a nine-o'clock press start. We're back in
production. The paper's going to look awfully good.
God damn! Let's just translate our glee into some
damned good work and a damned good paper."

That ended the meeting, and within minutes
those who had attended it were at work. By twelve-
thirty, all the lights over the reporters' desks had
been turned on. . . .

Catledge, smiling almost continuously, had taken
up a position near the entrance of the newsroom.
"Hi, Abe," he said, shaking hands with Raskin, who,
smiling broadly and looking as suave and conserva-
tively tailored as a Morgan partner, was among the
first to arrive.

Raskin was followed by Nan Robertson, a reporter, who made an exuberant entrance. "Uh boy!
Home!" she said, shaking hands with Catledge, who
went on to welcome Milton Bracker, Mort Stone,
Peter Kihss, Seth King, Gay Talese, Homer Bigart,
and many others, including Ruth Adler, an attractive, white-haired woman, who edits the paper's
house organ.

"I can't believe it," Miss Adler said after kissing
Catledge on the cheek and looking around the room.
"The place hasn't changed a bit."

Television crews had arrived and were setting up
their equipment.

"Do you want to say anything for publication?"
Catledge asked Orvil E. Dryfoos, the publisher, who
had come into the room.

"No," Dryfoos replied. "I just want to publish."

We did publish, and the next morning's *Times* was a joyous event
for all of us. But our joy was short-lived, for two months later, on
May 25, Orvil Dryfoos died of heart failure at age fifty.

XXIV

Executive Editor

THE strain of the 114-day strike no doubt contributed to Orvil
Dryfoos' death, but he had been in delicate health for several years.
He suffered a heart condition and had given up smoking and tennis
some years earlier. Not long before his death, I was approached by
a close friend of the Sulzberger family about becoming assistant to
the publisher, in order to relieve Dryfoos of some of his burdens.
I said I would do whatever was best for the paper, but nothing came
of the idea.

Dryfoos' early death left the paper, for the first time since Ochs
bought it, with no member of the publishing family who was carefully trained to take over as publisher. There was some speculation
at the time that Ruth Sulzberger Golden, publisher of the Chattanooga *Times*, or John Oakes, Mr. Ochs' nephew and our editorial-
page editor, might be chosen for the job. There was never any doubt
in my mind, however, as to who the next publisher would be. This
was a dynastic situation and the rules of dynasty would prevail. I
was correct, and three weeks after Dryfoos' death, Arthur Hays
Sulzberger announced that the new publisher would be his and
Iphigene Ochs Sulzberger's only son, thirty-seven-year-old Arthur
Ochs (Punch) Sulzberger. The only question in my mind was
whether AHS would insist on a regency, with Amory Bradford serving as the young publisher's chief advisor.

I can remember the first time I met Punch Sulzberger. It was at the Democratic convention in Philadelphia in 1936. His mother had brought Punch, who was ten, and his sisters to see the show. They came by our makeshift office and Punch spent some time examining the news ticker. He was far more interested in the mechanics of the thing than in the words coming out of it. That was typical of Punch, for he has always been mechanically inclined. He has a workshop in his home, and he generally has a few tools at hand wherever he goes. He several times fascinated my wife and me by repairing and revising the electrical wiring in our apartment. His mechanical bent has been put to good use at the *Times*, for publishing a newspaper is a mechanical process as well as an intellectual one.

Punch had a good deal of trouble in school. He was the youngest of the Sulzbergers' four children, and the only boy. His nickname came from his father's remark, at the time of his birth, that he had "come to play the Punch to Judy's endless show." Judy was his sister Judith, three years his senior. The Sulzbergers were extremely active people, and intimates of the family thought Punch never got all the attention he needed. I remember a trip I took with AHS to the Pacific in 1944; he spoke affectionately of Punch, who was then in the Marines, but not in the way he would have if he had been expecting his son to have a major role at the *Times*. Later, Jimmy James told me that Punch was not interested in the paper, only in tinkering with radio sets.

After the war, Punch earned a B.A. at Columbia and worked briefly as a reporter for the *Times* before he was recalled to the Marines during the Korean War. When he returned to civilian life he spent a year on the Milwaukee *Journal*. His father was pleased to have him go to Milwaukee because, among other reasons, the *Journal* had a plan of employee ownership of the paper that he wanted Punch to study. Sulzberger was acutely aware that eventually, after Adolph Ochs' trust ended with Iphigene Sulzberger's death, the ownership of the *Times* would be drastically changed, and he wanted to examine, and wanted Punch to examine, other forms of ownership.

Next, Punch worked as a reporter in our Paris bureau. Punch was then married to an attractive, vivacious young woman named Barbara Grant, and they had two children. Their marriage began to break up while they were in Paris. Both their mothers flew to Paris and tried unsuccessfully to help. I happened to be making a trip to Paris, and AHS asked me to make myself available in case Punch wanted to talk to me. I found there was nothing I could do. Later, after Punch and Barbara separated, he wanted to leave Paris, but AHS was not sure it would be wise for Punch to come to New York. There seemed to be no clear-cut opening for him at the paper. I suggested that Punch be assigned to Rome, where Arnaldo Cortesi, our bureau chief, a worldly and compassionate man, could keep an eye on him. Sulzberger thought this an excellent idea, and asked me to put it to Punch and Cortesi as my own. I did, and Punch went to Rome for a time.

He eventually returned to the New York office, where he was given the title of assistant treasurer, although his duties were ill-defined. Orvil Dryfoos was clearly in line to be the next publisher. Amory Bradford was the top man on the business side of the paper, and his attitude toward Punch was "Go away, boy, you bother me." Punch's duties were of the most menial sort; he seemed to spend much of his time wandering around the building inspecting things— to what purpose was never clear to me. I several times told Dryfoos this was a degrading way to treat a future owner of the paper, but Dryfoos would throw up his hands and say he didn't know what to do with Punch.

Punch and I spent a good deal of time together in those days. We were both separated from our wives, and he became part of the group that gathered in my office for a drink and conversation at the end of the day. Others in that group included Nat Goldstein, then head of circulation, and Irvin Taubkin, our promotion director. I liked Punch, and I was also concerned about him. He was an immensely pleasant young man, witty and good-natured, and I thought he had far more ability than he was given credit for. I became something of an uncle to him, providing a dry shoulder when he needed one. It happened, when we both remarried, he to Carol Fox Fuhrman in December of 1956, I to Abby a year later, that our wives became good friends and we continued to be very close.

Just before Punch's selection as publisher was announced, I witnessed a scene of some importance to my future at the *Times*. Amory Bradford then obviously hoped to be named president, and in effect publisher. AHS wanted Punch to be publisher, with Bradford in the background as a kind of regent. Punch, however, had different ideas, for he had not forgotten Bradford's attitude toward him in recent years. Punch called me up to his office one day. I'd been there hardly a minute when his mother came in.

"Darling, I'm sorry, but that's the way your father wants it," she was saying.

"I won't take it then," Punch declared. "I'm going to see him."

He dashed down the hall to his father's office, and returned in five minutes. "It's all settled," he told us proudly. His mother obviously was delighted at the way he had asserted himself.

I saw AHS a little later and he explained what had happened. "I wanted him to work with Bradford," he said. "But, hell, I can't get along with Bradford, so why should I expect him to?"

Bradford resigned shortly after that. Bradford told me that he thought he should leave because he was losing his resilience. I thought his expression accurately described his situation. When he first came to the *Times* we were rather close, and I visited occasionally with him and his wife, from whom he has since been divorced. But the increasing pressures of his duties at the *Times*, and especially the strains of the strike, had set off a streak of temperament in him which made him hard to deal with. On the occasions I have run into him since he left, he has always been most gracious and friendly. I can't say that I was sorry to see him go. If he had stayed, I would probably have left. It was clear that Punch would lean heavily on the advice of some older man. Now it seemed that I would be that man.

Punch came to power with no circle of contemporaries to advise and assist him. No one had expected him to be publisher and few people had bothered to cultivate him. Goldstein, Taubkin and I, and a few others of my early-evening circle, were his "gang." It was inevitable that Punch would develop advisors of his own age, but for the time we were the people he turned to.

Punch soon proved to be a more aggressive publisher than either Sulzberger or Dryfoos had been. Those two, having married into the newspaper, saw themselves as trustees, but Punch had a sense of proprietorship that they had lacked. He was less inclined to delegate full authority or to accept without questioning the advice of his editors, and this sometimes seemed to indicate lack of confidence. Adolph Ochs used to say, "I always question the obvious," and Punch was like his grandfather in that regard. He liked to ask questions and challenge assumptions, and some editors who did not know him well thought this implied dissatisfaction with their work. He had the impatience of a man who is underrated and wants to prove himself.

During the three weeks between Dryfoos' death and Punch's appointment to be publisher, we several times spoke of what he would do in the job. We reviewed an idea that I had previously discussed with both him and Dryfoos, that of uniting the daily and Sunday departments under one editor. As it was and had been for years, the managing editor and the Sunday editor reported separately to the publisher. In a sense, the publisher had been functioning as an executive editor. Punch, however, likes neat organization, for Punch is a very neat person. His clothes are always neatly pressed. When we traveled together, his last act as he left his hotel room would be to empty all the ashtrays, pick up all the papers, make sure everything was in perfect order. He wanted his newspaper to be in perfect order, too, and doted on charts and computers and efficiency experts. The daily-Sunday split seemed untidy to Punch and he proposed to remedy it by making me executive editor.

A key figure in his plan was Lester Markel, who had been our Sunday editor for forty years. I think that at one point Markel had hoped to become managing editor. He had been a brilliant and pioneering Sunday editor, and as independent as he was brilliant. Under Markel, the Sunday department was virtually a separate principality, not even always following the style of the daily *Times*. There was something of a philosophical difference between Markel and me, in that I regarded the Sunday *Times* as supplemental to the daily *Times*, but he tended to regard it as a primary publication. Questions arose, for example, as to whether the Sunday review of the news should assume the reader read the daily paper, or set out to tell him everything. The Sunday paper relied on many of the daily paper's staff members to write for it, and I often had to settle disputes as to which side had priority on a writer.

I once told Markel, "Lester, you've often been a headache, but you've never been a bore." Markel's long-time assistant, Dan Schwarz, once wrote a good description of him: "He was the best of bosses. He was the worst of bosses. He was domineering, stubborn, inconsistent, indecisive, arrogant. He was stimulating, inspiring, sympathetic, idealistic, brilliant. 'I'm not looking for admiration,' he would say. 'All I want is respect.'"

I had been dealing with Markel since I was a young reporter in Washington. I sometimes contributed to the Sunday *Magazine* in those days and regularly to the Week in Review section. When the Depression hit, Markel had to quit paying for contributions to the Week in Review. You got your by-line and that was all. I was young and ambitious but by-line-less, so for twenty-six weeks in a row I contributed to the Week in Review without extra pay. When Markel was able to start paying again, he saw to it that I got all the Sunday assignments I wanted.

Markel was famous as a demanding editor. Usually he demanded that you write a piece his way, not yours. This was especially true of magazine articles. I never had much trouble with him, except once when he asked me to write a piece to be called "The Fascist Menace of Gerald L. K. Smith." The difficulty was that after traveling with Smith for several days I concluded Smith wasn't a menace, Fascist or otherwise. He loved to hear the sound of his own voice, but he had no organization and no administrative ability. I couldn't take him seriously, and I wrote the article that way. Markel wouldn't accept it, and I wouldn't change my mind, so the article was never published.

However difficult he was to deal with, Markel did what Adolph Ochs had asked him to do many years before: he produced a superior Sunday newspaper. The Sunday *Magazine* was a model for other newspapers. The book review became the most influential in America. The Week in Review section pioneered news analysis and depth reporting. He made our Sunday entertainment section one of our most attractive and popular features.

Sulzberger had inherited Markel, he respected him, and he was willing to grant him the autonomy he demanded. Dryfoos had thought of a joint daily and Sunday editor and actually discussed this idea with me several times, but he was willing to wait until Markel was ready to retire. When Punch took over, however, he was less patient.

Punch found it difficult to deal with Markel. He felt frozen out of the Sunday department. The problem was not the quality of the Sunday paper, which was high, but more one of diffuse organization. Punch, like Dryfoos, wanted a single editor over the entire paper. There was no reason to think that Markel, after years of reporting to the publisher (if to anyone) would now agree to report to me, so the corollary of Punch's plan to elevate me to executive editor was to remove Markel as Sunday editor.

The announcement was made on September 1, 1964. I was named executive editor. Markel was shifted from Sunday editor to associate editor, in which post he would no longer direct the Sunday department. At the same time, Scotty Reston stepped down as Washington bureau chief to concentrate on his column. Tom Wicker became the new head of that bureau. Clifton Daniel replaced me as managing editor, and Dan Schwarz became the new Sunday editor.

The news that I was to be executive editor came as a surprise to most people at the *Times*. Even Daniel, the new managing editor, was not informed in advance. He was angry about that, even though he was delighted at his promotion. But Punch had wanted to keep the change quiet until he was ready to make his move. He was wor-

ried about Markel's reaction. Punch called me to his office when he
had it all worked out and showed me a memo he'd prepared for
Markel. He wanted to present Markel with a *fait accompli,* which he
did, in a last-minute, face-to-face encounter. Markel was shocked,
less at the decision, I think, than that he had not been consulted.
He became very difficult for a time, as was understandable. It was
an abrupt end to a distinguished career, one that had begun under
Punch's grandfather. I agreed with what Punch wanted to accom-
plish, but I can't say I was wholly pleased with the way he handled it.
But he was a young man, and young men can be cruel, sometimes
without even knowing it.

Dan Schwarz, the new Sunday editor, was a talented, soft-spoken,
wonderfully agreeable person with whom I could work in perfect
harmony—and had since we first met back in 1929. He was the
ideal man to help me break down the barriers between the daily and
Sunday departments. I began spending one morning a week with the
Magazine staff and meeting as much as possible with the Sunday
editors. I found them a bright, lively bunch of young people, brim-
ming over with good ideas and intellectually daring. They hadn't
been happy with their isolation from the rest of the *Times,* and they
were glad to be brought into the mainstream. They gobbled up stories
and story ideas I'd bring back from trips. The Sunday paper had
been good, but in the mid-sixties it became much better.

Both Schwarz and I believed the *Magazine* needed to be more
lively. For example, the lead article for an issue in November of
1966 concerned the movie *The Sound of Music* and why it was the
biggest money-maker in movie history. This was perhaps the first
time the *Magazine* had ever led off with an article on entertainment,
and the change was the result of a conscious decision on Schwarz'
part. Punch questioned the change, but I knew Markel was needling
him and this led me to write a memo to Punch stating some of my
thoughts about the *Magazine's* development:

> We are making a conscious and deliberate effort to keep the Maga-
> zine varied, both in content and display. We don't want it to be too
> solemn; neither do we want it to be fluffy and fickle. Above all, we
> do not want it to be predictable. It seems to us highly desirable to
> whet the reader's curiosity. We want him to ask, "What in the
> world are they going to print next week?" We want to avoid stereo-
> types, to vary the mixture, to keep the reader on his toes by show-
> ing him that we are on our toes.
>
> This does not in our view change the basic purpose of the Maga-
> zine. Our purpose remains exactly as it has been all along—to

explain the news, before, when, and after it develops. At the same time, we want to broaden the meaning of the word "news" to cover activities in our lives and in our society that perhaps we have not considered the term "news" to cover before.

Punch himself had been the instigator of a big improvement some months earlier. In December of 1965, for its Christmas issue, the *Magazine* ran its first color cover, and Punch sent me a memo which said: "I really like the color cover on the Magazine section. How much more would it cost if we decided to do it fifty-two times a year?" I learned that Markel had believed that color covers were impractical. But Dan Schwarz thought differently and, encouraged by Punch, color covers became a regular feature.

We made other changes in the Sunday sections. The unsigned articles in the Week in Review were replaced by signed news-analysis pieces. I resisted this change at first, because I liked the institutional quality of the unsigned pieces, but I was persuaded it was a needed change. Punch also opposed dropping the summary of the news in the first pages of the Review—I told him I suspected it was because he used it for his week's reading. Markel took some of the changes as personal affronts and made his displeasure known from his new office on the fourteenth floor. But they were changes for the better, and in time Markel accepted them with good grace and applied himself energetically to his new responsibilities.

With Punch as its publisher, the *Times* became a lively place to work. He was energetic and impatient, filled with ideas and criticisms, filled also with wit and high-spirits, and soon his memos rained down on me just as his father's had. He often called me "Professor," and despite the quarter-century difference in our ages there was nothing formal about our relationship. I was constantly delighted by his puckish humor, which pervaded even the critical notes he sent me.

One, in early 1965, read:

Turner:
   I realize that you are planning some day to retire to a floating home, but it seems to me that we have had more than our fair measure of such advance publicity. Earlier in the week we had a floating home on the second front. We repeat it again today and also on the women's page.
      Let's lower the anchor and step ashore
      quickly.

                                                    Punch

Another time, one of our young lady reporters sent Punch a joyous note when she received a check for her first Merit Award. Unfortunately, her note began "Dear Mr. Sulzburger." Punch sent this on to me with the comment: "No more goodies for —— —— until she learns to spell my name."

More important than Punch's humor was his decisive style. It was seen in his handling of Markel, and in many other matters. In January of 1964 he stopped publication of our West Coast edition, which Dryfoos had started sixteen months before. I had been among the supporters of the West Coast venture, but I had underestimated the problems it would face, and I agreed with Punch that we could not go on losing thousands of dollars a week on it. Punch again showed his pragmatism in 1967 when he folded our European edition (or, to be precise, merged it with the Paris *Herald Tribune*). His father had begun the international edition in 1948, so folding it was a painful move, but, again, a necessary one, since the edition was losing more than a million dollars a year.

Punch was willing to halt losing projects, but he was more interested in starting successful ones. The one that interested him most was the possibility of starting an afternoon paper in New York after the *World-Journal-Tribune* failed. Abe Rosenthal and a dozen-man staff were assigned to produce dummy editions in the summer of 1967. I was against the plan, but at Punch's request I kept my opinions to myself, so the new paper's advocates could have every chance to make their case. My worry was that if we launched a new paper Punch and others of us would inevitably give it a lot of our time, and the *Times* might suffer. I was not sure there was an audience for it, either of readers or advertisers—the people who wanted our sort of paper already had it in the *Times*. Eventually Punch came to share these doubts, and others about the economics of the proposal, and the plan was dropped.

Along with reshuffling his top editors, Punch was building a first-rate team of administrators and business advisers. One of the most influential is Ivan Veit. Veit, a short, dark, able executive, started with the *Times* as a classified-ad taker in 1928 and now holds the title of Vice President. Veit is active in the paper's program of acquisition and diversification, which has included, among other things, the purchase of two golf magazines, one in the United States and the other in England; a microfilm company; a programmed-learning firm; and an expanded book-publishing operation.

Other key members of Punch's administrative team were Harding Bancroft, the soft-spoken aristocratic executive vice president;

Francis Cox, a former CPA who is now vice president in charge of finance; and Andrew Fisher, vice president for sales and production, a graduate of Amherst and the Harvard Business School, whose fascination with charts and computers equals Punch's own.

All of these men are able; none towers above the paper's business affairs as General Adler and Amory Bradford once did, partly because the paper's affairs are getting more complex, partly because of Punch's inclination toward committee rule and corporate organization.

Two fine examples of "developed news" occurred during my years as executive editor. One was the series on the Central Intelligence Agency that we printed in the spring of 1966. The other was Harrison Salisbury's dispatches from North Vietnam later that year.

The CIA series really began at a daily news conference in early September, 1965, when our foreign news editor told us about an amazing story out of Singapore. Lee Kuan Yew, Prime Minister of Singapore, had charged that a CIA agent had offered him a $3.3 million bribe to cover up an unsuccessful CIA operation there in 1960. It developed that not only was the charge true, but when the State Department denied it, Prime Minister Lee produced the letter of apology from Secretary of State Dean Rusk to prove it.

I was astounded. "What is this CIA?" I asked my colleagues. "For God's sake, let's find out what they're doing. They're endangering all of us."

I had thought the CIA had been brought under checks after it engineered the Bay of Pigs disaster several years earlier. Now, my doubts and those of other editors began to return, and before the meeting was over we had decided to begin a world-wide investigation of the agency and its activities. I felt strongly that we had an obligation to our readers to go beyond routine reporting, to let them know what the intelligence agency was up to. Eventually, the question of the "national interest" would be raised in connection with our CIA series. But to my mind the national interest demanded that the public know more about the CIA, not be kept in ignorance. We told our correspondents in Washington and around the world to seek out all the facts they could about the CIA's operations. The fact-gathering continued through the winter, and in the early spring a team of writers headed by Tom Wicker began to shape our material into five long articles.

By that time, the CIA was well aware of our project. Word was passed from Paris that Charles (Chip) Bohlen, the distinguished Foreign Service officer who then was our ambassador to France, was disturbed by our undertaking. Bohlen, an expert on Russia, considered the CIA an invaluable tool in our government's struggle against Communism. This bothered me, for Bohlen is an old friend of mine, but we were on different sides of the fence in this instance.

Then Secretary of State Dean Rusk called Punch one day. Punch guessed Rusk wanted to talk about the CIA series. Punch didn't feel well enough informed about the series to discuss it with Rusk alone. He came down to my office, and we had Rusk's call put on the "squawk box," so we might have a three-way conversation. Rusk and I knew one another slightly, well enough to know we were both Presbyterian-reared sons of the rural South, and we made a joking allusion to that fact.

"Turner," Rusk said, "you and I speak the same language. As my father used to say, I hope you'll give this prayerful consideration."

"Mr. Secretary," I replied "as my mother used to say, I will give it prayerful consideration."

That was good for a laugh, but what Rusk had to say was deadly serious. He did not suggest, specifically, that we kill the series. But he did make it clear that he believed publication of the series might upset delicate U.S. intelligence efforts all over the world, might endanger agents, might offend allies, encourage enemies, and otherwise harm the national interest and perhaps the national security. My own feeling was that Rusk was afraid of what *he* might learn if we printed all we could about the CIA, so often had the Department of State been in the dark, or even duped, by the CIA's espionage activities.

Punch and I agreed we must take the greatest care with our facts on this series. At the suggestion of Daniel and Salisbury we decided to call in John McCone, the former CIA director, and let him read the completed series. He checked back with Washington, got the CIA's version of certain events, and then he and I and E. C. Daniel sat down in my office and went over the series line by line. We changed certain facts when we were persuaded we had been in error or that danger to an agent or an operation might result. When we'd finished with the facts, the CIA challenged the "tone" of the articles, and some of our conclusions, but we said we'd make the decision on those things.

Punch was sufficiently concerned by Rusk's arguments against the series that on April 19 I sent him the following memo:

Punch:
  We have completed the editing of the C.I.A. series. Every point raised in connection with them by Mr. McCone has been carefully

considered and in almost every case the piece has been revised or modified in line with his suggestions. Here and there where he raised points in which nothing but pure value judgments were involved we have preserved our own language. The series now is ready for release and I propose we release it if and when we have an adequate news peg.

I don't know of any other series in my time which has been prepared with greater care and with such remarkable attention to the views of the agency involved as this one. Articles involving much greater consideration of national security, such as for example Hanson Baldwin on the Defense Department and Frankel on the State Department, have been published without the extreme care which we have taken in this case. We have taken this care to meet the points raised by an agency which certainly is of no greater importance as far as security is concerned than those mentioned above.

My editorial judgment is that this series should be published. If there are policy judgments against publication I am afraid they'll have to be made by you.

T.C.

Two news pegs were soon forthcoming (a man on trial for slander pleading that he was a CIA agent, and the news that the agency had planted agents among Michigan State University scholars working in Vietnam) and the series began on April 25. There was not much controversy about it, once it appeared in print. The CIA was not happy, but there was nothing factual for it to take issue with.

Our purpose in working with McCone was not to protect the government but to protect the *Times*. Any newspaperman is liable to error, and when fifty or a hundred newspapermen file stories from around the world on an espionage agency the possibilities of error are very high indeed. It is better to correct errors before you make them than to apologize for them afterward. In this case, there was the risk that the CIA would use one error to attack the entire series. Obviously there was the risk the government would lie or distort the facts in an effort to protect itself, but Daniel and I realized that, and we reserved the right to make the final decisions ourselves. Even with the degree of self-censorship we exercised, the fact remained that we had published the most revealing mass-circulation account ever written about the CIA and the agency was far from happy about our disclosures.

Another outstanding example of news coverage came late in 1966 when Harrison Salisbury began his dispatches from Hanoi.

I've mentioned Salisbury's helping Clifton Daniel and me improve our cultural coverage, but that is only a tiny part of the contribution he had made to the *Times* since he had joined us in 1949. Salisbury is a journalistic one-man band. He can report, he can write, he can edit, he can see story ideas, he can direct others. He can do all these things because, besides having natural talent, he has a passion to excel. He wants anything he does—a five-paragraph story or a five-hundred-page book—to be done better than anyone else would do it. Fortunately, his skills often enable him to attain that goal.

A lean, quiet man, something of a loner, Salisbury came to us after an outstanding career with the United Press. We had an opening in Moscow and Jimmy James said he'd hire him if he could get a visa to enter Russia. He returned with the visa in a couple of weeks and for the next five years he was our correspondent in Russia, doing an excellent job under the most difficult circumstances. He won a Pulitzer Prize in 1955 for his reporting from Moscow, but to my mind his finest work came during his controversial trip to North Vietnam in December of 1966 and January of 1967. Not since Herbert Matthews found Castro in the Sierra Maestra in 1957 had any journalistic adventure so seized the world's imagination. And Salisbury's work was of even more immediate import, because of his reports that, contrary to U.S. government claims, our planes had been bombing civilian targets in Hanoi and other North Vietnam cities.

It was no accident that Salisbury turned up in North Vietnam for this remarkable piece of reporting. To Salisbury, it was the culmination of a career that had taken him all over the world. To the *Times*, it was a reflection of our policy of giving our readers as complete news reports as is possible, regardless of barriers erected by our government or others.

We had been trying to get a correspondent into China ever since the Communists took it over. At one point, in the mid-fifties, the Chinese indicated they would admit some correspondents and six of our men were on their list, Salisbury and Cy Sulzberger among them. I was delighted at this news, and I proudly reported it to the publisher, Arthur Sulzberger. He was not so gleeful. He said perhaps he should talk to John Foster Dulles. He did, and Dulles said the reporters must not go to China. The Department of State in those days did not recognize the existence of Communist China and did not want the press suggesting to the people that perhaps China was there, after all. Dulles said that if any U.S. reporters went to China he would have them prosecuted under the Trading with the Enemy Act. I was outraged. I wanted to send our men to China and make an issue of it. But Sulzberger would not allow this. He said, in his good-humored way, that my mistake had been in ever mentioning it to him in the first place. He was quite right. At that point, he was so great an admirer of Eisenhower that he would not have dreamed of going against the administration's wishes on what it claimed was a highly sensitive issue of foreign policy.

In the summer of 1966, Daniel suggested that Salisbury make a trip around the periphery of China. This trip provided some excellent stories and it also whetted his hunger for a trip to North Vietnam. And on December 15 he received a cryptic cable saying that a visa was awaiting him in Paris. He arrived in North Vietnam on December 22 and stayed until January 17.

His dispatches from Hanoi were a sensation. "Contrary to the impression given by the United States communiqués," the first one declared, "on-the-spot inspection indicates that American bombing has been inflicting considerable civilian casualties in Hanoi and its environs for some time." The series of dispatches went on to document the bombing damage to civilians and to declare that the bombing had stiffened, rather than reduced, the North Vietnamese will to fight.

According to Salisbury, the U.S. government had again lied to the people about the war in Vietnam. Thus, it was not surprising that the Pentagon, the State Department, and various of their allies in Congress and the press set out to question both Salisbury's accuracy and his patriotism.

I'm sorry to say that we in New York compounded an editorial slip that gave Salisbury's critics something to harp on. In his first dispatch, Salisbury gave no attribution for figures on the civilian casualties he reported. Quickly, with an air of triumph, U.S. government officials declared that Salisbury's casualty figures were the same as those put out by the government of North Vietnam.

Obviously his figures came from the North Vietnamese government. Where else would he get such figures in North Vietnam? He did not claim to have counted the bodies himself. The criticism was silly, but it had a certain effectiveness when put to people who had not thought through the situation. To end the issue, we noted in later articles that the figures came from North Vietnamese officials. I was sorry that we had not anticipated the objection, but we were so excited by Salisbury's series that we simply didn't think of it.

I think, too, that we erred in not explaining with the first report the circumstances of Salisbury's visit, instead of simply shocking our readers with a Hanoi dateline.

But the dispatches would have been controversial whatever we had done. I was greatly impressed by the mail we got on the series. There were hundreds of letters, most appreciative, some bitterly unfavorable. But, favorable or unfavorable, there was a high emotional element running through almost all of them. Those who opposed the war blessed us for exposing another instance of U.S. duplicity. Those who supported it denounced us as allies of Hanoi.

I was glad to read the letters that said Salisbury's articles would bring us closer to peace, but I knew that was not the purpose of his visit. The purpose was to go where the news was and report the truth, whomever it helped. Our critics assumed that a loyal American had no business in the capital of a government whose soldiers were killing our soldiers. These critics did not realize that if newspapermen talked only to our friends and allies they would give our readers a widely distorted picture of the world.

I think one reason for the interest and excitement about Salisbury's dispatches was simply that he did what he did alone. In an era of group journalism, junkets, handouts, briefings, Salisbury had gotten his story on his own, and a sense of old-fashioned adventure came across to the reader. And, despite the official denials, most readers knew that Salisbury had reported the truth about the bombing. In time the government stopped the bombing, in response to pressures that Salisbury's series had helped increase.

There could be little doubt that Salisbury had scored the biggest news beat of the year. Many people assumed that his feat would win him a second Pulitzer Prize. I was still serving on the Pulitzer advisory board and thus I was present when the board (with me abstaining, as was the practice when one's own paper was nominated) narrowly voted against giving the Pulitzer Prize to Salisbury. I was terribly upset by this vote, because I was convinced that several of my colleagues made their decision on political rather than journalistic grounds; indeed, they made no bones about it. They supported the war, so they voted against Salisbury. Joseph Pulitzer, Jr., publisher of the St. Louis *Post-Dispatch* and chairman of the advisory board, was so upset he called for a second, secret ballot, but the result stayed the same. As upset as I was, I kept absolutely quiet even as my colleagues stole embarrassed glances at me. I was afraid to let myself speak; tears were forcing their way into my eyes.

Salisbury shrugged off the Pulitzer decision as he had the earlier politically-inspired criticism of his dispatches. He could afford to.

He knew, we knew, and everyone in the newspaper business knew
what a fine job he had done.

As the 1960's began, I was dissatisfied with our local coverage.
The city was changing rapidly but our coverage of it seemed to me
to be standing still. Early in 1962 I broke the cultural-news staff
away from our city desk and made it responsible directly to me, but
that was only a partial solution. It was about this time I began to
think of Abe Rosenthal as a man who might rejuvenate our local
staff.

Abe began his career on the *Times* as our City College correspondent in the early 1940s. By age twenty-one he had earned a
place as a reporter, and he soon became one of our best. I remember
in 1946 I suggested to our city editor a feature on the life of a UN
delegate. Abe, then twenty-four, drew the assignment and turned in
a sparkling account of a day in the life of Andrei Gromyko. As an
editor, you find that most newspapermen excel either at gathering
the news or at writing it; Abe is, like Harrison Salisbury, one of those
rare fellows who is equally skilled at reporting and at writing.

Abe spent eight years in our United Nations bureau, then went
abroad as a foreign correspondent. He served in India, Poland, from
which he was expelled by the government, and Japan. He won a
Pulitzer Prize for his reporting from Poland, and wherever he went,
he sent back stories of a sensitivity and insight that made foreign
nations spring to life for his readers.

I believe Ted Bernstein first suggested that we bring Abe back
to New York. Ted was thinking of bringing Abe back as a reporter,
but as we discussed the idea we began to think of Abe in terms of
an editor, finally as city editor. He appealed to me as good talent-
breeding stock. Questions arose because Abe had had no administrative experience, and because he'd been away from New York for
several years, yet we knew what an inspired reporter he was and we
hoped those drawbacks might prove to be pluses. I discussed the idea
with Daniel and Dryfoos, and both were enthusiastic.

There remained the necessity of persuading Abe, who then was
stationed in Japan. In the spring of 1962 I saw him during a round-
the-world trip, the purpose of which was to visit foreign correspondents in general and Abe in particular. I didn't intend to make Abe
a firm offer immediately. I wanted to test his reaction to the idea,
and I wanted to get to know him better.

I knew that Abe might not accept the job. Previously, after he'd
been expelled from Poland, I'd visited him in Vienna and offered him

an assignment as a European troubleshooter, based in Geneva. Abe had turned down that offer, saying he wanted to go to Japan. I was displeased, as I always was when a correspondent turned down an assignment, but later I realized that Abe was right. He does his best work when he settles down in a country or a city and becomes part of it. He soaks up the mood of a country, comes to love it, and transmits his deep involvement back to his readers. There are reporters who are cut out to be troubleshooters, flying from country to country, but Abe knew he was not one of them.

After I had been in Tokyo a few days, Abe and I and our wives began an automobile trip across Japan. Abe and I were riding in one car and our wives in another when I first mentioned to him the possibility that he might return as Metropolitan Editor (for I had decided the title should be changed from City Editor to one that more accurately described the job). Abe is an emotional person and one who shows his emotions. I could see he was flabbergasted at my suggestion. He said he was tremendously complimented, yet he spoke with an air of disbelief. He also seemed worried. One reason for this was that, unknown to me, he was in the midst of conversations with John Oakes. John wanted Abe to join the editorial staff, and Abe wanted to write a signed editorial-page column about Asia.

We continued to discuss the idea of his coming to New York during the rest of my stay in Japan, but neither of us made a commitment. Abe expressed the hope that if he took the job the cultural-affairs staff could be brought back under the metropolitan editor's jurisdiction. He said he felt the job had been downgraded by the loss of that staff. He also questioned whether he could do a proper job of telling the New York story if he didn't have the cultural coverage under his direction. I said that was something we could talk about further. He had expressed a reluctance to give up his by-line, and I told him he'd learn, as I had, that as an editor he'd have not one by-line but dozens—one for each member of his staff.

When we arrived in India a few weeks later, Abe met us and we continued our talks while he showed me around that vast country. While we were staying at the Imperial Hotel in New Delhi, I received a letter from Dryfoos telling me, among other things, that John Oakes had agreed to let Russell Baker, of our Washington bureau, begin a humor column. I mentioned this news to Abe and I've rarely seen such a reaction. He almost went to pieces. His usually cheerful face was deflated like a balloon pricked by a pin. He fell into a terrible state of depression. I hadn't even known Abe aspired to a column, but now I did. We both understood that if Baker got a column no other new column was likely to be started for some time.

"Abe," I said, "columnitis is a worse disease than cancer."

My jokes didn't help much, but in time he got over his disappointment. He didn't accept the metropolitan editor position on that trip, but after I'd returned to New York he informed me he would.

Abe entered the new job that fall. The incumbent city editor, Frank Adams, was made our chief local editorial writer. He had urged that Abe serve one year under him, but neither Abe nor I liked the idea. I feared that if Abe spent a year in a subordinate post he might get in the old ruts. I wanted him to start fresh, as he had in Japan and India and Poland, not knowing anything but where his desk was. As it turned out, Abe succeeded beyond our wildest expectations. Returning to the city after a decade abroad, he saw the city with fresh, curious eyes, and his vision was soon reflected in a younger, livelier, more imaginative local staff. The only problem was that Abe's talent and ambition soon propelled him out of the job. Within six years he had advanced from metropolitan editor to assistant managing editor to managing editor. However, one of his protégés, Arthur Gelb, ably replaced him as metropolitan editor.

As 1968 began, and I entered my fourth year as executive editor, I felt that much progress had been made. The Sunday paper was constantly improving, and no longer operated in isolation from the daily. Daniel was performing ably as managing editor. Salisbury was extremely effective as a writer–editor–idea man, for he was all those things as assistant managing editor; Rosenthal had breathed new life into our local coverage, and people like Clive Barnes, Charlotte Curtis, and Craig Claiborne had been highly successful in their respective fields. There remained one trouble spot on my agenda, however, and that was our Washington bureau. My efforts to deal with it led to one of my sharpest disappointments.

XXV

A Tale of Two Cities

WHEN I became an executive of the *Times,* one of my fondest hopes was to help achieve a closer relationship between our Washington bureau and the editors who got out the paper in New York. I had been aware of the estrangement between the two offices ever since I had become a Washington reporter in 1929. Over the years, the bureau had developed an identity of its own and become quite set in its ways. The Washington reporters often achieved considerable prestige, and frequently resented questions asked of them by worka-day editors in New York. They felt they understood Washington politics, and the New York editors didn't. They saw themselves as the victims of constant nitpicking. The New York editors often took the line of least resistance, and let the Washington bureau do much as it pleased. In general, New York editors, from the top down, had not tried consistently to establish the sort of straight-line administration that I thought desirable and even necessary. And so I began seeking ways to make New York needs and attitudes felt in Washington.

As for the bureau's needs and attitudes, I thought that as one who had worked in Washington many years, I was in the position of a reformed sinner. I could remember vividly my frequent outrages when the New York office dared touch my copy or question, no matter how indirectly or slightly, my "superior" knowledge of Washington or the national scene. Once I got to New York, however, I could see how often my reactions had been mistaken, and sometimes downright silly. As a New York editor, I didn't stop to lecture Washington but sought to meet the problem in day-to-day, incident-by-incident articulation of my hopes. I counted on my friendships with the individuals back in Washington, and especially with Arthur Krock, to make it easier to bring the two offices closer together, as indeed it did.

Krock understood the problem and had tried to do something about it when he first became head of the bureau in the spring of 1932. He brought one of the assistant managing editors from the New York office down to Washington to establish a desk system, the purpose of which was to improve liaison between New York and Washington. Still, the apartness continued. Krock came to view himself, and sometimes referred to himself, as the *Times*' "proconsul" in Washington, and a similar view of him prevailed in New York. There, recognition of his ability, his reputation, his natural independence combined to inspire awe, especially in the minds of editors on the lower level, where most of the editing is actually done. The New York editors were far more in awe of Krock than they needed to be, or even he wanted. Often in those days I'd step in if a difference arose and my experience was that if I called Krock we could resolve the problem amicably; the difficulties arose if problems started at a lower level and reached us as issues. Then Krock could be expected to—and with his sense of loyalty, did—resolve any doubt in his own mind in favor of his Washington staff. I understood Krock's attitude, and in the old days I had often profited from it.

Krock, as the Washington correspondent, developed over the years a dual role. He was both administrative head of the bureau, or bureau chief, and its chief writer and columnist. Both jobs carry great prestige in Washington. In the mid-fifties, when Reston was tempted by a lucrative offer from the Washington *Post*, Krock voluntarily relinquished his role as bureau chief to Reston, while continuing as columnist. In Reston the bureau got a chief who was both a gifted leader and great reporter. This latter talent inspired his staff and attracted youngsters of like abilities to the *Times*.

In 1964, at the time of the package deal whereby I became executive editor and Clifton Daniel became managing editor, Reston chose to give up his responsibilities as bureau chief while continuing as a columnist. He recommended that Tom Wicker, then our White House correspondent, be named to replace him as bureau chief, and Punch and I readily agreed. Wicker was then in his late thirties, a personable, sensitive, and highly intelligent North Carolinian who had come to us from the Nashville *Tennessean* in 1959. He soon made a great name for himself in the Washington bureau by his brilliant reporting, a prime example being his story from Dallas on the day of President Kennedy's assassination. I admired Wicker's talents and liked him personally. He and Punch, who were about the same age, struck it off well, as did their wives.

Wicker became Washington bureau chief in September, 1964, and within a year the New York editors, as well as Punch, began having second thoughts on the assignment. Wicker was finding it extremely difficult to carry on the role of top administrator in the bureau while keeping up his aggressive pace as a reporter. The situation simmered for many months, then finally exploded in early 1968. A lot has been written about that affair; what follows is an account of how it looked from where the executive editor sat.

Hardly the day passed in late 1966 and all of 1967 that Punch and I did not discuss the Washington problem. Clifton Daniel, too, was at my door almost daily with some report about the performance of the bureau, some favorable but many sharply critical of the bureau's management. Punch was urging me to "do something," and even urged several times that I take a more direct hand in the day-to-day dealings between New York and Washington. I took the position in this case, as I did in general, that as executive editor I should not grab the wheel from the hands of people who were driving the car—the managing editor and his assistants.

My feelings about the bureau can be most accurately expressed by quoting from a memorandum I sent to Punch in May of 1966. I began by saying that no problem had caused me more concern in the past year than that of the Washington bureau. "The problem began," I wrote, "with the fact that the reins of the Washington bureau were rather suddenly dropped by a man with the highest reputation and skill. In turn they were given over to a younger man who, while talented and very personable—and one on whom we wanted to count heavily in the future—lacked the breadth of experience and knowledge which the job required and with which it had been done so skillfully before."

I noted that Wicker was well liked by the bureau, and I suggested that part of the problem was Tom's instinctive desire to be liked by his associates; it detracted from his leadership and made him unnecessarily defensive toward New York. As a result, I said, the bureau as a unit was not doing the job to which we had become accustomed and which, individual by individual, it was entirely capable of doing.

There were contributing factors. Daniel and his assistants performed aggressively, and Daniel was more sharp-spoken than I had been. Wicker often interpreted this as needless harassment, and sometimes he probably was correct.

Another factor, as seen from New York, was that our Washington bureau had more and tougher competition in the mid-sixties than it had ever had before. The much-improved Washington *Post* was becoming a respected rival, and the television newsmen and news magazines were beginning to get some of the news breaks that once we could have counted as ours. We were "following" too much, and if Daniel and his assistants were harassing the bureau, I was harassing the managing editor. Also, the volume and complexity of news were increasing while our space was not, and so there was a sheer necessity for closer editing in New York; this too was often interpreted as nitpicking. I was perhaps the champion nitpicker of them all, but I did my picking with the managing editor and he in turn with the desks and the desks with the bureau.

For all these reasons, we needed the best possible leadership in Washington and we didn't think that Wicker, for all his talents, was providing it. The consequence of all of this, as Punch and I analyzed it time and again, was that too many good political stories were going elsewhere, too many questions were left unanswered in our stories—and there was too much resistance in Washington to answering them.

What was to be done? I decided to take a more direct hand and made several suggestions to Wicker to see if we could get things on a better footing. I thought what he needed most of all was administrative help, so he could continue to report and give leadership to the bureau, without so much attention to detail. We wanted him to travel more. I made several suggestions about sending executives down from New York, as had been done when Krock first took over the bureau. Harrison Salisbury's name was mentioned. Wicker's reaction was that his bureau would take this as a sign that New York felt he had failed.

In 1965 we did send Robert Phelps, a highly competent copy editor, to serve as an administrative deputy to Wicker. This move helped some, but the basic problem remained.

In a memorandum in May, 1966, I proposed a plan of action to Punch, as he had urged me to do. My plan was that, at the time of Krock's retirement early in 1967, we make Wicker a columnist, as he very much wanted to be, and at the same time turn over direction of the bureau to someone else. But Wicker didn't like my idea, when he got wind of it. He wanted the column but he wanted to retain the position of bureau chief—Krock and Reston had held both posts simultaneously, why couldn't he? He felt that even though he would gain the distinction of becoming a regular columnist, to give up the bureau chief's job would reflect on his abilities and lower his prestige in Washington.

Punch and I both sympathized with Tom's feelings, but we concluded that we'd better proceed according to plan. The one big question left was whom we could put in as bureau chief. We considered several names, but could not come up with anyone we thought sufficiently "ripe" for the task. I went down to Washington to get the feel of the situation, and I found resistance on the part of bureau members to our leading candidates for the job, resistance strong enough to seem to threaten a morale problem that would make things worse than they were. Meanwhile, Wicker was becoming quite nervous. When I returned from Washington and reported my impressions to Punch, I recommended that we not only continue as we were but that I so inform Wicker to ease his nervousness. Punch was highly pleased that I was recommending that Wicker stay on and urged me to tell Wicker immediately.

So Wicker became a columnist and continued as bureau chief, but the situation did not improve beyond a temporary lift in the spirits of Wicker and his closer associates. At the time, I could see no better solution, although in retrospect I think I may have made a mistake not to push harder for a solution then.

The matter simmered through 1967. Around the first of February, 1968, Punch asked Reston and me to come to his office late one afternoon; he wanted to discuss the Washington bureau problem again. I told both of them frankly that I was unwilling to enter a Presidential-election year without a resolution.

By then we had a new candidate for a place in the Washington bureau. He was James Greenfield, a former reporter for *Time* and a former State Department official under President Kennedy. Greenfield, who was then an officer in an airline company, was a close friend of Abe Rosenthal, who had recruited him for the *Times*. Greenfield joined us as assistant metropolitan editor and showed himself immediately to be innovative and industrious. On several occasions, his Washington contacts proved useful to us.

Rosenthal and Daniel began immediately to push Greenfield for assignment to Washington, even appointment to direct the bureau. The idea appealed to Punch, who was not one to be awed by suggestions of new approaches. Reston also seemed reluctantly to agree, since we did not seem to have anyone else ready for the job at that time. So it was decided at that late-afternoon meeting, or at least I certainly thought it was decided, that we would proceed to install Greenfield as bureau chief in Washington at an early date. The one big question left was how the transfer should be handled. Greenfield's name had been discussd quite thoroughly before. During those discussions Wicker had said he was willing to take him as a deputy, even with the view of future advancement, but he was unwilling to surrender the post of bureau chief to him at that time. Other members of the Washington bureau objected to Greenfield both as a "Kennedy man" and too recent an arrival on the *Times* staff.

But we had made our decision and now, over the objections of both Reston and me, Punch took on the task of breaking the news to Wicker. Punch felt he owed that to Wicker as a friend. I feared, as I am sure Reston did too, that the combination of Wicker's sensitivity and Punch's affection would cause problems, as indeed it did.

Punch went down to Washington a day or two later and had a talk with Wicker. When he returned to New York he came to my office, obviously disturbed and shaken. The meeting with Wicker had not gone well; I gathered it had been quite traumatic for Punch but he gave no indication that he was pulling back from the Greenfield appointment. It was, however, left hanging; no immediate announcement was to be made despite Daniel's and Rosenthal's urging. Meanwhile, ferment was building in Washington.

It was the next day, I believe, that Wicker called me from Washington. He said he was going to New Hampshire to write some stories on the New Hampshire primary but before he left he wanted to post on the bureau bulletin board an announcement of his resignation as bureau chief. He said he was convinced, after weighing all considerations, including his conversation with Punch, that it was best all around for him to resign as chief. He preferred, however, to announce it as his own decision. I persuaded Wicker not to do this. I thought that sticking a note on the bulletin board was no way to handle the matter. If Wicker resigned abruptly, it would hurt bureau morale. Also, there were other people we wanted to notify before any public announcement of Greenfield's appointment.

At Punch's suggestion I called Max Frankel, a leading aspirant for the job, to New York. We had lunch at Sardi's, and I told him of Greenfield's selection. Frankel was not surprised; he knew what was in the wind. But he was obviously displeased and suggested that if Greenfield was brought in over him he might leave the paper. Punch had also assigned me to give advance notice to Anthony Lewis, head of the London bureau, another candidate for the Washington job. Before I could get in touch with Lewis, however, the Greenfield decision began to come unglued. Reston apparently had a further talk with Punch and took a decided stand against the Greenfield appointment. I say "apparently" because I was not present when it took place and had no further conversation with Reston about the matter.

The climax came on Wednesday, February 7. I had put in a call to London, so that I could tell Lewis about Greenfield's appointment. Daniel and Rosenthal were waiting anxiously out in the newsroom to make the office announcement as soon as Lewis was informed. During the afternoon news conference in Daniel's office, I got word that Punch was in my office and wanted to see me immediately.

When I got there I found Punch pacing the floor and puffing hard on his pipe.

"Professor," he said, "I can't go through with it."

I could see without his saying so that he had become fearful of the consequences of Greenfield's appointment. He was obviously in great stress and I knew there was no further point in arguing the matter. My only reply at the time was to say: "Aren't you taking some people for granted?" He replied candidly: "You're absolutely right; I *am* taking you for granted."

I returned to the news conference and when it was over I asked Daniel and Rosenthal to stay behind. Then I told them.

"Gentlemen," I said, "I have bad news for you. The publisher has reversed his decision on the Washington bureau."

They were shaken. Rosenthal, over my objections and entreaties, placed a call to Punch but couldn't reach him. I urged both men not to speak to the publisher until they had cooled off—better still, not to speak to him about the matter at all but to hold me responsible. Rosenthal turned and walked swiftly out of Daniel's office. I feared he would rush up to see Punch. Instead he went over to Greenfield's desk and beckoned him to come out into one of the little interview rooms off the third-floor corridor. Within minutes Greenfield went back to his desk, picked up his personal belonging and left the building. He had resigned.*

I had no occasion to speak to Punch in the next few days, and didn't go out of my way to find one. I certainly saw no point to rehashing the affair, and am doing it now only because of the publicity given the episode then and later. Daniel and Rosenthal

* Greenfield, at Punch's instigation, returned to the *Times* less than two years later as foreign news editor.

continued in a state of frustration and depression, but I refrained from discussing the matter with them. I felt that the deed was done; right or wrong, we'd have to live with it in the interest of the *Times*. Rosenthal was the first to see Punch. Unable to swallow things whole, Abe made it quite clear to the publisher that he was angry at the way he had treated Greenfield and undercut his editors, but Abe's manner and Punch's attitude toward him were such that they parted friends, the incident behind them.

Punch called me to his office to tell me about his talk with Abe.

"You're not going to run out on me, are you, Professor?" was Punch's first comment as I entered his office.

"Of course not," I said. "I don't see how that question could cross your mind." I thought he knew by then that resigning in protest, or threatening to, was not my style.

I volunteered no comment on the situation, only responded to his questions. He asked, of course, what I thought. I told him I thought he had hurt himself with his staff, but that in time it would pass. He never pretended that he'd handled the matter well; he later spoke of it as a fiasco, which it was.

I was naturally depressed by the whole affair, and felt considerably let down. It was not a case of my selling him a plan for the Washington bureau which he had to return as questionable merchandise. He had seen the need for action, had urged it, and had actively participated in formulating the plan. At first I concluded that he had bowed to the threat, implied if not real, that leading members of the Washington bureau would resign if he appointed Greenfield as bureau chief. I had no such fear, and I also felt that even if all the aggrieved reporters had quit, the *New York Times* would still have come out.

Yet Punch had had a problem which in time I came to understand and appreciate. He had believed he was running the risk of losing Frankel and Wicker and possibly Reston. The possible alternative of losing Greenfield, who was a new recruit, and even Rosenthal and Daniel, was preferable to Punch. I suppose he knew I wouldn't quit, and of course he knew my retirement was near. Obviously I didn't agree with Punch's decision, but I tried to understand the pressures that led to it, and I never questioned that the decision was his to make.

There remained the question of Punch's relationship with his managing editor, Daniel, after the Greenfield matter. Punch and Daniel were friendly, but they were different sorts of men, and no real intimacy existed between them. Punch once told me he felt there was an invisible sign on Daniel's office that said, "Publishers, Keep Out." For about two weeks after the Greenfield decision, Punch and Daniel didn't speak. Then, wanting to settle things, Punch went to Daniel's office one afternoon and asked him to state his feelings. Daniel did so, and as he spoke he became angry and berated Punch mercilessly. The confrontation took place in a small office off Daniel's main office. When I and the other editors arrived for Daniel's afternoon news conference, we could hear Daniel's voice through the door. The words were not clear but the message got through. We were embarrassed, and Abe Rosenthal started the meeting without Punch and Daniel. Finally they joined us, both visibly upset.

There was later speculation, inside and outside the *Times*, that this confrontation resulted in Punch's later decision to transfer Daniel from managing editor to associate editor, thereby removing him from authority over the news department. I think the die was cast long before, and for reasons more basic in the two men's personalities. One of Punch's concerns at this time was that I might unexpectedly retire or otherwise leave the executive editorship and that he would then have to face the question of whether to make Daniel my successor.

This concern undoubtedly led Punch to make still another unexpected decision. He came to my office one afternoon about two months later and told me he'd decided to go ahead with a reorganization of the news department's high command. He proposed that I accept the position of vice president of the Times Company, and turn over the executive editorship to Scotty Reston.

I was visibly shaken by the suddenness of the move, and by the manner in which it was announced to me. Perhaps by then I should have become accustomed to Punch's abrupt actions. Punch, on the other hand, was surprised at my surprise. "I thought you'd already heard," he said. "I told Gruson, and apparently he's been telling everybody."

It seemed that Punch had been playing golf with foreign correspondent Sydney Gruson in Florida a short time before. Gruson was threatening to leave the *Times* to work for *Newsday*—eventually he did leave—and Punch, in the course of trying to dissuade Gruson, told Gruson about the upcoming changes. Punch asked Gruson to keep them secret, but Gruson let the word slip out and, for at least a day before Punch spoke to me, it was common knowledge in the newsroom. Furthermore, Punch had discussed the changes at a board meeting that morning. Somehow the news never reached me.

However, although I was startled by the move, the decision itself did not surprise me. Punch had often said he wanted to talk to me about the future of the newsroom, although he'd never really done so. And he had always said he would favor Reston as my successor, unless we could settle on a younger man who was satisfactory to Punch, which Daniel was not. I think Punch knew that had he asked my advice I would have urged him to reconcile his differences with Daniel and make him my successor, for I regarded him as by far the best qualified for the job. But Punch, I am sure, would have been unwilling to do this and would have persisted in his compromise solution. In effect, what he did was to bring Reston in for an interim period, during which Abe Rosenthal received further training; then, when Reston decided to return to Washington after a year, Daniel was moved out of the news department to an associate editorship, and Abe became managing editor.

A day or two after Punch spoke to me, I told him I would accept the position of vice president. We also agreed I would serve on the company's board of directors.

A few minutes later, Arthur Hays Sulzberger phoned me and asked me to come up to his office on the fourteenth floor. When I arrived, I found Punch in the corridor outside his father's office. I entered, and Mrs. Sulzberger embraced me and said it was wonderful to have me on the board of directors. AHS was seated in his wheelchair behind his desk. He bade me have a glass of sherry with him. After a moment he lowered his head and said in an emotion-filled voice, "I want you to know this is not the way I wanted it."

I was extremely moved by his concern, and I assured him that everything was all right. A few minutes later I left. Punch was still pacing in the hall outside.

"Is everything all right?" he asked.

I told him everything was fine. And it was.

XXVI

The Meeting Is Adjourned

I SERVED as a vice president of The New York Times Company from June 1, 1968, until January 1, 1970. I maintained my staff and my suite of offices down the hallway from the *Times* newsroom, and I functioned as a senior adviser to Punch Sulzberger and to my successor as executive editor, Scotty Reston. When Reston came to me minutes after our new jobs were announced, he told me he would count on my advice in his new job, and I promised to give him any help I could. He did often seek my ideas in the months ahead, but I tried to avoid volunteering them, for I did not want to be a kibitzer now that I had ceased to have responsibility for the daily operations of the news department.

As executive editor, Reston continued to write his thrice-weekly political column. I told him he might find it difficult to serve those two demanding masters, but he was determined to make the effort. The column had for years been his source of independence and he could not bring himself to give it up. When, inevitably, his column began to suffer, and he felt compelled to choose between it and the editorship, his decision was to return to Washington and write the column. At that point, Abe Rosenthal became managing editor, and the transition from Arthur Hays Sulzberger's generation to Punch's generation was complete.

During my term as vice president, work was completed on the new home my wife and I were having built in New Orelans. I was spending more and more time in New Orleans, and Punch and I agreed I should resign as vice president. He asked that I remain on the board of directors and as a consultant to the paper. These duties require me to visit New York a few days each month, but beyond that I began my retirement on the first day of 1970.

Once I settled down in New Orleans, I accepted quite a few invitations to speak, and I also began work on this book. As I struggled with the chore of speechwriting, I sometimes recalled the most popular speech I ever delivered. It was the conclusion of a dinner, in April of 1960, when I succeeded Russ Wiggins as president of the American Society of Newspaper Editors. Our scheduled after-dinner speaker canceled on us at the last moment and we somehow got as his replacement two officials from the State Department. Those two gentlemen droned on for an hour apiece, amid many moans and dirty looks from the editors assembled. Finally they finished and it was time for Russ Wiggins to introduce me for *my* speech. I carried a huge pile of papers to the lectern with me, poured myself a glass of water, adjusted my spectacles, looked out over my captive audience, and shouted:

"The meeting is adjourned!"

That four-word speech earned me a standing ovation, and I would like to wind up these recollections with something like the same alacrity.

I have written a lot about the problems I confronted as editor of the *Times.* This was inevitable, for problem-solving is an editor's job. Yet, as I look back, it is not the problems I recall but the countless pleasures of my association with the *Times.* It was an honor and a joy to be associated with people like Arthur and Iphigene Sulzberger, with Jimmy James and Arthur Krock, with Orvil Dryfoos and Punch Sulzberger, with Ted Bernstein and E. C. Daniel and Harrison Salisbury, with Nat Goldstein, with Scotty Reston and Abe Rosenthal, and with many more I could name. I loved seeing the *Times* come out each morning, knowing that my efforts and ideas had helped make it what it was. I was proud to be associated with the traditions of the *New York Times,* an institution that has done so much good for the city and the nation it serves.

I remember vividly the first time I returned to the *Times* in the spring of 1943 after my ill-fated fling with the Chicago *Sun.* When I walked into the lobby of the *Times* building, I felt a sudden thrill, a shiver of pride, just at seeing the elevator operators with "The New York Times" inscribed on their caps. That was more than a quarter century ago, but today, as I return to the *Times* each month for board meetings, I still feel the same thrill, and the same sense of gratitude to my fellows and my fate.

Index

The abbreviation TC is used for Turner Catledge.

311

70 71 72 73 10 9 8 7 6 5 4 3 2 1